Jungle Combat with
the 112th Cavalry

ALSO BY ROBERT PEYTON WIGGINS

Chief Bender: A Baseball Biography (McFarland, 2010)

*The Federal League of Base Ball Clubs: The History
of an Outlaw Major League, 1914–1915* (McFarland, 2009)

Jungle Combat with the 112th Cavalry

Three Texans in the Pacific in World War II

ROBERT PEYTON WIGGINS

McFarland & Company, Inc., Publishers
Jefferson, North Carolina, and London

LIBRARY OF CONGRESS CATALOGUING-IN-PUBLICATION DATA

Wiggins, Robert Peyton.
  Jungle combat with the 112th Cavalry : three Texans in the
Pacific in World War II / Robert Peyton Wiggins.
        p.   cm.
  Includes bibliographical references and index.

  ISBN 978-0-7864-6150-9
  softcover : 50# alkaline paper ∞

  1. United States. Army. Cavalry Regiment, 112th — History.
2. World War, 1939–1945 — Regimental histories — United
States.   3. World War, 1939–1945 — Jungle warfare.
4. World War, 1939–1945 — Campaigns — Pacific Area.
5. Wiggins, C.W., 1916–2002.   6. Wright, Alonzo, 1914–1991.
7. Wright, Robert Locke, 1922–2007.   8. Soldiers — Texas —
Biography.   I. Title.
D769.325112th .W44   2011
940.54'12730922 — dc22   2011001108

BRITISH LIBRARY CATALOGUING DATA ARE AVAILABLE

On the cover: *top* Troops on maneuvers in New Mexico while
stationed at Fort Bliss, June 1941; *bottom* Loading troops of the
112th Cavalry into LCTs at Talasea, New Britain, for transportation
to New Guinea (U.S. Army photographs courtesy
of the Texas Military Forces Museum)

Manufactured in the United States of America

*McFarland & , Inc., Publishers
  Box 611, Jefferson, North Carolina 28640
  www.mcfarlandpub.com*

Table of Contents

To
Dale Walter Wiggins

3rd Battalion, 116th Infantry Brigade Combat Team,
29 Infantry Division
Operation Iraqi Freedom, 2007–2008

Preface and Acknowledgments

The war to end all wars did not end for the survivors of the 112th Cavalry Regiment with the surrender of Japan in 1945. The cavalrymen bore the haunting memories, the scars, and endured the nightmares for years. There were fond memories, too, mainly of the comradeship with their fellow troopers.

This is mainly the story of three men from that regiment's G Troop: two brothers, Pug and Pickett Wright, and their future brother-in-law, C.W. Wiggins. After they returned to normal lives in northwest Texas, memories of the 112th Cavalry would always be with them. These men's children and grandchildren heard them talk of the horse cavalry and the war, but those stories were foreign to the younger generations.

Wives and children retained a few facts from their conversations about the war. They knew the three served with the U.S. Army in the South Pacific under General MacArthur and that Pickett Wright had been wounded after he was missing from his regiment for several days. Names of places like Arawe, Aitape and Woodlark were as alien as the names of the craters on Mars. Their children did notice that when these former cavalrymen talked to each other, there was a special bond, a comradeship indigenous only to men who had endured that life or death struggle together in combat.

The story of the 112th Cavalry Regiment in World War II is not well known, even in Texas. Most of the plaudits have been reserved for the state's federalized infantry division, the 36th, that fought its way up the Italian peninsula, across France and into Germany. More than one former cavalryman from the 112th commented that theirs was a "bastard regiment" and it always received the less attractive assignments compared to the regiments from infantry divisions that served in the same theater, the 1st Cavalry Division, the 32nd infantry, and the 43rd Infantry.

The 112th was the last American mounted regiment to serve overseas (New Caledonia), it participated in three campaigns and six major operations, and its troopers spent 434 days in combat. Even after the regiment was dismounted and gave up their distinctive uniforms, the 112th was distinguished from other National Guard units by the men's sidearms and it had about half the personnel of a regular U.S. Army infantry regiment.

The 112th Cavalry was the first U.S. Army unit in the Pacific theater of operations to use bazookas and flame throwers in combat against the Japanese (Arawe), it first used amphibious "Alligators" and rocket-firing DUKWs ("ducks") in an amphibious assault (Arawe), and the regiment became the first to routinely utilize helicopters to evacuate wounded (January 1945 on Luzon).

The nucleus of the 112th Cavalry was a cadre of young men from rural Depression Texas. Many had only a rudimentary education and left school at an early age to help support their families. The comradeship they developed after having served together three years or longer before their first combat experience contributed to a special esprit de corps among the cavalrymen. Officers at the squadron and even the regimental level knew many of their men on a first name basis and that familiarity only added to troop cohesion. Replacements came to the regiment in sporadic increments instead of in large groups of draftees that restocked many an infantry regiment.

The genesis of this volume came in 1987 when I began working on a history of my mother's family. That November Uncle Robert "Pickett" Wright related the story of the "Missing Patrol" from his bed in a Lubbock hospital.

Each time I spoke with another uncle, Alonzo "Pug" Wright, about his wartime experiences, each question posed would elicit a plethora of information. As a narrative began to take shape, an adventure of that time in American history began to unfold. These three men had participated in the demise of the horse cavalry, then fought in and lived through the largest war in human history. However, this volume is not a traditional memoir nor is it a unit history. It is the story of a particular troop of cavalry as told through the perspective of a family, particularly the three men who served in Troop G, 112th Cavalry Regiment.

Employing each of our heroes' experiences, their story takes the 112th Cavalry from its time at Fort Clark, Texas, to the final days of the battle for the Philippines. The main sources for this story are the personal accounts of the three main subjects, Texas farm boys who were thrust into an extraordinary situation. No efforts have been made to glamorize their story.

For each of them, the experience with G Troop meant different things, and each man's memory of events is somewhat different. Whenever possible, attempts were made to confirm their recollections with secondary sources, but when unable, their remembrances are taken at face value. Historical accounts along with comments by fellow troopers and family are added to supplement the accounts of the main characters.

Important to note are the special contributions of two other G troopers. Lionel Carter, publisher of the newsletter *Reunion Review,* provided copies of his publication as far back as 1960. In addition to the valuable articles and letters in the *Review,* Mr. Carter's personal memoirs, "Carter and the Cavalry," is a useful chronology and supplement to my narrative. In response to a few questions, Tony Frangella of Chicago graciously provided an audio cassette tape with his recollections of the "missing patrol" and his experiences with G Troop in the Philippines.

Scott Powell's dissertation, "Learning Under Fire: A Combat Unit in the Southwest Pacific" (Graduate Studies of Texas A&M University, August 2006), provides a basic combat history of that unit. Dr. Edward Drea's Leavenworth paper, "Defending the Driniumor," is invaluable as a chronological narrative on the 112th's participation in the fight for New Guinea. Other sources are credited in the notes and bibliography.

I would like to thank my wife Deborah for her assistance in the proofreading of the manuscript and her computer skills that far exceed my own. Bob and Jean Gates, photo archivists at the Texas Military Forces Museum in Austin, deserve acknowledgment for their invaluable assistance in the acquisition of U.S. Army photographs for the 112th Cavalry Regiment.

Members of the Wright family — Pug, Pickett, Dorothy Wright Whitney, and Rita Wright Morrison — contributed photographs to my collection over the years. And of course, this volume would have been impossible to complete without the contributions of my father, C.W. Wiggins, and my two uncles, Alonzo "Pug" Wright and Robert "Pickett" Wright.

1

A Long Way from Home

Papua New Guinea, September 1944

The Driniumor River was peaceful now, but over the previous month and a half it had been the site of a living nightmare for the soldiers of the 112th Cavalry Regiment. These cavalrymen had defended their position on the river since the second of July, under constant attack or threat of attack from the seldom-seen Japanese enemy. Amidst one of the densest tropical rain forests in the world, they subsisted in primitive conditions, in dugouts, foxholes or log-encased gun positions. Malaria-bearing mosquitoes, bugs of all types and the tropical humidity were always with them. Even the smell was odious. Decaying vegetation emitted an unpleasant odor and unburied bodies began to decompose in a matter of hours.

Dead friends were wrapped in their ponchos and buried, to be dug up later for a proper funeral. Some bodies, however, could not be found in the jungle, while others simply washed down the river and out to sea.

Alonzo "Pug" Wright and C.W. Wiggins had served together and been friends since they joined the 112th Cavalry Regiment in February 1941. Together they had sailed halfway around the world. At one point or another they had battled cavalry horses, disease-bearing insects, and the Japanese Army. Organized of mostly Texans, the 112th Cavalry was a close-knit group, many of their number having been together for almost four years. They left their horses behind on New Caledonia in May 1943 and became jungle fighters for General Douglas MacArthur. Now, this deadly river had cost the regiment almost a quarter of its number as killed or wounded. Among the latter was Pug's younger brother Robert.

And with C.W., or "Bull" as he was known in the army, returning to the

United States, most of Pug's old friends from Texas had left the regiment. But the older Wright brother's ordeal was to continue — his next stop, the invasion of the Philippines! Four years earlier none of them could have envisioned what they were destined to endure.

* * *

When the Wright brothers and C.W. Wiggins arrived at Fort Bliss, Texas, in early 1941 the United States was at peace and military preparations were focused on a war in Europe that was in its second year. The recruits prayed their country would not be drawn into the foreign conflict and at least hoped their military obligation would be satisfied before the United States entered the war.

The military experience for the Wrights and C.W. began in the dusty Rio Grande country of Texas in the days when the United States Army still used horse cavalry. The men of the 112th Cavalry had various reasons for joining the military. Some enlisted in the army for adventure, or for patriotism, some even signed up to get out of trouble with the law. Many young men enlisted to satisfy their one-year military obligation before the United States' inevitable entrance into the war against Nazi Germany.

The United States government reinstated the draft in October 1940 and the option of volunteering for one year in the Army to satisfy one's military commitment seemed to be an acceptable alternative to awaiting conscription. This provided a strong incentive for a young man who wanted to complete his military obligation and had no thoughts of a career in the army. The Japanese attack on Pearl Harbor on December 7, 1941, would dash any plans for a short enlistment.

Times were simpler before the war. Most Americans had little money, but many did not consider themselves poor. The most important things were family, hard work, and religion. Texas was more than 55 percent rural in 1940 and country music was an important part of their social lives.

Both Pug and C.W. came from similar Southern agrarian backgrounds. Each left school at an early age to work on the farm and neither anticipated military service. But there the similarities ended. The freewheeling and adventurous Pug Wright came from a family of fourteen children. One of only two children, C.W. was quiet, serious, and prudent.

If not for the impending war in Europe, there was nothing in C.W.'s background to suggest any tradition of military service. C.W.'s most recent military ancestor was his great-grandfather Robert Morton. Married with two daughters at the time of the Civil War, Mr. Morton served with the 45th Virginia Regiment during that conflict. The venerable old man whom C.W. remembered as balding, hawk faced, and with a long white beard, died at the age of ninety-two in 1923. Six-year-old C.W. watched them place Mr. Morton's body in a nineteenth-century hearse pulled by a team of white horses before taking him down a country road to be buried amid a grove of trees.

C.W.'s grandfather, Seaborn Wiggins, left Georgia at the age of twenty-one and settled in Parker County, Texas, in 1885. Without a plan he got off a train in Weatherford, Texas, and began to look for work. Mr. Morton hired the newcomer from the East to help work the farm. Seaborn courted his employer's youngest daughter, Rebecca, and they married the following year. The newlyweds acquired a piece of land nearby Morton's and their new home would eventually become known as the "Ole Homestead." Their second son, Walter, married Christine Wright[1] and settled down to farm like his father and his father's father.

Their first son, C.W. Wiggins, was born on December 4, 1916, in the same room of the Parker County farmhouse where his father was born twenty-five years earlier. Using only initials for the given name of a child was not uncommon in the South at that time and an aunt suggested Christine and Walter name the baby by using the first letter of each of his parent's names. Although his mother always called him C.W., everybody else called him Seeb, perhaps after his grandfather.

When C.W. was a small child his parents moved to Reno, a small community some four miles east of Springtown, Texas. Sons were essential to help work the farm, but after Christine suffered a miscarriage, it appeared Seeb might be an only child. C.W. was five years old when his brother, Welden, was born at Reno, Texas, in 1921.

Though his younger brother was outgoing and rowdy, Seeb was a shy youngster and spoke only when necessary. When it came time for C.W. to begin the first grade, there was no school near the Wiggins farm so he went to live with Grandpa John Wright.

"I stayed with Grandpa and Grandma when I was in the first grade because they said it was too far to ride to school," he recalled. "I rode Jack, a grey mule, to the Hopewell school with my aunts Nola and Mozelle — three of us on the same mule. Every weekend Mom and Aunt Ava came after me. In the second grade I went to Agnus — rode two-three miles on a mule by myself to school."

For most of the year, life around the farm was monotonous. On special occasions, the whole family piled into their mule-drawn wagon for a day of shopping and sightseeing in Weatherford. The county seat of Parker County boasted a population of around 6,000 in 1920, but its size ballooned on Saturdays with the influx of area farmers.

When the family arrived in Weatherford, they would park in the wagon yard on the edge of town and mingle with the numerous other country folk who had come to town for the day. The team mules were led away to be fed and watered then stabled. The wagon yard was a natural place to congregate for the local gossip and to listen to the windy tales of the tobacco spitting and whittling crowd.

When the Ringling Brothers Circus came to Weatherford in the early 1920s, Walter, Chris, and the boys, along with Uncle Iva and Aunt Ava, piled into the wagon and made the trip to the county seat. The Wiggins made their way through the crowds to see the circus animals unloaded from the train and watch the parade to the grounds where tents would be set up. On the family's return trip to the farm, they were caught in a blue norther. When the wagon broke a wheel, Walter and Iva left their freezing family and rode the mules back to town for another wagon. The women and kids spent an anxious evening shivering under a mattress in the disabled wagon until the men returned.

When C.W. was nine years old, Walter loaded his family and possessions on the train going west and joined his older brother Benjamin on a farm near the central Texas town of Loraine. There, C.W.'s childhood was similar to thousands of other Texas farm children of the twenties and thirties. Seeb rode a mule to the two-room country schoolhouse south of town, but formal education was practical only when farm work permitted.

The terrain around their new home was substantially different from that of Parker County. Farmers had to rely on fate for rain and the landscape was broken by the numerous windmills that towered above the short mesquite trees and hills. Long dry spells were inevitable.

Many of the old plank farm houses were so porous they hardly kept out the icy northern winds. During the winter, the Wiggins family huddled around a roaring fire in the pot-bellied stove or snuggled in bed beneath a plethora of home spun quilts. In summer, a person could sweat through the night inside or sleep on the porch and fight off the mosquitoes. Conveniences like electricity, indoor bathrooms and the like were luxuries of the future. In winter or summer, in bad weather or the middle of the night, family members had to walk outside to use the odious outhouse.

The sometimes violent West Texas weather produced spring tornados, fall northers and dust storms. When the afternoon sky turned black, adults and kids scurried to the safety of the damp and musty cellar, a rectangular hole in the ground covered with timbers and earth. Only the dim glow of a kerosene lantern broke the darkness inside when the door was closed.

A young C.W. learned horsemanship at an early age and eventually earned his own mount, a red bay mare. The family supported themselves by raising the usual farm animals: chickens, hogs, and cattle. They grew grain and cotton, yields of which were inconsistent because of Depression prices and the infrequency of rain on their terraced fields. Using as much as possible from what they grew, rural families depended on the sale of cotton and eggs for necessities as the Depression deepened.

In those days, boys wore overalls and took to the fields as early as four years of age picking cotton. Farming in the unpredictable climate of West Texas was a risky business. Just after the last frost in late April or early May, cotton seeds were sewn eight to eighteen inches apart in rows separated by about four feet. Once the plants emerged from the earth, the Wiggins thinned out the plants with a hoe and fought the constant growth of weeds and plant-eating insects. When weeds and invasive Johnson grass grew up amidst the cotton plants the only sure way to get rid of it was to "dig 'em out," C.W. and his brother spent many summer days toiling with a hoe in the fields. Walter had to keep a close rein on the restless boys. Their father did not have any use for "foolishness" like squabbling or pranks.

When the cotton bolls opened and became fluffy, the whole family went into the fields to pick them. The pickers worked, stooped over, shoving the white bolls into the large homemade canvas bags they pulled along the rows. Because it was essential to get the crop out of the field as early as possible, workers toiled from daybreak to sunset, a twelve-hour day that today would be described as "hard labor."

Cotton profits were volatile because of the potential for drought, hail storms or even too much water at the wrong time. The 1920s had been a boom for the cotton grower in Texas as the price per pound usually stayed above twenty cents. It rose to an incredible forty-five cents a pound in the fall of 1929 before the bottom fell out of the market and it would be five years before the price rose above ten cents a pound.

Despite having few material goods, C.W. remarked to a cousin many years later, "I don't think kids today have as much fun as we did." His closest playmates were his three cousins, the sons of Uncle Ben. Swimming in the nearby creek, smoking cedar bark and riding the plow horses were among their favorite pastimes.

C.W. was not enthusiastic about some of his father's passions — shooting and raising wolf hounds for hunting. "Before the war, Dad, Ben and several other men hunted wolves and coyotes on that Spade Ranch. I went a time or two, stayed up all night — just to see those ole dogs run."

As he grew older, C.W. assumed more of the duties on the farm. Mules were used to pull plows and cultivators until Mr. Wiggins purchased a tractor shortly before the War. Grandfather Seaborn had instilled a strong Baptist tradition in his family and C.W. accepted this faith at an early age and, as an adult, patterned his life along Christian values.

"When I was about fifteen or sixteen," he recalled, "I got baptized south of Loraine in an old water tank. They ran that windmill all day to get it full and that water was real cold. They baptized several people and we all like to froze to death."

By the late thirties, broadcasts on the Wiggins' wind-charged radio told of the war in Europe and Japan's invasion of China. C.W. was only two years old when his father's younger brother sailed to Europe to join the American Expeditionary Force in an earlier foreign war, but Uncle Iva Wiggins arrived only days after the Armistice ended World War I and he participated in the occupation along the Rhine River.

Rather than risk awaiting a wartime draft, C.W. decided to fulfill his one-year military commitment by enlisting in the Army. He turned his Model B Ford automobile over to his father to trade and bade his hometown girl-friend good-bye, assuring her he would be away only one year. She did not wait for his return.

C.W.'s father drove him to the county seat at Colorado City where he joined the group of volunteers from Mitchell County.[2] A neighbor and friend, Van Sawyer, was among the enlistees, as was another Loraine boy, Williard Cranfill, whom C.W. knew only by the nickname "Pooch."

After three days of tests in Lubbock, Texas, C.W. and the others were sworn into the Army of the United States on January 29, 1941. At five foot six and 114 pounds, C.W. was not much bigger than the weapons he would have to carry, but due to his background in physical labor he was stronger than he looked, able to carry a greater proportionate weight than larger men. The only deficiency in the physical exam was a far-sighted condition that necessitated the use of eyeglasses for reading.

While completing forms at the induction center, C.W. was told he had to have a first name, not just initials! He stammered "Christine" in his Texas twang. It was recorded "Christaine" and for the next four and a half years, as far as the Army was concerned, his name was Christaine W. Wiggins.[3] C.W. never attempted to have the spelling corrected.

The Mitchell County recruits boarded a train at the depot in Lubbock for the trip to El Paso. Their destination was the reception center at the sprawling military complex known as Fort Bliss. C.W. remembered that "they kept me scared to death!"

When Corporal Ed Price came over with a truck from the 112th Cavalry Regiment, C.W. began his tour with that horse cavalry unit. That assignment linked C.W.'s destiny with that of a pair of brothers, Pug and Pickett Wright, who were among a group of recruits that had gone through the Lubbock induction center a week earlier.

The older of the two, Pug, was born Alonzo Wright in Berry, Alabama, on February 23, 1914. He was the sixth of fourteen children, but large families like his were not unusual in the rural South back then. He was mainly of English extraction, although his mother asserted she had some Dutch and American Indian blood.

The Wrights had lived in Fayette County, Alabama, since the 1840s. Pug's great-grandfather, Robert Wright, homesteaded there in 1854 when he reached the age of twenty. Fifty years later, his grandson and namesake, Robert R. Wright, eloped with Donna Frost, daughter of a farmer from nearby Corona.[4]

Pug could hardly remember his great-grandfather Tom Frost and it was even harder for him to visualize the graying Methodist circuit preacher as a Confederate cavalryman during the Civil War. His great-grandfather Robert Wright had been in the cavalry too, with the Union Army.[5]

Known as Pug from an early age, Alonzo remembered going to the coal mines with his father and sitting on a boiler to keep warm. He started going to school at Carbon Hill, Alabama, and later went to a one-room brick country school. Robert R. Wright tried his hand at farming, mining, construction, and even worked for a Carbon Hill garage assembling Chevrolet automobiles. The family left Alabama in 1924 and moved several times while gradually working their way west. Times were hard so Robert R. and his eldest son Earl often had to leave the family and find work wherever available.

Pug was twelve years old when he and his family were caught up in the great Mississippi River flood of 1927. "We lived three miles from Little River, which ran through Lepanto (Arkansas) and twenty one miles from the Mississippi," Pug recalled. "During the big flood of '27, we were nearly washed out. Everybody had to have a boat. Someone had to row out to milk the cow until they eventually brought her up to the house and tied her up to the back porch. When they milked her, they had to move her up on the porch. The water lacked two inches running into the house. We had to row a boat to Jonesboro for supplies."

Not long after the flood, Pa Wright and his cousin heard about harvest jobs in the southwest. The large family and their possessions were loaded in a Model T truck with a covered back made of roofing material and they headed for Oklahoma. There were no highways then, mostly just dirt roads some no better than trails. "Every time we would come to a hill, all the kids would have to jump out and push the ole truck over the top," Pug remembered.

By 1933, the family had worked its way to Texas where Robert R. Wright became friends with a Denton banker. The banker leased Pug's father a large farm twelve miles down a gravel and dirt road north of Childress, Texas. White's Creek meandered through the property and emptied into the Red River.

The country was deep into the Great Depression when the Wrights moved to the farm in Childress County. Farming back then meant hard work and very little money. That first autumn on White's Creek, the Wrights went into their fields and pulled the unharvested cotton bolls that had "just cracked." It was estimated they salvaged about 600 pounds of usable bolls the Wrights called "hickory nuts" and sold them in town for $15, important money for that time.

Unlike many families in the Depression, they did have plenty to eat. Mr. Wright and the boys cultivated feed grain and cotton while Ma and the girls tended a vegetable garden. The younger children milked the cows and turned the separator for the milk and cream to be sold in town along with their excess eggs.

The uncultivated area around White's Creek was rich with wild life. The Wright boys hunted and trapped rabbits and quail for the family's table, while the farm's hounds pursued the numerous coyotes to keep them away from the livestock. White's Creek not only yielded catfish and perch for the dinner table, it became a gathering place for most of the kids in the vicinity. They cleared a picnic area, laid out a baseball field and strung a trolley wire to an old cottonwood tree that would provide sky rides across the creek on a cultivator seat hanging from a pulley.

The Wrights built up their holdings and Pug recalled that "one year — with two hired hands, it made eighteen mouths to feed (and) we butchered 3700 pounds of hogs. We leased more land and had 100 head of cattle and 200 horses."

Pug learned to ride and break horses in those days. The boys organized rodeos with their unbroken horses and mules to entertain family and friends.

In addition to his horsemanship, Pug honed his homespun style of story telling through the experiences of his youth. When asked about his first girlfriend, he mused "It was in Arkansas when I was ten years old. I would hold her parasol when she needed a fresh dip of snuff."

Some of his favorite stories involved his older brother Alfred. "Alfred was a rodeo cowboy — a bronco buster — and he dressed well in new western clothes, hat and boots. He always traded everybody's things. But once he traded his boots for two pigs. The pigs died of colic and Alfred took them down to the creek and buried them. He put up a tombstone (that read) 'Here lies my boots!'"

Other stories involved a pair of the farm's mules, Shorty and Guts. Both were red and their monikers came from their appearance. Guts was pot bellied and Shorty was simply not as tall as the other mules. Pug chuckled about the time the rodeo cowboy was thrown by the plow mule. "Alfred thought he had it made and was slappin' that mule on the neck. Ole Shorty bucked him right off."

"Alfred would ride one of them mules to court his schoolteacher girl-friend," went one of Pug's stories. "Next morning, we couldn't plow because he hadn't come home yet and one of the team was missing. Pa was fit to be tied." Of course they had other mules, but the stories were better with just the two.

By the late 1930s, bands like *The Lite Crust Doughboys* and Bob Wills' *Texas Playboys* had popularized a new style of country music called "Western Swing." Pug had played the guitar since an early age and, along with four of his brothers, organized a cowboy band, self styled *The Famous Panhandle Cowboys.* The novice musicians wore black cowboy hats and black scarves as the style of the day dictated. They played for local dances, in stores, and at the courthouse gazebo on Saturday nights.

"We played at Bob Brown's service station across the street from the (Childress) courthouse," explained Pug's brother Edgar. "We played inside and the music went outside through a loudspeaker. Anybody that was goin' down that street had to hear it. There was Butch (their brother Andrew), Pug and me."

In 1936 Pug and his younger brothers Ed and Aubort went on tour with the Texas Centennial Rodeo through North Texas and Oklahoma. They didn't get paid, just the privileges of the rodeo. Three square meals and the excitement of the tour were pretty good rewards during those hard times.

Robert Locke Wright and his twin brother Aubort were born on April 23, 1922. Aubort was nicknamed "Cotton" as a toddler because of his curly white hair; and Robert acquired the inevitable sobriquet "Pick-it." His mother and older sister often called him by his middle name, Locke.

Pickett was eleven years old when his family moved to the farm near Childress. Along with his brothers and sisters, he walked the four miles to White's Creek's two-room schoolhouse. When it closed, they had to catch the bus to River Camp School. There, Pickett began his lifelong love affair with baseball. The River Camp team was made up of "five Wright brothers, five Mooney boys and one other boy who was the catcher. We won most of the games we played," he boasted.

Pickett displayed a fearless nature as a young boy and always sought to be included in the adventures of his older brothers. The Wrights' farm was within easy walking distance from the Red River that could become a dangerous torrent by a sudden cloudburst. The rushing current of the river would wash out depressions in its bed, creating a swirling effect, so swimmers had to be careful not to be sucked under by one of the whirlpools.

"We'd swim down that creek (White's) about two miles to the river and then have to walk back," Pickett remembered "We rode logs in the Red River. It would hit a whirlpool, spin you around and off you'd go! Pa would just roar, 'You damn boys are gonna get killed in that river'"

According to his twin brother, "Pickett like to got drowned over there, too. If he hadn't had some help he would've. I think it was Fletcher D. Childs who got his head up out of the water. It's a wonder all of us didn't get drowned."[6]

The near drowning was not Pickett's only narrow escape from tragedy while a teenager. The farm's cotton field went right up to the edge of White's Creek. Pickett was turning the family's new *Oliver* tractor around at the end of the cotton rows when the tractor began to slide down the embankment of the creek. He just escaped serious injury by diving onto a cattle trail worn into the bank. The tractor tumbled into the creek and broke in half.

Seven years younger than Pug, Pickett idolized his older brother. He was only fourteen when he went with Pug to work on brother Earl's farm near Fort Worth and later he joined his brothers as a guitarist in their cowboy band.

The younger Wright boys were anxious to go into the military when war fever enveloped the country in 1940, but their Pa asked them to wait until the crops were harvested in the fall. Pug and his brother Ed were subject to the daft so they joined the Army. When seventeen-year-old Robert heard that his brothers were going into the Army, he too went to the enlistment office. After being told that he would have to have parental consent because he was underage, Robert convinced his father to sign for him. Robert's twin brother Aubort and older brother Andrew also wanted to join the military, but Mr. Wright convinced them to agree to stay home for another year and help work the farm. When the elder Wright suffered a minor heart attack during the war, his son Andrew received a hardship discharge from the coast artillery in order to work the farm.

After three weeks of rowdy going away parties, the three Wright brothers joined seven other new army recruits at the Childress railroad depot to catch the train bound for the induction center in Lubbock.[7] The train stopped at Estelene, Texas, where it picked up four more recruits, a group that included Orvil Weddel and Howard Richardson.

Pug, Ed, and Robert Wright were sworn into the United States Army in Lubbock on January 24, 1941, and their group took the train to Fort Bliss. Recruits were housed in tents, pending assignment to a unit. The three brothers decided they wanted to go to the 36th Infantry Division (formerly Texas National Guard) that was garrisoned at Brownwood, Texas.

"We all wanted to go to Brownwood," Pug explained. "Then they called our names that morning for the cavalry. There were three of us and I asked which one? And he said, 'Both of you!' Me and Pickett said all right and went to our tent to pack out — this was before daylight — and we got to thinking. What's gonna happen to ole Ed? So we bailed out and started back up there to have him go too — and he met us half way: 'Don't go up there and fool with him,' he said. 'I'm goin' to Brownwood!'"[8]

The 112th Cavalry Regiment could trace its origin to 1918, when the regular cavalry units serving along the Rio Grande River were withdrawn for duty in the World War. The governor of Texas was to organize two cavalry brigades to replace the units that had been protecting the border from infiltrators and Mexican bandits, but World War I ended two months before the new state regiments were ready. On July 20, 1921, the new 5th Texas Cavalry was designated 112th Cavalry, Texas National Guard, with headquarters in Fort Worth. The regiment was part of the

"Rarin' to Go"—112th Cavalry Regiment pin and shoulder patch insignia.

56th Cavalry Brigade which was used for martial law several times: in hurricane-ravaged Galveston, in the East Texas oil fields, and in the boom town of Borger. As another war became imminent, the 112th was expanded by three troops and inducted into federal service on November 18, 1940.[9]

At that time, a cavalry regiment was composed of six troops of horsemen (a cavalry troop was significantly smaller than a regular infantry company), a headquarters troop, and a weapons troop. Each regiment was divided into two combat squadrons of three troops each. At full strength, a troop was composed of 150 officers and men, divided into three rifle platoons and a weapons (or machine gun) platoon. The full complement of the regiment was 1,650 men —1,191 of them mounted, 179 pack animals, and numerous trucks, ranging between a fourth ton and two and a half ton. There was a twenty-eight man band, attached medical personnel, and a chaplain.[10]

Because the 112th Cavalry was originally a National Guard outfit, its recruits came from a specific geographic area. Many of the troopers knew each other before going into the army and often brothers and cousins served alongside one another in the same troop. Most of the 112th's original contingent came from Dallas, Fort Worth and surrounding counties. The sixth and final troop organized was Troop G, recruited from the Abilene area. G Troop's first commander was Captain Clyde Grant, who would work his way up from a second lieutenant to colonel in command of the regiment. Grant would become one of the most respected officers ever to served with the National

Guard cavalry regiment and was universally respected by the men he served under and by the men that severed under him.[11]

At the first of December 1940, the 112th and 124th cavalry regiments of the 56th Brigade were transferred to El Paso's Fort Bliss where they began a thirteen-week training program, designed to bring them up to regular army standards. There were barracks for the base's permanent units like the 1st Cavalry Division, but when not on maneuvers, the 56th Brigade was bivouacked in a tent city on part of the reservation's 404,000 acres. The troopers of the 112th spent several weeks there without heat, electricity or running water. They had to construct their own mess halls, latrines and stables which left limited time for training. Only a minority of the men had horses and when sufficient mounts were eventually provided, the cavalrymen had to shoe and break them to the saddle. The regiment was also seriously under strength and new recruits were brought in from among new enlistees and draftees. This wave of recruits came from the state of Texas, which sustained a sense of camaraderie and preserved a National Guard identity. The Wright brothers were part of this group of selectees.

When the Wrights arrived there, Fort Bliss was a beehive of activity, the station for artillery, cavalry, infantry and air corps units, as well as incoming inductees awaiting assignment. A lot had changed since their older brother, Earl Wright, was stationed there with the 82nd Field Artillery in the late 1930s.[12]

While at Fort Bliss, the home for the men of the 112th Cavalry was a community of pyramidal tents. The canvas tents received this designation because they resembled four-sided pyramids. They were sixteen by sixteen feet with a center pole of twelve feet in height and comfortably housed four troopers who slept on cots. Most had a wooden floor that supported a small gas stove in the center of the tent. The flaps on the four sides of the tent were usually raised to permit what breeze there was, but even with them down the frequent sandstorms kept the occupants choking with dust.[13]

Pug recalled that his assignment to G Troop began when a corporal from a machine gun platoon came over to the reception center and picked him for his squad. Pug had been with the 112th for only three or four days when this same corporal suggested Wright go into town with him. Pug explained that he was still in basic training, but eventually agreed to go. Back then, El Paso was a bustling city of nearly 100,000 residents and was the gateway to Ciudad Juarez, Mexico; and it cost only nine cents to ride the trolley anywhere in the city. When the two troopers came back to camp about one in the morning, they had obviously spent a large amount of time in the city's cantinas.

"It was cool," Pug remembered. "Anderson decided he was gonna light that stove — we had them little ole square gas stoves. Well, that hose hooked to it had a leak and it caught on fire — it caught ole (Elmer) Wilson's pillow on fire. He bailed out.

"They had poles out there and buckets hanging on 'em. Anderson kept telling me to put the fire out. 'Naw, you set it, you put the son-a-bitch out!'"

By now, smoke was pouring out the door of the tent and the whole troop was aroused. Troopers hurriedly began emptying the fire buckets on the smoking tent and First Sergeant Bud Reeves stomped up to see what caused all the commotion.

"Go on out! Go on out!" Anderson instructed. But Pug responded, "Naw, you're my corporal, you go out and I'll follow."

When the corporal stuck his head out of the tent, there stood First Sergeant Reeves towering above him. The large hands of the "top kick" grabbed the delinquent by the collar and shook him. When Pug exited the tent, he received the same treatment.

Alonzo "Pug" Wright (author's collection).

The next morning, Pug and his corporal were on extra duty in the mess hall. Their job was "table orderly," a particularly boring task of taking the dirty dishes from the dining room's tables to the kitchen, scrubbing tables, and sweeping the floor.

"So they put us to pickin' them dishes up." Pug recalled. "You took them and set 'em in a cubbyhole then the KPs would take 'em and put 'em in water. Ole Anderson stacked the dishes up — I stacked mine up. He walked out in the aisle with them plates and I was behind him. He got nearly to that cubbyhole. Instead of puttin' 'em up there, he just pitched 'em. When he did, them s.o.b.'s hit the floor and broke all to pieces. Well, I walked up there and I just throw'd mine in the same pile. The mess hall sergeant went over and told the first sergeant to get us out of that mess hall. We was breakin' all the dishes!"

First Sergeant Reeves gave the two rebellious troopers some shovels and took them behind the CQ (company headquarters). He said, "I want you to dig a hole — 6 foot deep, 6 foot square — right here!"

"So we started diggin' — and that was early in the morning, about eight o'clock. You talk about hard ground. We dug on that hole until about eleven o'clock. When we got done, Anderson said, 'Go around there and tell 'em we got this hole dug.' I said naw. 'No, you go around there, that s.o.b. will chew me out.' So he explained me how to do it. Go knock on that tent door ... and stand at attention while talkin' to him."

Pug did as he was told; "Sergeant Sir, We got that hole done."

Reeves looked the recruit over and told him to dig another one right beside it and fill the first hole up. Pug's encounter with First Sergeant Reeves cost him seven days extra duty and when he got to Fort Clark the new recruit was put to work with a saw in the wood yard.

The group of Mitchell County recruits arrived at Fort Bliss a week after the Wrights. C.W. Wiggins, Van Sawyer, as well as Herman Stokes and Vaughn Mitchell of Colorado City, and Silas "Spider" Moody of San Angelo went to Troop G. Pooch Cranfill was assigned to Troop A.

The newest troopers were issued the cavalry uniform of the day. The typical uniform included the usual khaki shirt with riding breeches that were fuller at the outside of the upper leg and reinforced at the inner leg for horseback riding. Headgear included the felt service hat with chin strap and a 112th Cavalry insignia pin in front (a rearing black horse on yellow background). Once the regiment received an overseas assignment all insignia had to be removed from the troopers' uniforms. The men who joined the 112th after July 1942 may never have seen the unit's insignia.

The basin style helmet of the World War I doughboy was used until it was replaced by the World War II style pot-shaped helmet in mid–1941. Their outfits were completed by laced boots and spurs. The saber had been abolished as a cavalry weapon in 1934.

Unlike the infantry, cavalrymen were issued side arms (Colt .45s) that later distinguished them from regular infantry while in the Southwest Pacific. Once the regiment was dismounted no replacement .45s were issued.

Recruits were initially trained with the bolt action Springfield 03 rifle, so called because it had been the U.S. Army's standard rifle since 1903. But late in 1941, it would be replaced by the main army weapon for the next war, the .30 caliber M1 rifle. After a shot was fired, the M1 automatically ejected the shell and inserted another. A shooter could expend an eight-round clip in 20 seconds. The weapon was accurate at 500 yards and had a maximum firing distance of 3500 yards. After they went overseas officers were given the lighter M1 carbine, about which C.W. commented, "It wasn't much more than a .22!"

Each soldier's serial number was engraved on his pair of dog tags and at no time were these to be removed from one's person. C.W. learned the importance of these little metal tags around his neck right from the start. The first time he went to headquarters to pick up a pass to go to town, First Sergeant

Reeves asked him for his serial number. "I reached down and pulled out my dog tags and started to read," he remembered. The First Sergeant abruptly stopped him and told him not to come back until he learned it. C.W. never forgot that experience and without hesitation he could recite his eight-digit army serial number fifty years later.

Seeb was assigned to a rifle platoon in G Troop. His first platoon sergeant was Lester Dorton and the squad leader was Corporal Jack Taylor of Abilene. These assignments didn't last long, however, for commanders and non-commissioned officers in rifle platoons were constantly being shuffled or transferred.

Wiggins was not one to call attention to himself. His philosophy was simple: Keep your mouth shut and never volunteer for anything. Of course this wasn't difficult for someone whose twelve-year-old aunt had to act as his spokesman in his first grade class because he wouldn't respond to the teacher. It wasn't long before C.W.'s quiet and serious demeanor made an impression on the other G troopers.

"We called him 'Bull' because he didn't take nothing off nobody," said Pug. "And (he) never had a fight, I don't guess. C.W. was quite a guy. Everybody liked him. He didn't talk much, but when he got mad he was like a bull!"

One of the Abilene cowboys first tagged him with the nickname "Bull" — "Bull" Wiggins. "The way it happened," C.W. stated, "me and Joe Bynum were wrestling around there in the barracks. I bent over and charged him — butted him in the stomach with my head. He started callin' me 'Bull' and it spread like wildfire!"[14]

Serving in the same rifle platoon with C.W. was the younger Wright brother, Robert "Pickett" Wright. Less verbose than his older brother, baby-faced Pickett was initially influenced by the hard drinkers in 1st platoon, but as he matured, Robert caught the eye of his superiors and would be the leader of a squad of men when he went into his first combat.

On February 6, 1941, the 112th Cavalry Regiment departed Fort Bliss for garrison duty at Fort Clark, Texas. When the troop train left for Fort Clark, Pug Wright was not on board, because he was still on extra duty for Sergeant Reeves.

2

Fort Clark

The 112th Cavalry's train traveled some 450 miles to the southeast from El Paso before it reached the assigned destination. As the troopers emerged from railway cars, it may have seemed they were being deposited in the middle of nowhere. There was no depot, only a few shacks and some shipping pens, surrounded by endless barren prairie. It was later learned the place was called Spofford and everything that came in by rail for Fort Clark had to be unloaded there and taken to Brackettville by truck. C.W. Wiggins, Pickett Wright and the others were herded into army trucks and headed out on the narrow road for the final ten miles of their trip. The surrounding country was desolate—desert spotted with short mesquite and chaparral. The landscape was broken by an occasional windmill.

The trucks finally arrived at the entrance to Fort Clark. Across the road was Brackettville, Texas, a town of less than 2000 that was supported by the free-spending soldiers and nearby ranchers. The military vehicles passed through the fort's gate, crossed Las Moras Creek Bridge, and drove up the gentle slope past a row of limestone buildings, parade ground and post hospital before stopping next to a row of typical two story wooden army barracks.

Just north of the stone barracks, the elevation drops abruptly to creek level. The Los Moras Spring issued cold, clear water that eventually flowed into the Rio Grande River. Massive Live oak, pecans, and white oak grew seventy to eighty feet along the creek's banks. Despite its location in south Texas, Fort Clark is 1133 feet above sea level and has an average daily temperature of 84 degrees. It falls off in the evening, making the nights cool and pleasant. The winters are mild, but summer days could be oppressively humid for men at work.

Founded as a cavalry post in 1852, Fort Clark was only twenty miles from the Rio Grande, a river that separated Texas from Mexico. Established to protect the Texas frontier from Indian depravations and Mexican bandits, the fort had been home to some of the United States Army's most illustrious figures. Colonel Ronald S. Mackenzie, Lieutenant George S. Patton, and General Jonathan Wainwright served there. During the Civil War it was occupied by the Confederates and U.S. Army units at Fort Clark had tracked the Comanche, the Apache, and Pancho Villa's raiders. The fort's famous Seminole Negro scouts earned four Medals of Honor.

The old fort still sported numerous nineteenth-century stone buildings built of limestone taken from the nearby quarry. The most commanding structure at the post was the three-story commissary building that boasted a modern ice plant. Across the road and a block west was the guard house. Officers' quarters made up the west side of the spacious parade ground and to the north were stone barracks that housed A, B, and C Troops. The parade ground was cut in half by a row of buildings that included the post theater, adjutant's office and the hose house. The only church on the post was Catholic so men of other faiths had the option to attend Sunday services in Brackettville.

While the three original National Guard Troops of the regiment received the better stone barracks, the later organized troops were left with regular two-story wooden army barracks. However, even these provided the first electrical conveniences and indoor plumbing many of the rural Texans had experienced. Of course the central heat and the warm water for the showers came from a wood fire that had to be stoked and fed to keep it going. A wood detail to feed the fires was an everyday function.

In the barracks a man said good-bye to privacy. Men ate, bathed, slept, and went to the toilet alongside others. It didn't bother Pug Wright much, because in his case, he had more personal space than back at the farm. There were so many children in his family, the boys all slept in one room and the girls slept in another. He once complained that "there were so many boys, we had to sleep head-foot, head-foot. You always had to smell the other fellow's feet."

Certain types of individuals emerged in the barracks society: the loudmouth, the brown-noser, the gold brick, and there were those you couldn't trust. Newly arrived troopers soon learned who not to loan money.

New men were indoctrinated in traditional army jargon. They quickly learned the meaning of such terms as top kick (first sergeant), dog robber[1] (officer's orderly), mess hall (where meals were served); and latrine (toilet). There were also terms unique to the cavalry like farrier (a horseshoer) and saddler. The unaccustomed also had to adjust to the constant and crude use of obscenities by the non-commissioned officers (NCOs) and fellow troopers.

That spring, G Troop acquired a new troop commander when First Lieutenant Lloyd Leonard was transferred from Machine Gun Troop. Pug maintained that Leonard "couldn't laugh; he was sarcastic! He always called me 'Wright' and Pickett 'Robert L.' He would say, 'Wright! Why can't you be more like Robert L.' His ole lady looked like (First Lady) Eleanor Roosevelt. She ran the troop while we were in the States." Wright added that it only took some wise guy at formation to holler "Eleanor" to raise Leonard's ire.

Once settled in at Fort Clark, C.W. was issued his most essential piece of cavalry equipment, a sorrel mount called Tiger. "Prior to going in (the army)," he recalled, "I had a mare named Daisy I had raised from a colt. I liked horses until I went into the army, then I hated them! You had to feed 'em before you ate — you had to groom 'em before you ate!"

Each cavalry horse had its own serial number tattooed inside the ear. The animals received a field ration of nine pounds of oats and nineteen pounds of hay each day, along with a daily ounce of salt. The Army preferred geldings because stallions fought and mares kicked. However, C.W. remarked, "The best horse I had in the cavalry was a black mare."

The new recruits were stuck with either aging cavalry horses or unmanageable broncos. If an officer or a non-commissioned officer liked the mount of a trooper of lower rank, he could appropriate that horse for his own. But one particular horse in the troop that no one wanted was named "Squirrel Head." The veteran Abilene G Troopers always made it a point to warn new recruits that "Squirrel Head" had once killed a man!

Pickett remarked, "After he killed a guy, they sentenced ole Squirrel Head to death. A new guy got into his stall. Bird Dog Lane rode him right before they took him out and shot him."

Even though C.W. and the Wrights had ridden often, they still had to learn how to ride cavalry style, called posting. The rider had to sit erect in the McClellan saddle, rise up and down in the stirrups, and touch back in the saddle along with his mount's trotting gait. Troopers also learned to mount cavalry style, in counted sequence. Upon the command "prepare to mount" the rider put his left foot in the stirrup then swung into the saddle when the command "mount" was given.

Men and horses were trained to ride in column, four abreast. Each fourth man became a horse handler when the other three dismounted for combat. While in the field, horses were hitched to a picket line where they were given a nose bag of grain. Hay was left on the ground at night.

Unlike C.W. and Pug, many of the new troopers had never ridden a horse before joining the cavalry. C.W. laughed about the time a newly transferred soldier from Detroit was told to go over to the corral and pick out a horse. "The Troop had two mules that pulled the 'S' (Manure) wagon. This guy went over to the corral and tried to put a bridle on one of those mules!"

Pug remembered the poor horsemanship of a pair of brothers from the Midwest who were with G Troop when he arrived: "They were both big, about 18–19 years old and they had never seen a horse — except hooked to a milk wagon. They put one of 'em on a runaway horse down at (Fort) Clark. That ole horse would just bite down on that bit and you couldn't stop him when we'd go jumping hurdles. We'd come in at 11:30 and that kid would come in about 1:30–2 o'clock. That horse had run away just as soon as he went through them hurdles!"

Day after day, duties at Fort Clark followed the same pattern, much the same as the cavalry of the 1800s: mounted and dismounted drill, target practice, inspections, parades and extra duty. At the

C.W. Wiggins beside stables at Fort Clark, Texas (author's collection; Wiggins family photograph).

specified times, the bugler blew the appropriate calls that regulated the day's routine.

A typical work day at Fort Clark began at 7:00 A.M. with reveille, announced by the firing of the artillery piece next to the guard house. After the horses were fed, mess call was sounded at 7:45. When "boots and saddles" was blown at 8:45, the troopers fell out in front of the barracks and marched to the stables. The remainder of the morning was spent grooming horses or performing mounted drills. At noon, the mounts had to be unsaddled, brushed again, and fed before the men ate. After noon mess, the afternoon was spent in training or on the firing range practicing with rifles or a machine gun. The post had a spacious rifle range just west of the fort, its range limited only by the post boundary three miles away. Riflemen received

Pug Wright "horsing around," officers' row, Fort Clark, Texas (author's collection; Wright family photograph).

points, increasing in value the closer one got to the center, or bull's eye, of the target. If the shooter completely missed the target, the marking trooper inside the pit waved "Maggie's Drawers."

"We had stable guard, regimental guard (duty), and K.P. every week," Pug Wright explained. K.P., which included cutting logs for the wood burning stoves, lasted from 5 A.M. to 9 P.M. The army's cooks particularly enjoyed having someone to boss around and left no doubt about their enjoyment of their victims' misery as they cleaned pots and pans, scrubbed the floor, peeled potatoes, or suffered through the absolute worst chore of chopping a seemingly endless number of onions.

Stable duty began at 6 A.M. and lasted a whole day. After the 200 or so horses of the troop were watered and fed, the three privates and a corporal rotated guard shifts until the following morning. When the troop took their mounts out for drill, the men on stable duty had to clean out the stalls with pitchforks and load the manure and wet hay into the "shit" wagon before placing new hay in the stalls. Work in the stable and horse stalls continued all day so it would be ready for inspection when the next day's shift arrived.[2]

"The last time I saw my platoon sergeant was on stable guard," Pug said. "He told me, 'If that O.D. (officer of the day) comes down here, tell him I've gone to the latrine.' I said OK. Sure enough, at 2 o'clock the next morning, the officer of the day showed up. And he wanted to know where sergeant of the guard was. I said, 'He just went to the latrine.' But he had gone A.W.O.L. He was gone about a week. They busted him back down to a private. I think he transferred to the air force. Jack Taylor replaced him as my sergeant."

For recreation, troopers could catch a movie at the post theater or request a pass to go into Brackettville or other nearby towns. "Brackettville had a hardware store, a grocery store and them two honkytonks, the Hilltop and the Lone Oak," Pug explained. "In peacetime you were off. You had three nights you couldn't go to town (because of the routine extra duty). Of course, that $21 a month, you spent that the first payday night. If you didn't go to the PX (Post Exchange) and get your toiletries the first day you didn't get them."

Pug noted that Uvalde, Del Rio and Eagle Pass were all within a forty-mile radius. "Me and Pickett played (our guitars) with that regimental band down there at schools, picnics at Eagle Pass, Del Rio. We knew seven school teachers over at Eagle Pass. If you got stranded, we'd just call one of them and they'd pick you up. Pickett had a girlfriend at Carta Valley.

"Some of the guys had cars down there (at Clark): Van Sawyer had a car, Spider Moody had a car, and another ole boy from Childress I ran around with had a Chevrolet. The Abilene guys, every weekend, they got into their cars and went home. Guys like me and C.W. couldn't."

At the bottom of each pass was the notation: "You have been repeatedly warned about the dangers of venereal disease ... if you have had sexual intercourse, you will report to the Station Hospital for prophylactic treatment. Violation of this order will result in disciplinary action!"

Lieutenant Jesse Stallings was commander of the machine gun platoon for much of the time Pug, and later C.W., were assigned to it at Fort Clark. Stallings was nicknamed "Dude," because of his gentlemanly style and tall slender build.

Each of the troop's four machine gun squads was composed of a corporal, two machine guns, six men with horses, and two packhorses to carry ammunition, although G Troop did not pack ammunition on horses during field exercises. Each man learned how to fire his gun, take it apart, clean it, and put it together again. When on maneuvers, Pug and the other troopers in his platoon had to repeatedly pack, unpack, assemble and disassemble the .30 caliber machine guns for transportation on the packhorses. One member of the machine gun crew led the packhorse. His job was to quickly dismount, unstrap and remove the receiver, tripod and ammunition from the pack animal, then lead the squad's mounts away.

Near the end of May, 1941, the 112th Cavalry Regiment received orders to decamp for Fort Bliss and prepare for the Louisiana Maneuvers, scheduled for that August. The troopers were loaded into the regiment's GI trucks for the two day trip to El Paso. A night was spent in bivouac on the grounds of old Fort Davis, in ruins since its abandonment by the army in 1891.

Once they reached Fort Bliss, the regiment was assigned a bivouac area for the summer "in these hot tents out in the boondocks!" Amid withering temperatures, field exercises with its sister regiment, the 124th Cavalry, would be the order of the day. After G Troop settled in, Pug and Pickett received a visit that night from their brother, Aubort, who was there awaiting an assignment following his enlistment.

"There was a little radio station there," Aubort recalled. "and the three of us were scheduled to play there on the following weekend. But then I shipped out and Pug had my guitar!"[3]

Pug was proud of the newly acquired guitar and also his new horse, selected from one of the 6500 mounts at Fort Bliss. "I took that Lazy Joe horse — he had a Lazy Joe Brand — and every mornin' when I got on him, he'd buck me off. So (Hollis) Hutchins, my buddy, had one that would rear up and jump just as far as he could and then run. Well, he'd tear that column of four horses up and so they stopped us from riding in column. They put me and him to riding patrol between the 112th and the 124th Cavalry. We just rode at will and one day one of those Yankees let a packhorse get away and I run him down. I chased him about two miles. He bucked until he bucked all the guns off his pack, even his feed, a pack of oats. I caught this horse, so they made me lead him from then on."

As was the custom in the cavalry, when a sergeant took a liking to Lazy Joe he took him for his own mount. Pug had to pick another horse from the remounts. This horse, named Happy Jack, served Pug for the remainder of his tenure at Fort Clark:

"Ole Happy Jack had been in the army about 16–17 years," Pug noted. "As long as somebody led him he was okay. He had four stocking feet, blaze face and that packhorse had three stocking feet and blaze face — both of 'em looked just alike."

The regiment operated in the mountains around Fort Bliss and trained for the traditional cavalry missions — scouting, screening, and escort. Toward the end of its training, the 112th rode in parade along with the 124th Cavalry Regiment and the regiments of the 1st Cavalry Division. Pickett remarked that it was the largest assemblage of horsemen in United States Army history (at least since the Civil War) and never again would anywhere near this number of U.S. cavalrymen ride in review together.

"There were men and horses as far as the eye could see," he boasted. "G Troop passed right in front of the review stand!"

"It took all day," recalled a veteran trooper named Herb Campbell. "About 12,000 men and horses once around at the walk with all units saluting and dipping guidons. Then around at a trot, then around at a gallop. This was a sight to see.... Of course, at the gallop, all you could see was a big cloud of dust, about five miles in circumference.[4]

Veteran Abilene G Troopers warned the newcomers about the arduous Louisiana maneuvers of 1940, and in August the regiment was scheduled to take part in the 1941 edition. Nineteen divisions, 342,000 men of the United States 2nd and 3rd Armies were to take part in the largest peacetime exercise in U.S. history. It also would be the last hurrah for the 56th Brigade along with most of the United States' cavalry. Never again would the Army's horsemen participate in maneuvers anywhere approaching these numbers.

General Walter Krueger's 3rd Army was to "invade" the United States and the 2nd Army was to "defend." The boundaries for the exercise were the entire state of Louisiana. The 3rd Army attacked north from Lake Charles on September 15. The 56th brigade, which included the 112th Cavalry, was to be the eyes and ears of Krueger's army while covering its left flank along the east bank of the Sabine River. To the brass, this would be the U.S. Army's main training exercise prior to war. For the men, it was an exercise in mud, mosquitoes, and misery.

One 3rd Army officer wrote: The maneuvers were "where I don't think any human beings have been for over fifty years. We found snakes all over the place, rattlers; we killed fifteen, twenty rattlers a day, and we were just torn apart by ticks. A lot of men had poison oak.... It was a hundred degrees in the daytime and forty or thirty at night. You would go down and take a shower and by the time you get back, you were just as dirty and sweaty as you were when you left. Because of dysentery, all of the mess equipment had to be scalded before and after we ate."[5]

After picking up the horses at the Shreveport train station, the 112th operated in the Mansfield area, which the Texans described as 'the sticks.' "The day began at 4 A.M. and ended at 10 P.M.," recalled C.W. "The red bugs (chiggers) were terrible! All we had to put on 'em was kerosene. They just drank it and kept eatin'!"

Despite the hardships suffered by the men, Louisiana was even harder on the horses. The animals lost weight and developed sores; large numbers of mounts broke down from exhaustion. Many of the trails were wide enough for only one horse so there would be a long line of cavalry, each trooper following the man and horse in front of him with no idea where they were going.

"Our horses were rode to death," said C.W. "Ole Tiger broke down so bad, I couldn't even lead him. I hung around an old country grocery store for days until a truck finally came after me and the horse. I didn't see that horse again after that. But, I would have rather been there than with the troop."

The adventurous Pickett Wright tired of the incessant rain and mud; "We

G Troop detraining near Shreveport for 1941 Louisiana Maneuvers (author's collection; Wright family photograph).

were ridin' rear guard. So many men were fallin' out we just left." Pickett and two other troopers rode to nearby Alexandra, Louisiana. They deposited their horses in a corral outside the city and spend three days in town.

"On the way back, we were captured by this dang artillery outfit," he bemoaned. "We sat down with these mess kits. I told them, 'I'm going to leave here as soon as we finish eating.' When we finished, we made a run for the horses. This captain yelled, 'You can't leave, YOU'RE CAPTURED!' It took us three days to find G Troop. Every farmhouse we stopped at, we had chicken. Louisiana must have been full of chickens at that time."

So many troopers were dropping out there was no reason not to believe their story about being captured, so Pickett and the others escaped censure. However, one of Pickett's wayward buddies was one to press his luck and he disappeared.

The breakdown in the unit's effectiveness during the maneuvers led to the replacement of the regiment's commander, Colonel Clarence Parker, with Colonel Harry Johnson, formerly of the 124th Cavalry.

Another casualty of the exercises was C.W. It happened while he was riding in the back of a truck, sitting with his back against a partition between him and some cavalry horses. He was eating a triple-decker sandwich when

Unit of 112th Cavalry crossing a bridge during 1941 Louisiana Maneuvers (courtesy of the Texas Military Forces Museum, U.S. Army photograph).

one of the horses leaned across the dividing wall and bit C.W. on the head, breaking the skin. C.W. looked up at the grinning horse and couldn't resist giving the animal a sound thrashing even though abusing a mount was a severe breach of cavalry regulations.

Like C.W. and Pickett, Pug had his own troubles in Louisiana.

"They charged us for everything we lost in Louisiana," he said. "I got docked $360. Might have been deducted from my check, but it was so little, you couldn't tell anyway! I lost my tent poles, lost my tent, I lost my bridle, I lost my saddle, but they found my horse. I put him in the sick pasture down there. We lived three days in a stack of peanuts. When he got back (to Fort Clark), Happy Jack got well, got real fat."

"In Louisiana we had C-rations," Pug recalled. "They came out with ten in one and all the new rations during World War II. And they cooked bread in ovens. It was just like a football — cooked with that thick crust on it so it would stay fresh. Once ole Tucker, he just throw'd one loaf from one truck to another and hit ole Willingham right between the eyes; and boy, the fight was on!"

"There were rumors we were goin' back to Clark," Pug chuckled. "So I got loose and went to town. Got pretty well lit, got to drinkin'. I came in, two or three of us, about 1:30 or 2:00 in the morning. I went down through there wakin' everybody up and I told 'em 'Pack Out! We're goin' to Clark!' Half of 'em didn't believe me, so they went to R.D. Jones — R.D. was just a private then and asked him if that was so. R.D. said, 'Anything Pug Wright said, I'll back it a hundred percent.'

"So they all started reelin' up their tents. By daylight, they had everything packed, loaded, ready to go. That damn first sergeant came out and bawled them out at formation. He wanted to know who told 'em — 'Pug Wright passed the word down last night!' So he put me on the shit list again."

The maneuvers ended on September 28, but it was almost a week before the whole regiment returned to Fort Clark. When G Troop's trucks drove up in the troop area, Pickett's wayward buddy that went A.W.O.L. in Louisiana was there waiting for them. "When we came back, he came out across the parade ground to greet us," laughed C.W. "They threw him in the brig for two or three days then let him out."

As punishment for telling G Troop to fall out in the middle of the night, Pug Wright was given the extra duty of cleaning the cook's field ovens.

"We had two hats," Pug recalled, "but the one I wore all the time was old. That crease in the top of that Smokey Bear hat, well, it had holes in it. I was cleaning in those stoves out there and ole Sergeant Dorton came by and took his knife and run it in the holes and cut the top out of my hat. 'You s.o.b., I'm gonna stand inspection tomorrow evening with that hat!' He just laughed.

"The next evening at retreat inspection, I pulled my hair up through the top of that hat. I was in the back platoon, machine gun, which was the last one inspected. Ole Leonard came down that line. He'd come up to a guy makin' half rights. He walked up in front of me and made a half right and his eyes popped out. 'Wright! What's wrong with your hat?' I said, 'It's got a hole in it.' He said, 'After the formation, you go by the supply and tell Sergeant Harris to give you a new hat.

"That ole supply sergeant, after we got overseas, he would steal our mess kits we'd left hanging in the bushes and issue them back to you, just to aggravate you. He just acted like he was paying for all that supply. So I walked in that supply and said, 'Sergeant, the Captain told me to get a new hat; this one's got a hole in it.' 'You ain't gonna get a new hat in here!!' Of course he knew we had another one.

"The next day at retreat, I fell out with that hat (and) I pulled my hair up through it. Ole Leonard came down through there — he was Irish in the first place — and when he turned around his face got so red. 'I thought I told you to get a new hat!' 'Sergeant Harris said he didn't have one.' He said, 'You go back by that supply room after this formation. He WILL have a hat.'

"Just as soon as he got through inspection, he went to the orderly room. He must have called ole Harris. I went by that supply — 'Sergeant Harris, the Captain told me to get a hat again.' He throw'd me two hats, three pair of breeches and said, 'Just take ever damn thing in here!' "

While the cavalry was in Louisiana, the United States Congress extended the one-year enlistees term of service to eighteen months. However, the Army also instituted a policy to discharge soldiers that met certain criteria and were over twenty-eight years old.

Among those discharged were the G Troop Top Kick, the troop farrier, and a member of Stallings' machine gun platoon. General Krueger inspected the regiment in October, but C.W. was home in Loraine, his first leave since joining the army. The extension of his enlistment meant he had slightly more than nine months to go before his "one year commitment" was up.

That same month, the regiment received a large contingent of replacements. These fifty or so men, fresh from basic training at Fort Riley, Kansas, were spread out among the seven troops of the 112th. Most of the newcomers were from Illinois and Michigan. Among the Texans, there was still a heritage of sectionalism passed down from their Confederate ancestors. This led to resentment and suspicion of the Northerners. These feelings passed with time and lasting friendships developed between the Texans and midwesterners. C.W. counted the burly, astute Ray Czerniejeski and Frank "Harbo" Harbiezwski, the large easy-going Pole from Michigan, among his closest friends in the regiment.

At five foot six inches, the top of C.W.'s head barely surpassed the top of Harbiezwski's shoulders. One wartime photograph shows Harbo holding C.W. aloft with one arm and another trooper with the other.

The 112th Cavalry also received a new commander that November. Harry Johnson was promoted to brigadier general and was replaced as regimental commander by Colonel Julian Cunningham, a regular army officer. Cunningham secured his commission in 1917 and served the Army in multiple capacities. He had been involved with a number of units, from National Guard outfits to the Philippine Scouts on Luzon. Cunningham was a senior umpire during the Louisiana Maneuvers and obviously was not impressed with what he saw of the former National Guard cavalry units.[6]

Forty-nine-year-old Colonel Cunningham came with the reputation as a demanding, aloof, and fiery army officer. At first, subordinates either feared or disliked him. However, Cunningham's men grew to respect him and he had a genuine fondness for them. His adjutant, Lieutenant Colonel Philip Hooper, recognized Cunningham's affection for his men and saw that emotion first hand when the regiment experienced casualties in the Pacific.[7]

The newest troopers from Fort Riley arrived just in time to replace the men recently released from the Army because of their age. However, the ex-cavalrymens' freedom lasted only about two months before an event occurred that would result in their recall and forever affect the lives of all the members of G Troop.

The December 6, 1941, edition of the Fort Clark newspaper, *The Centaur*, was all about preparations for the Christmas holidays. Elaborate plans were being made by the regimental morale officer for a big dance at the airport hanger and army trucks were to bring girls from Del Rio, Eagle Pass and Brackettville for the party. More interesting to many of the troopers was the news that fifty percent of the command would be granted Christmas furloughs and all men in the regiment were to receive ten days of leave.[8] Within twenty-four hours these plans would have to be put on hold.

"On December 7, I was in the G Troop mess hall at Fort Clark when they announced that Pearl Harbor had been bombed by the Japanese!" C.W. recalled. So much for getting his discharge in July, he was now in for the duration.

Pug Wright was in Piedras Negras (just across the Rio Grande), Mexico, that fateful Sunday. "That night we came back (across the border) and rented us a room in Eagle Pass. Next morning, we walked out of there and an old lady and old man — in a big ole car — stopped us in the street and said they bombed Pearl Harbor and that ole lady was cryin'. I patted her on the back and I said, 'Don't worry about it, we'll whip them before breakfast!' "

The next day, Pug and Pickett were walking from the troop area to the Post Exchange when Captain Leonard stopped them and announced the news that war had been declared against Japan and Germany. While President Roosevelt was declaring over the radio that the United States was at war, the 112th Cavalry was on alert and confined to post until further notice.

All leaves were cancelled and most of the regiment was distributed to locations deemed potential targets of saboteurs or spies. Various troops were dispatched to guard the international bridges at Del Rio and Eagle Pass, the major railroad bridges on the Mexican border, and the area's airports. Troop G received the assignment to man Fort Clark.

Rumors abounded over the next few weeks about where the regiment would ultimately be sent, anywhere from Alaska to Panama, although Australia or the Philippines appeared to be the most likely travel destinations. Barracks bags were packed and unpacked, depending upon the latest scuttlebutt.

"They issued one round (of ammunition) to each man right after war was declared," Pickett remembered. "This rookie was put on guard at the front gate. The corporal of the guard told him that when anyone came through the gate, holler three times then shoot! The colonel's driver always just slowed down and waved when he came through because everyone knew the colonel's car. Ole Cunningham came through in his car and his driver slowed down. The boy on guard hollered three times. The driver sped up and that guy fired a shot into the turtle of Cunningham's car. They took up the ammunition the next day!"

Eventually the hysteria subsided, furloughs became available on a limited basis, and Fort Clark gradually returned to a normal routine, although the base was always on alert. If the guardhouse cannon fired three times, the men had to report back to their troop area, whether on duty or on pass in Brackettville. Then there were the boring weekly orientation lectures on the causes and implications of the war. Amazingly, the Army was slow in implementing infantry training, which would obviously supplant the cavalry in a modern war.

When the 113th Cavalry Regiment (Iowa National Guard) moved in and established camp on the old polo field across the street from G Troop, there was the usual banter back and forth between the rival soldiers. C.W. didn't go in for such horseplay, but he and Pickett Wright became interested observers as the rivals challenged one another across the road.

Pickett recalled that after the 113th Cavalry set up across the road from G Troop's barracks, "one of our guys who had a big mouth was out there hollering insults at them. This big Swede came out and wanted to know who was calling them names. The loudmouth snuck back into the barracks, but Ole Hillison walked out and said, 'I did! What are you going to do about it?'"

As it turned out, Hillison wasn't part of group that had been bad mouthing the Iowans. Corporal Brigham Young ordered the leader of the group involved in the "good natured heckling" after a day of celebrating pay day in Brackettville to go straighten things out. Hillison had not been part of the "celebration" of the previous evening and offered to settle things with the newcomers for his good friend who started the quarrel.

"Hillison didn't weigh over 140 pounds," continued Pickett. "That Swede hit him right between the eyes and knocked him cold. His nose and both eyes were blackened and he was in bed two or three days."

By the time Brigham Young rousted the troublemaker from his second floor bunk, Hillison was back in the barracks holding his hand over a swollen right eye. Young made the loudmouth go through the chow line, get his food, and bring it back to the barracks for Hillison before he got his own.[9]

In January 1942, 1st Platoon, G Troop, received a new second lieutenant. Contrary to the military's sense of military decorum, this new officer did not let rank intrude on his friendship with the men in his platoon and he spent more time with the privates than with other officers. First Platoon underwent another change a month later when John Coppinger of Abilene replaced Lester Dorton as platoon sergeant.

Not much of interest happened in G Troop during the first few weeks of the war until the day in March that Captain Leonard decided to demonstrate the proper way to jump a horse over an obstacle. The troop commander had grown impatient observing his men's poor technique in jumping their mounts over hurdles. He stopped the exercises and told the assembled troopers that every man and horse would be required to jump the hurdle individually until they jumped it properly. "And remember this," he said, "if a horse misses a jump, it is not the horse's fault but the rider's fault!"

While the entire troop looked on, their captain mounted his horse, trotted out a ways then turned his mount and galloped toward the hurdle. "The horse's front feet failed to clear the hurdle," wrote Lionel Carter of First Platoon. "The horse cart wheeled and then fell on its back, Captain Leonard was thrown from the saddle and landed on his shoulder about ten feet in front of the fallen horse." An ambulance was called for and the captain was carried away with a broken collarbone and a ruffled ego. The troop solemnly rode back to camp without completing the exercise.[10]

The day after Easter Sunday, Fort Clark was assaulted by a vicious wind storm. Large trees were uprooted and one crashed through the roof of one of the wooden barracks. The porch roof that ran the length of A Troop's brick barrack was torn off and flung onto the orderly room. Following the wind and dust, the rain fell so hard that it obscured the view of the Iowans' mangled pyramid tents across the road from Second Squadron's barracks. The storm abated in less than an hour and the curious ventured from their buildings to view the damage. Miraculously, no one was seriously hurt.[11]

The first six months of the war in the Pacific went badly for the United States. The Japanese overran most of New Guinea and New Britain, and Australia was under air attack. In the Philippine Islands, American forces on Bataan capitulated on April 9, 1942, and the island of Corregidor was under heavy bombardment. The commanding general in the Philippines, Douglas MacArthur, escaped by P.T. boat and on May 6 General Wainwright surrendered the remaining U.S. forces in the Philippines.

Since war was declared, the troops of the 112th had been taking turns guarding the three major Southern Pacific railroad bridges near the Mexican border. G Troop's turn came the third week in April. With a grain of sarcasm, C.W. remarked, "They thought someone would come out of Mexico and blow 'em up!"

On April 22, 1942, C.W.'s platoon loaded into trucks and set out for outpost duty. They traveled west across country similar to that around Fort

New Pecos River Railroad Bridge. The bridge guarded by 1st platoon, G Troop, was dismantled and in 1948 was rebuilt across the Wabash River in Indiana (author's collection; Wiggins family photograph).

Clark — desert with frequent rises and depressions. The only flora was short mesquite, chaparral and cacti.

One G Troop platoon, plus a machine gun squad, went to the bridge spanning Devil's River, a second platoon plus a machine gun squad went to the Meyers Canyon Bridge, and Pickett's First platoon drew the Pecos River Bridge assignment.

After a dusty trip of seventy-five miles, the troop's trucks carrying Pickett's platoon arrived at the edge of an immense canyon, over 300 feet deep with the meandering Pecos River flowing between the bases of a mighty railroad bridge. At that time, the Pecos River High Bridge (built in 1892) was one of the world's longest — 2,180 feet long and 321 feet above water. In most places, the sides of the 200 foot wide canyon were almost a straight drop. The confluence of the Pecos and the Rio Grande was just to the south of the bridge and Judge Roy Bean's legendary "Jersey Lilly" saloon was only eighteen miles farther west.

The G troopers assigned to the High Bridge took over the wooden-floored pyramid tents evacuated by A Troop which had preceded them there. Kitchen equipment was also provided for the mess hall, which had a cement floor. Guard posts and sand-bagged machine gun positions were located on both sides of the bridge and all trains had to stop before crossing from either direction.

Another guard post was down at river level under the bridge. It took over thirty minutes to transverse the steep incline to the post down below. Pickett enjoyed river level duty, because he was free from inspections and had time for pastimes like fishing. He also made friends with a man who ran a pumping station along the river. The civilian guard and his wife who had a little house under the bridge often gave the cavalrymen on river duty home-made cinnamon rolls and coffee.

Guard duty at the bridge was a boring assignment. Trains were searched and cleared before crossing; hobos had to be pulled off and returned to the nearest town. In addition, Captain Leonard made sure the men had plenty of routine drill and extra duty to keep them busy. He also held a full dress uniform inspection at the end of the day's details.

Pecos River Bridge duty could be dangerous. When the freight trains stopped for water, a trooper climbed atop the boxcars and made a running check to evict stowaways undetectable from the ground. The boxcar hopping cavalryman had to make sure he jumped off before the train got underway. One night, a member of the platoon completed an evening of drinking in a nearby town and hitched a ride on a freight train back to the High Bridge. As he walked alongside the tracks after detraining the wobbly soldier stumbled and, in and the attempt to break the fall, his left hand clutched the rail. Almost instantaneously, the moving train crushed four of his fingers.[12]

"Once, some idiot shot a train, because they found bullet holes in the boxcars," C.W. noted.

"Most of the time I was up there at Meyer's Canyon," he added. "We had them little trolley cars and every chance we'd get we'd go to Sanderson and go to a show."

Pug's squad was assigned to the bridge over Devil's River, now part of the Amistad Reservoir. Unlike the guards at the Pecos River or Meyers' Canyon, they took along their horses for use in mounted patrols.

"We had a four mile patrol up at Devil's River," recalled Pug, "two miles from the railroad bridge to the highway and two miles down to the Rio Grande. And right under that highway bridge was a beer joint. And the two guys that rode up there in the morning, well, they'd switch at dinner and ride to the river and let the other two go to the beer joint. You'd go down to the river and fish (then) you'd go the other way and you'd drink all day."

While at Devil's River, Trooper Olei's runaway horse ran away once too often and was struck by a train. "We burnt that old horse — gave him a military funeral," Pug noted.

Robert "Pickett" Wright posed behind a .30 caliber heavy machine gun at Pecos River Bridge, 1942 (author's collection; Wright family photograph).

"Dude Stallings was our commander out there," he continued. "He had a '41 Ford convertible and we'd climb up that telephone pole on that railroad and tie that field phone up to them wires and talk to them operators in Del Rio. And we'd get ole Dude dates (and) he'd go get them in that new convertible. Boy, it was classy, and Dude was classy, too. He'd bring them ole girls up there — drive 'em right up under that bridge. He'd have two or three in that convertible. They never stayed too long."

First Lieutenant J.D. Stallings was one of the most interesting officers in the regiment. A year younger than Pug Wright, Stallings already had a colorful past. He grew up on a ranch near Bryan, Texas, and became an accomplished rodeo performer at an early age. The adventurous young cowboy joined the Texas National Guard while in his mid-teens. J.D. played "Smoky" the cowboy in the Texas Centennial production, "Cavalcade of Texas" at a Dallas amphitheater and he worked as a stunt rider for Republic Pictures in the late 1930s, becoming noted for his falls from a horse at a full gallop. Stallings worked his way up from a private in Machine Gun Troop, completed Officers' Candidate School and became a platoon leader of G Troop, 112th Cavalry, after the regiment transferred to Fort Bliss in December of 1940.[13] Pug and his platoon's lieutenant also had something in common: they were two of the best story tellers in the Troop and the pair's "tall tales" became legendary among fellow G Troopers.

When the regiment returned to Fort Clark in June, C.W. discovered he had received a raise. As a new recruit, he made only $21 a month and got a $2 clothing allowance. Now, as a private first class, C.W. saw his monthly check jump to $50.

Wiggins also found himself in another platoon. For the remainder of his service with the 112th, C.W. would be a member of machine gun platoon. His new platoon sergeant was an old friend, Jack Taylor, C.W.'s former corporal in the rifle platoon.

Assigned to the same machine gun with C.W. were Alabamian Legion Goodson and an Abilene teenager named Doyle Tucker.[14] Like C.W., Tucker was one of the smaller men in the 112th. Pug remembered that he "couldn't have been more than seventeen when he went in. His daddy got killed in Abilene. Colonel Grant talked him into joining (the army)."

The blonde curly-haired Tucker would spend almost three years with C.W. on the same gun crew, but during the same period several different troopers served as the third man on C.W.'s gun. Among that number were Goodson, Clyde Summers and Frank Harbiezwski at various times. There also was another machine gun crew with which C.W.'s life now became closely intertwined — the trio of Pug Wright, Dewey Johnson and Mudcat Patterson.[15]

After returning from outpost duty, G Troopers began spending less and less time with their horses and more attention was devoted to infantry drill consisting mostly of long hikes in combat gear. Years later, C.W. lectured his grandson who was small for his age, "They didn't think I could do anything because I was too small. When we started those long hikes with full gear I sure showed 'em. When those big guys started stumbling along I said, 'We're fixin' to separate the men from the boys!' "

One large trooper who was gasping for air snarled at the untiring smaller man carrying the same amount of load, "You little s.o.b.! If we fall out, we'll beat the crap out of you!"

C.W. knew it was an idle threat. Bull Wiggins didn't take abuse from anybody.

The weapons that C.W. and Pug would take into combat were Browning air-cooled .30 caliber machine guns. One could fire 450 to 600 rounds a minute and the weapon had an effective range of 1800 yards. Each three man crew consisted of a gunner, an assistant gunner (he fed the ammunition belt into the machine gun) and an ammo bearer. One man was responsible for carrying the thirty-one pound gun; another man carried the tripod that weighed fifteen pounds; and the ammo bearer brought along the 250-round link belt.

Bill Garbo, later a member of G Troop's machine gun platoon, explained that the light machine guns were prone to be unsteady because of the tripod. "You can put the tripod down, put the receiver on the tripod, put the belt in, crank one in the breech, and start firing, but immediately that machine gun will start vibrating and moving about.... You can't steady it as well as a rifle. Even though you have an aiming mechanism on it, you do all this by line of sight — almost like shooting from the hip."[16]

In March 1942, all members of .30 caliber machine gun crews received additional training on operation of the weapon. Members of each squad fired 150 rounds on the machine gun range.

That June, the regiment received word that it would soon be deployed to the Pacific Theater of the war. Troopers were issued new equipment, including tropical uniforms, and they received inoculations for yellow fever and typhoid. However, the continual care of the horses interfered with the amount of time that could be devoted to infantry training.

Prior to shipping out from Clark for overseas assignment, the 112th received a contingent of replacements from its sister regiment in the 56th Brigade, the 124th Cavalry.[17] G troop received a dozen or so of the transfers, including Malcom Tarleton of Ralls, Texas, who joined C.W.'s squad in machine gun platoon.

When the 9th Cavalry arrived at Fort Clark at the end of June it was just a matter of time before the 112th shipped out. On Sunday, July 5, the cavalry horses were turned over to the 9th and the "Buffalo Soldiers" assumed control of Fort Clark two days later.

The inevitable happened on July 8, 1942, when the 112th received orders to prepare to move out. That afternoon, the regiment was loaded into trucks for the trip to Spofford, where they boarded a troop train heading west.

Due to security, the Pullman cars' window shades remained drawn and no one was allowed to get off at stops except once for exercise. After a two and a half day hot, sweaty ride through New Mexico, Arizona and Southern California, the regiment's troop train arrived at Pittsburg, California, early in the morning of July 11. There was another truck ride to their temporary home, Camp Stoneman.

3

San Francisco to Down Under

Located in a valley at the foot of the Diablo Mountain Range, Camp Stoneman was the staging area for the San Francisco port of embarkation. During World War II, this sprawling military complex eventually increased its facilities to quarter over 38,000 soldiers.

The 112th Cavalry Regiment was housed in new barracks amidst all types of military units. There was a great deal of hostility between outfits and ridicule was especially directed at the horse soldiers, perhaps because of the cavalrymen's uniforms — Smokey the Bear hat, riding breeches and spurs.

An artillery outfit in adjacent barracks especially gave the Texans a hard time. One day, Troop G was marching in formation when things almost got out of hand. "That outfit kept callin' us 'horses,' 'horse manure' and everything else," Pug Wright recalled. "Ole Sergeant Currier stopped us out in the street. We were goin' to get that stopped real quick: A battalion of them and a troop of us. The first squadron bailed out and they were comin' down the street to help us."

Several of the more outraged troopers broke ranks and were heading toward the artillery men when Captain Leonard and an Army colonel intervened, preventing a riot. The cavalry and the artillery would have to continue their battles off base at the bars of Pittsburg.

During their brief stay at Camp Stoneman, troopers that received twenty-four hour passes could take the bus into San Francisco, a city of hills: Nob, Telegraph and others rising from the coast. The "City by the Bay" was also famous for its Barbary Coast, China Town, and the Golden Gate Bridge. During the war, San Francisco was alive with military personnel from all branches of the service.

Pug Wright vividly remembered first his pass to the City:

Headquarters and Service Troops preparing to board a Southern Pacific train near Pittsburg, California, for transportation to disembarkation point in San Francisco, 20 July 1942 (courtesy of the Texas Military Forces Museum, U.S. Army photograph).

"Me, Mac, and Smitty went down to the USO. This red-headed woman asked us to come to her place for a spaghetti dinner. She lived on Signal Hill in one of them apartment houses. It had buzzers you pushed for someone to come down and open the door. We pushed them all and finally someone came down. Another man was there with the redhead. We had the spaghetti dinner. Smitty kept eating flower pedals and at about twelve o'clock he finally passed out. I thought that woman had rolled him, took his money. We called a cab — carried him out and put him in the cab.

"'Take us to a motel, nothing fancy, all we need is a bed,' I told the driver.

"He took us down to Market Street Hotel. We got a room on the fourteenth floor. We carried ole Smitty up there and throw'd him in bed. Me and Mac left to see the sights.

"We went into this cafe and ordered steak. That steak was so tough my knife flew up and went down the back of my shirt. I complained and this fat waitress came over. I told her the steak was too tough. That's when that ole gal said, 'You guys must have been raised in Texas!' We told her, 'Naw! We RAISE cattle!' Some smart aleck sailor kept popping off, sitting at the bar. I threw a beer bottle and it hit the cash register right beside him. Mac got in his licks, but I didn't hit anyone or get hit. They threw us out of there and we walked right by two MPs who didn't say a thing."

Having spent their money, the trio of cavalrymen had to hitchhike back to Camp Stoneman the next day.

Pickett Wright remembered, "On that waterfront near Stoneman, they went down and battled every night." His good friend Private Richard Riggs was involved in one of these episodes just before the 112th shipped out.

"Ole Riggs was from Colorado and weighed about 220 pounds," Pickett recalled. "He joined us right before we went overseas. He and a buddy got in a fight in one of them bars at Stoneman. The other guy got a broken skull and Riggs always said he wished he had been the one with the cracked skull!"[1]

One night, Pug went to a poker game in Pittsburg with two of the recent transfers from the 124th Cavalry. "One of them was pretty rugged and was a good poker player," Pug remembered. "I guarded the door and they got a whole pile of money on that table. Ole Hector stepped back and picked up his chair and told Mac to rake it in! While he got the money, Hector fought 'em off and we ran out the door."

Other than the passes, the two weeks at Stoneman was military life as usual — extra duty, drills, ten-mile hikes. On Saturday, July 18, the regiment marched in review for Camp Stoneman's commanding general, a former cavalry officer. Private Lionel Carter of First Platoon, G Troop, proudly recounted that "Never before had we marched like that and never again would we march like that, with our boots polished to a mirror-shine that reflected light with every trooper in every troop in step, with our campaign hats bobbing up and down like gentle waves approaching a beach. We were indeed impressive. Our wonderful band played 'To the Colors' in swing, and we marched to 'Deep in the Heart of Texas' and 'The Eyes of Texas Are upon You.'"[2]

The regiment's executive officer, Major A.M. Miller, was also impressed. "I was posted in front of the whole command where I could see everything. I have never seen a finer body of troops nor a more perfect march pass in review — and I have seen a lot of things." [3]

After supper on Monday, the troop marched the mile and a half with full gear to the Southern Pacific train that would take them to a location across the street from Pier 41 in San Francisco. Moored to the dock there in the bay was the biggest object most of the Texans had ever seen. The 599-foot vessel that was to be the cavalrymen's home for the next three weeks was the USS *Republic* (AP-33). However, the ship was generally known as

Members of Troop F proceeding up the gangway onto the S.S. *President Grant* after midnight 21 July 1942 (U.S. Army; courtesy National Archives photograph SC-140757).

the *President Grant,* the name it was christened during World War I when the former liner was confiscated from Germany. The ship was to provide transportation for the regiment to an unnamed destination somewhere in the South Pacific Ocean.

In darkness and amid great security the men, with all their equipment, lined up by troop to be checked off as they ascended the gangplank. Sergeant Charles McDearmont of Machine Gun Troop recalled, "It was a quit and solemn night — nobody around but a few MPs. All one could hear were trooper's names being called out…. As each trooper stepped up to board the ship, the First Sergeant would call out his name, the trooper would answer with his first name and middle initial then proceed up the gangplank." [4]

Army Signal Corps photographs of the event show the troopers to be in khaki uniform, burdened with saddlebags, steel helmet, canteen, raincoat, a .45 automatic and holster attached to a cartridge belt, gas mask, and topped off by a barracks bag slung over the shoulder. The regimental roster of officers and troopers added up to 1547 men.

Formerly a luxury liner of the President line, the *President Grant* had undergone a transformation prior to becoming a military transport. Upon reaching their quarters, the troopers found that the staterooms had been ripped out and tier after tier of bunks separated by a narrow plank corridor had been installed.

After sunrise, July 21, 1942, the *President Grant* pulled away from the pier, sailed past Alcatraz Island and under the 4220-foot-long Golden Gate Bridge. The immense suspension bridge spanning the entrance to San Francisco harbor was the longest single span bridge in the world. For a soldier in the Pacific, the Golden Gate Bridge was as special to PFC Wiggins as the Statue of Liberty was to the soldier returning from Europe.

"I watched that bridge as long as I could — until it disappeared," C.W. remembered. "You can see the bridge longer than anything else."

"This cruiser (the USS *Helena*) stayed with us part of the way," he added. "It had some of those amphibious airplanes (seaplanes). They shot 'em off the back of that ship. When they came back, it had a crane that would pick 'em up."

The twenty-one day ocean voyage aboard the *President Grant* in a slow-moving convoy was not pleasant for C.W. and the other enlisted men of the regiment. The stench from overflowing garbage, body odors, and seasick troopers made the area inside the ship almost intolerable. There were fans in the living quarters, but they provided little relief from the heat and smell. After a couple of days, the men realized the advantage of sleeping outside on the ship's deck.

The enlisted men aboard the *President Grant* were served a breakfast of coffee, a boiled egg, toast and a square of cake, and oxtail soup the rest of the time. Years later, most all the troopers acknowledged how disgusting that soup was and the edibles in the ship's store were exhausted in only a few days.

C.W. cringed when he spoke about the oxtail soup: "It was miserable, but that's all we had — three times a day."

The further out to sea they sailed, any semblance of life disappeared and the seemingly endless blue extended to the horizon. At night, the ship was darkened, all portholes sealed and covered in case a Japanese submarine might be in the area.

"That ship had bombs, torpedoes, all kind of weapons on board," Wiggins observed. "If a torpedo had hit it, it would of blown screws all over that ocean!"

Aside from an enemy submarine alert, the trip was uneventful for the troops. The weather was pleasant, except for the rain. However, too much time in the sun on cloudless days could result in an uncomfortable burn.

Daily activities included mess, abandon ship drill and deck muster inspection. The moist salt air caused metal equipment to rust much quicker than normal. The machine guns were packed away, but the troopers' .45s and rifles had to repeatedly be cleaned to prevent corrosion.

Calisthenics and the occasional inspections broke the monotony, but the main feature of the trip was boredom. Of course, the gamblers had plenty of time to ply their trade at cards and dice, but most of the men just caught up on their sleep. They had plenty of time for reading — if they had anything to read.

No mail was delivered while the regiment was at sea except for one occasion. After a few days at sea, "mail call" was announced. The puzzled troopers assembled and each of them received an envelope of uniform size with a return address of the White House, Wash-

Colonel Julian W. Cunningham and Major Ruppert H. Johnson (1st Squadron Headquarters) converse at the pier 41, San Francisco while troops of the 112th Cavalry Regiment are boarding the *President Grant*; July 20 1942. (U.S. Army; courtesy National Archives photograph SC-140723).

ington D.C. The standardized letter began "To the members of the United States Army Expeditionary Forces" and read, in part, "You have embarked for distant places where the war is being fought. Upon the outcome depends the freedom of your lives: the freedom of the lives of those you love — your fellow citizens — your people." The letter was signed "Franklin D. Roosevelt."[5]

C.W. remembered having heard that the ship's captain didn't even know their destination. He opened an envelope each day which gave him sailing instructions.

A couple of weeks out from San Francisco, Captain Leonard announced the 112th's destination was New Caledonia. Halfway between Fiji and Australia in the South Pacific Ocean, New Caledonia is a cigar-shaped island, 240 miles long and 30 miles in average width. Its total area is about the size of New Jersey, but in 1942, the island had only 61,000 people, most of them French and natives of Polynesian and Melanesian origin. The average

Top: Troops of the 112th Cavalry Regiment at Grand Quay Docks, Noumea, after disembarking from the USAT General Grant. *Bottom:* Australian mounts of the 112th Cavalry, Dumbea Valley, New Caledonia. Troopers can be seen in the background bathing in the river (both photographs courtesy of the Texas Military Forces Museum, U.S. Army photographs).

temperature of New Caledonia ranged from 66 degrees in the winter to 78 degrees with high humidity during the hottest month, February. The climate was ideal except during the rainy season which began in April.

On August 11, 1942, the *General Grant's* passengers spotted the outline of New Caledonia emerge on the southwest horizon. The curious troopers crowded on deck as the big ship eased into the harbor at Noumea, the capital and, with a population of 13,000, the only town of any size on the island. The regimental band struck the Bob Wills country tune "San Antonio Rose" then "The Eyes of Texas" as the regiment disembarked down the gangplank.

"They unloaded that ship for a week," C.W. noted. "As they did, you could see it rise in that water."

Outgoing mail was scrutinized by military censors and all mention of geographic location or military unit designation was blacked out. One trooper wrote a letter home with the instruction, "Give my love to Callie." "Callie" was a prearranged code for New Caledonia. Through this coded letter to a family who knew the Wrights, Pug and Pickett's parents knew where they were stationed soon after their arrival in New Caledonia.

G Troop set up pup tents in a coconut plantation near Noumea for a short stay. After a little over a day, the regiment was loaded in trucks and headed out on the country's only paved highway, a narrow, twisting road along the coast. Fringing the shoreline were the first of many coconut trees the Texans would see and they marveled at the huge spider webs that stretched from tree to tree.

The convoy finally turned off the main road and entered the picturesque Dumbea Valley on a road lined on both sides by tall palm trees. The regiment established camp next to the Dumbea River, only a few feet deep and easily crossed by hopping along the large rocks in its bed. In places, the river formed deep clean pools, which made ideal swimming holes. The men had no bathing suits nor were any needed.

Their homes for the next nine months would be the regiment's pyramidal tents. Troopers utilized the nearby timber for the framework of their six-man floored tents, moved cots in, and prepared for a long stay. Everything seemed so peaceful compared to the violence raging to the north in the Solomon Islands.

While in New Caledonia, the 112th Cavalry Regiment fell under the control of the Navy's Southern Pacific Command and more specifically Major General Alexander Patch, commander of the island's defense force. The 112th would be part of the "American Division," made up of National Guard infantry regiments and regular army artillery battalions.

The outcome in the battle for Guadalcanal was still in doubt and the Allied high command knew that New Caledonia was directly in the path of

Japan's plan for conquest. The Allies were preparing to make a stand in New Caledonia if the Solomon Islands chain fell into the hands of the Japanese. The Army was in the process of building twelve airfields there, but the island would be difficult to garrison. There also were numerous suitable landing beaches along the coast for an invading force to utilize.

"New Caledonia had a string of mountains right in the center of it," Pug related. "There was no way you could take a truck and get to the north side of it without going plum around the end of it. There was a pack mule outfit out of El Paso there. They were put there and we were put there for defense. We could go across the mountains and intercept them (the enemy)."

The cavalry did have at least two physical enemies already present in New Caledonia — mosquitoes and horses!

C.W. remarked that "We wore a head net, but the mosquitoes were sometime so thick you had to wear your raincoat because they would bite right through your clothes. They were bad on the other islands, but not as bad as New Caledonia! I always took my Atabrine. The main thing is — it tasted horrible!"[6]

Some troopers would not take Atabrine because it tasted so bad. This became such a problem that officers were assigned to the chow line to oversee the administration of the pill directly into the recipient's mouth. The clerk would then check the trooper's name off and move to the next man.

After the Atabrine pills came the army chow that wasn't much better tasting. PFC Lionel Carter remembered that eating powdered eggs was bad enough, but the green shade along the edges of the huge container in which they were cooked left them hardly palatable.

Then there was the time on New Caledonia that affable Frank Harbiezwski found worms in his oatmeal. He looked down at the concoction in his mess kit and announced, "I'm Catholic! I can't eat meat on Friday." First Sergeant Dallas Currier overheard the remark and put the devout private to work digging a garbage pit for the kitchen.[7]

Naturally, hungry troopers were always on the lookout for alternatives to army chow. Pickett remembered the time one of the men in his squad killed a calf and had it hanging up in the troop area. Colonel Cunningham came by and called Captain Leonard out.

"'G Troop out here has steak while the rest of 'em are eatin' spam!' he barked.

"They had to bury that calf. I guess the army had to pay for it," noted Pickett.

The cavalrymen expected a shipload of horses from Australia soon after their arrival. Word made the rounds that the transport bringing the mounts was torpedoed and all the horses had drowned.[8] A second shipload of horses would have to be sent.

C.W. was more skeptical than Pug about the cavalry's prospects of defending the island. "I wish the second load of horses had been sunk. Biggest waste of time — cavalry in New Caledonia."

Although C.W.'s new mount was already tame, many of the 1600 "Aussie broncos" (a mixed breed known as Walers) were wild and unbroken to the saddle. These Australian horses were smaller and ornerier than their North American counterparts. The troopers had to first catch and halter the animals then lead them barebacked for several miles a day until the horses would tolerate a saddle. After the horses became accustomed to a saddle, the regiment's "bronco busters" would go to work breaking in this new batch of cavalry mounts.

"Those range broncos looked like wooly mammoths," noted Sergeant Ben Moody of F Troop. "Once we got them clipped, the day came to mount all 1,500 of them. Talk about the world's biggest rodeo. There were horses and men in every direction and many a broken arm.... Maybe 15 to 20 sailors saw the first one, but word got around and next time there were 500. From then on, every time we mounted up we had an audience."[9]

Pickett Wright broke his own horse. "My mare would rear up and go back every time I mounted her. Once she reared up and threw me. My foot got hung in the stirrup and I couldn't get it loose. Ole Big Foot (Thomas) saw me and stopped her — tore his hand up pretty bad. After that, when they said "mount," I mounted her cowboy style."

Later it was decided the regiment should hold a mounted review for Admiral Halsey. Band member Charles Brabham recalled that Troop A began the show. "First time around at the walk was pretty good, but at the command 'trot' and as the band started playing 'Gary Owen' it turned into a rodeo."[10]

In mid–September 1942 the regiment staged an inter-troop competition and track meet with the usual accompanying gambling activities. There were long and short distance running events and non–Olympic contests like the "tug-o-war" and "piggy-back" race. The latter especially stood out in Lionel Carter's mind:

"I remember ... the 'piggy back' race; and I can see in my mind's eye, 140 plus pound 'Bull' Wiggins with his arms wrapped around Ray Czerniejewski's neck and Ray pumping his arms up and down like he was running some sort of dash, winning the event easily." [11]

After the wagers were settled up, there were plenty of losers among troopers who had not actively participated in the games. Pug recalled that C.W. always had plenty of money because he didn't drink or gamble and there was very little else to spend money on in the South Pacific unless you could get a leave to Australia.

Tents of the 112th Cavalry Regiment Dumbea Valley, New Caledonia (U.S. Army photograph; courtesy of the Texas Military Forces Museum).

"I borrowed money from ole C.W.," Pug remarked. "He charged fifty cents on the dollar. C.W. always made payroll and collected what was owed!"

Pug remembered that one thing they didn't have to buy while overseas was cigarettes. "Cigarettes were nine cents a pack until we went overseas, and then we got 'em free — U.S. Army cigarettes. The only kind we could get was 'Piedmonts'— from Australia."

That September, G Troop was assigned guard duty at one of the air bases near Noumea. The sentries could only stand and watch as the bullet-riddled planes came in on a wing and a prayer from combat in the Solomons.

Pug was on guard at a radar station one night when a Navy officer drove up to his post and ordered the cavalryman to open the gate. Pug refused on the grounds that he was "a guard, not a gate opener!" The irate officer's complaint reached Captain Leonard, but Pug's behavior had been appropriate. "I made PFC in New Caledonia," he chuckled, "either because I played my guitar at church or because I wouldn't open that gate for a naval officer at the Naval Radar Station."

The scourge of officers, Pug was popular among the enlisted men in the regiment. Years later, G Trooper Lionel Carter, four years Pug's junior, wrote:

"Nothing ever seemed to bother Pug. He always gave a happy-go-lucky appearance but that was only a thin veneer that concealed the man underneath who was in complete control of his emotions and his life. Without ever knowing it, nor even intending to do so, he pulled me up by my bootstraps and gave me an example I could try to emulate although I knew I could never duplicate."[12]

The greatest danger to the Americans on New Caledonia may have come from their fellow troopers. "There was a guy if you went to relieve him on guard duty and he'd been asleep, he'd wake up and shoot at you," Pug remembered. "I don't think he hit anybody. If he got the first shift up there at that airport, he stayed all night. Nobody would go relieve him!"

Noumea wasn't much of a hot spot for night life so the soldiers stationed there had to create most of their own entertainment. One of G Troop's machine gunners had operated a still back home and he employed that skill in New Caledonia. His homemade brew provided refreshments for the always thirsty troopers. Other diversions were the movies provided to the army. In early September the regiment began showing movies on a regular basis.

"They had a movie screen set up (on a hill near town)," C.W. recalled. "The first time I heard 'White Christmas' was in that Bing Crosby movie I saw there. I got stampeded at a show in New Caledonia — never knew what caused the riot."

The Wright brothers and most of the regiment were there watching a movie when the crowd panicked. Pickett recalled that "an ambulance up on the hill started up. All of a sudden, everybody started running and they kept yelling 'Horse Stampede!' When I bend over to pick up my shelter half, I got knocked down. And every time I got up to run, I got knocked down again. If I had left that shelter half on the ground I would have been able to get out."

Some soldiers were badly injured during the stampede as the rush crushed several men against the sides of parked trucks. C.W. and his two companions escaped injury, but "the guy that drove our truck lost the keys. We were walking back to camp along a road when an army truck came along behind me just as I crossed this narrow bridge. I walked right off that bridge. It was about ten feet deep with a gravel bottom. They thought that truck had hit me!"

Though not a pacifist, C.W.'s personal convictions left him uncomfortable with the prospect of killing fellow human beings and he would have preferred a non-combatant position. "While I was overseas, I had a chance to be the chaplain's 'dog robber.' They called it 'chaplain's assistant,' but it was just an orderly. (Captain) Leonard wouldn't allow it; 'I didn't train those men to be orderlies!' he said."

In February 1943, the battle for Guadalcanal ended with the Americans victorious and the threat of a Japanese invasion into New Caledonia passed.

Top: Pack train of the 112th Cavalry, Dumbea, New Caledonia. *Bottom:* Comedian Joe E. Brown performs for the troops on makeshift stage in New Caledonia (both photographs courtesy of the Texas Military Forces Museum, U.S. Army photographs).

Two battle-tested U.S. Marine battalions bivouacked on the Dumbea near the 112th.[13] Marine instructors passed on the lessons they had learned in the Solomons directly to the cavalrymen. The troopers were instructed in hand-to-hand combat, threw hand grenades, and practiced the use of the bayonet. As time went by, the regiment began to spend more time on dismounted drills and tactics. It was finally obvious there would be no place for horses in this war.

Later that month, the men of the 112th enthusiastically attended their first USO show. It starred the wide-mouthed comedian and former vaude-villian, Joe E. Brown, and featured a hillbilly guitarist named Johnny Mar-vin. Brown charmed C.W. and the others with his stories, baseball pantomime, and characterizations. Unlike many acts in the war zone, Brown did not tell off-color stories or use profanity. Corny by today's standards, the comedy show was a welcome distraction for the entertainment starved troopers.

Pickett's platoon leader put on Wright's jacket and went to the show with the enlisted men. "I looked behind us and two rows back there stood Cap-tain Leonard and ole Major Hunnicutt," Pickett recalled. "I poked the lieu-tenant and said, 'You've got company!' He left in a hurry!"

Pug's favorite story about the lieutenant over 1st Platoon was the time he led a patrol out into the New Caledonia bush. Instead of completing the assigned exercise, he sent Pug and another trooper out to watch for officers while the rest of the patrol went to sleep. The two sentries also fell asleep and they all got caught!

Pickett's lieutenant also had a mischievous nature, particularly when it came to a fellow platoon lieutenant who was a by-the-book officer. Pickett remembered the night his lieutenant opened the flaps on his victim's tent and left a shining flashlight to attract the hordes of ever present mosquitoes. He removed the flashlight, closed the flaps and hurried to Wright's tent to lie in wait for the other officer to return and be assaulted by the hungry insects. A short time later, Pickett's favorite officer was transferred from G Troop.

During March and April 1943 mounted exercises became increasingly infrequent and troops went on long marches on a weekly basis. No longer would men be able to transfer the weight of their equipment to their horses and thereafter would always bear the entire burden on their own backs and shoulders.

The Texans experienced their first tropical "rainy season" that April when it rained virtually every day. The Dumbea swelled from a gentle stream to a raging torrent. The tents leaked and nothing ever had time to dry out.

On April 16, the 112th Cavalry paraded in an event that marked the last mounted review ever by a regular U.S. cavalry regiment outside the States. Hopes the cavalrymen had of sitting out the war in New Caledonia were dashed on May 13, 1943, when the regiment left the horses behind and departed for Australia. G Troop was the last to leave New Caledonia, boarding the transports *Sands* and *Humphries* a day after the rest of the regiment had sailed.

Pickett and C.W. were amazed at the poor condition of the two World War I era destroyers provided for their regiment. C.W. related that a sailor told him that when they chipped some rust off the hull of their destroyer, it sprang a leak.

A 105 mm gun on the deck of his transport aroused Pickett's curiosity so he asked a sailor if they fired it. With a straight face, the sailor responded, "Only in an emergency, because when we fire it, it causes a leak in the ship!"

By the spring of 1943, General Douglas MacArthur's American and Australian forces had wrestled southwest New Guinea from the Japanese. The next target was Rabaul, a strong Japanese naval and army base on the eastern end of New Britain that operated as the main staging area for the enemy's operations in that sector of the Pacific Ocean. The part of the plan to place an American force in Western New Britain by the end of the year would commence with the occupation of the isolated islands of Woodlark and Kiriwina.[14] Airstrips then would be constructed there to bring Rabaul within the range of American fighter planes and bombers. In the early planning for the operation known as "Cartwheel," Admiral Halsey volunteered to provide the ground units for the occupation of the two islands. That April, the 112th was transferred to Lieutenant General Walter Krueger's Sixth Army for a planned amphibious landing on Woodlark Island, about midway between New Guinea and the Solomon Island chain.[14]

Between May 20 and June 21, the 112th Cavalry was in training at Townsville, Australia, a town on the northeast coast of the continent. Cradled in a pocket between a high bluff and the sea, Townsville was the second largest city in Queensland and outlet port for a vast agricultural plain. The area's most prominent landmark was Castle Hill, almost 1000 feet high, dominating the center of the city. Although the climate there is considered tropical, the 112th arrived at the beginning of the mild season.

Townsville's pre-war population of about 30,000 people was swamped by tens of thousands of Allied military personnel. Planes from the large air base were a major factor in the Allies' victory in the Battle of the Coral Sea.

The 112th Cavalry was housed in a large camp with row after row of uniform army tents. During their one-month stay, the former horse soldiers were drilled in infantry tactics, as well as loading and unloading landing craft. All maneuvers fell under the watchful eye of Colonel Cunningham.

Still, there was enough free time to observe some of the wonders of the continent down under. Pickett recalled that one G trooper actually managed to catch a kangaroo, but then the unlucky American was beaten up by the powerful animal.

"These Kangaroos crossed the rifle range," C.W. recalled. "We got to shootin' at 'em; didn't hit a one. That son of a gun could jump over fifteen feet!"

"Wasn't just us," added Pug. "The other troops, E and F — a line of machine guns all lined up out there. A dog came across there after one of them kangaroos. We were firin' all together, everybody trying to concentrate on that kangaroo. They sure didn't kill that kangaroo, but killed the dog."

Once in Australia, the regiment officially passed from control of the Navy to General Walter Krueger's Sixth Army. The German-born Krueger, who had served as a private during the Spanish-American War, had the reputation as a soldier's general. After the war, Pug was serving in the 15th Field Artillery in Washington State when he again came under General Krueger's command. Once, General Krueger came around to inspect the artillery men, most of who had never been outside the United States.

"The quartermaster fixed this jacket for me," Pug remembered. "I had all my little overseas stripes on it and had three hash marks on it. On one side I wore the 4th Division patch and on the right shoulder I wore the Southern Cross — four stars in a blue background. Krueger came up there on inspection. Me and one more guy were the only ones in that battalion that had a rifle m.o.s. (Military Occupational Specialty). Then ole Krueger came down that line and was takin' them guns from 'em and inspectin' them. When he got to me that was as far as he got. He turned around to Captain Williams and said, 'Why ain't this soldier got a rating?'

"He's got one on the way, Sir! I've done turned one in for him' (the captain nervously replied). The next week I was Tech-5th grade (and) that was as high as I ever got."

While in Australia, the 112th Cavalry was redesignated "112th Cavalry Regiment (Special)," which meant that they would forthwith be utilized as an infantry unit. Gradually, the regiment lost almost all of its cavalry identity. Only the men's sidearms distinguished them from regular infantry outfits. The 112th was not issued shoulder patches overseas so its troops wore no visible unit insignia until the rearing horse insignia was restored in Japan at the end of the war.[15]

By June 21, 1943, all of the regiment except G Troop had been moved from Townsville to Milne Bay. "We literally awakened one morning to find that the rest of the regiment had cleanly pulled out and left us," recalled Trooper William J. McDonnell. "That day a group of Marine Corps signalmen and another group, of Air Corps surveyors, moved into our tent village. We were going somewhere and they were going with us."[16]

Major D.M. McMains also stayed behind with Troop G and would command the planned amphibious landing on Woodlark, scheduled for the early morning hours of June 23, 1943.

4

Woodlark

Monday, June 21, 1943, began early for G Troop. Two aging destroyers were awaiting them in the harbor at Townsville, Australia. Machine Gun Platoon and Third Platoon boarded the *Brooks*, while Pickett Wright's First Platoon and the Second Platoon were assigned to the USS *Humphreys*. By 4 A.M., all loading was completed and the troop-laden ships departed under the cover of darkness, destination unknown to the cavalrymen aboard. After a stop at the strong American base at Milne Bay, New Guinea, the ships sailed east at a high rate of speed, right into the teeth of a tropical rainstorm. The high ocean waves unmercifully jostled the unlucky troops inside the ships' bellies. Bull Wiggins was out in the elements, hanging on for dear life.

"I was up on deck, on lookout. I don't know what I was lookin' for! Them ole waves — that ship had to go into the waves; they'd go plum up over that ship's bow. I vomited until I had nothing left, then I went to gaggin'."

G Troop's objective was announced before the ships arrived at their destination. It was to be tiny Woodlark Island, 150 miles northeast of Milne Bay. Major D.M. McMains had orders to take possession of Woodlark with the hundred plus men of G Troop and his men were not told whether or not the island was defended by the Japanese. Engineer reconnaissance teams had earlier discovered that there were no enemy soldiers on the island, but the men of G Troop were not privy to that information.

"They told us to get our machine guns and everything out on deck," Pug Wright recalled. "Mac set his out there and a box of that ammunition — that ship was just going up and down and that water comin' over that front end of it — that ammunition box, it took off down that steel deck and went all the way to the back. He was just cursing up a storm. That ole captain up

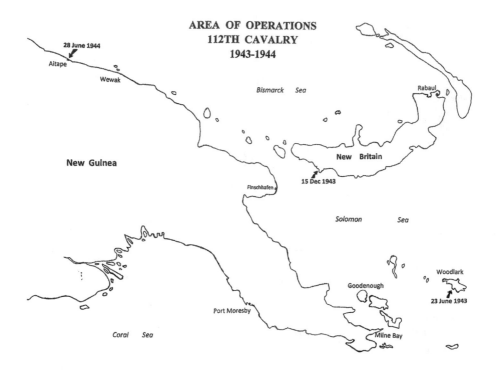

**AREA OF OPERATIONS
112TH CAVALRY
1943–1944**

28 June 1944

Aitape

Wewak

Bismarck Sea

Rabaul

New Guinea

New Britain

15 Dec 1943

Finschhafen

Solomon Sea

Woodlark

Goodenough

23 June 1943

Port Moresby

Coral Sea

Milne Bay

Area of operations: 112th Cavalry, 1943–1944 (drawn by the author)

in his roost hollered, 'You be quiet down there!' And ole Mac muttered, 'You s.o.b., go jump off into the water!'"

The sea had calmed by the early hours of June 23 when the cavalrymen began descending the cargo nets hung along the side of the transport. The big ships were running without lights, so only a bright moon silhouetted the troopers' boats. Sounds of the waves against the sides of the craft and the clang of the men's equipment broke the dark silence as the machine gunners worked their way down the cargo net into their six landing boats. The invading force turned toward the end of a small peninsula that formed a serviceable harbor. Inside the bobbing landing craft, tension was high with anticipation of encountering the enemy ashore.[1]

As the invaders approached the bay, there emerged an island similar to ones in the movies or travel brochures, white sand for a few yards then the peaceful forest of palm trees. Pug remembered that the first one on the beach was the troop mascot. He "was one of them Australian jobbers, part bulldog. He had a friend before daylight — found another dog. I don't know what happened to that dog, somebody might have eaten him."

The other dog was a female in heat and as the mascot satisfied himself he was "cheered by the entire troop" which prompted one cavalryman to comment, "Well, old Bowser got the first piece on this island!"[2] The little dog disappeared with his conquest and was never seen by the G troopers again.

"We went in and set up our machine guns in a coconut groove," Pug continued. "About four o'clock in the morning, somebody found a coconut and was hackin' on it with a machete. When he set that tripod up, that coconut was in the way and it wouldn't go down."

The occupation of Woodlark was the troopers' initiation into a jungle environment — the immense rain forest, swamps and malaria-bearing mosquitoes. On the opposite side of the cove, a sixty-foot bluff dropped off to beach level. A short way from the coast was a plantation house, occupied by an Australian family before the war. Further inland were slime-crusted swamps and mangrove trees, their extensive root systems rising from the muck in a spreading, entangled fashion. A sharp ridge that ran down the middle of the island was forty miles long and about ten miles across at its widest part.

The climate in the tropics is dangerously hot and humid. Rainy season was relative — averaging 150 inches of rain a year. The indigenous people, as in New Guinea, were Negroid, affectionately called "Fuzzy Wuzzies" because of their hairstyle that was similar to an Afro.

C.W. said, "When we came ashore at Woodlark, the natives took off into the jungle. The next morning, there was not one in sight at their camp on the beach. Some of the men got to sneakin' around in the trees. The army said not to give them cigarettes. Eventually, a few would come out and we gave them cigarettes. Then you couldn't get rid of them! They had little ole gardens and pigs. I don't know how they lived on that.

"Never saw any of the younger women," he added. "I guess they kept 'em hidden. Saw a few older ones. (During their deployment) one G trooper ran off. He was going to stay with the natives. They had to go after him. I've forgotten his name."

Seldom taller than five feet, most of the natives were friendly and generous. The mouths of most all of them were dyed a vivid red, the result of chewing a hallucinogenic nut that lent to their perpetual grin. The native clothing consisted of a waistband with a cloth skirt of grass for the bare breasted women. Shell earrings strung through pierced ears and stringed shells around their necks completed the wardrobe. The sago palm tree not only provided the leaves for thatched roofs on their huts, but the bark was used for floors and walls and the trunks were utilized for support beams. These thatched structures were usually built on platforms, four or five feet off the ground that could be reached by two-rung ladders.

G troopers dug foxholes to about waist deep and fixed gun positions on the beach in case the Japanese had any interest in the island. When Pug returned to his freshly dug machine gun pit, he was surprised to find a salt-water crocodile had crawled into the hole and broke its neck. They dug another position.

The next day, some of the troopers decided to have their picture taken with the crocodile so they pulled the big reptile out of the pit. One of the cavalrymen "stepped off" the length of the monster and determined it as seventeen and a half feet long. They propped the croc's mouth open with a heavy stick and took turns lying down next to its jaw to have a photograph taken. However, the pictures were never developed because the roll of film was confiscated by a military censor from the barracks bag of the trooper who was taking it to the States.[3]

A bivouac was set up in the old coconut plantation just off the bay. Troopers strung hammocks between coconut trees, off the ground to escape the annoying sand crabs and the dangerous adder snakes. The hammocks were encased in mesh netting because, at night, mosquitoes came out by the thousands.

"Those hammocks were pretty neat!" C.W. commented. "They had mosquito netting on top and you just zipped yourself up inside. The first time I got in one, it spun me over upside down. The night a herd of those wild hogs stampeded through there, a lot of those hammocks were turned over!"

After the stampede of wild pigs, the hammocks were raised farther from the ground. There was suspicion that troopers returning from guard duty frightened the hogs but no one ever admitted it.

Patrols began almost as soon as the cavalry arrived on Woodlark. Pug accompanied Lieutenant Stallings on a patrol by boat to scout a tiny neighboring island. No Japanese were found.

G Troop's landing on Woodlark came ten days before the scheduled arrival of the majority of the regiment and a construction battalion. Until then, their assignment was to cut truck trails out of the deep underbrush, leaving an overhead canopy of larger trees whose foliage protected the trails from Japanese observation planes. This method formed a tunnel effect around the roadways.

While felling trees, several troopers were attacked by large warrior ants that clamped onto the skin and would not let go even when its head was pulled off. This provided a dilemma for the soldier wishing to pick coconuts some thirty to fifty feet off the ground as Pug soon discovered:

"I climbed one of those coconut trees once; it was full of red ants! (After that) I was lazy — I just chopped them (coconut trees) down with a machete. Natives ate 'em green; said they had more nutritional value that way."

The natives were so adept at shinnying up coconut trees to get the fruit that, for a cigarette, they would gladly climb up a tree and shake down the coconuts. No one knew why they were immune to the stings of the ants. C.W. and other troopers also took advantage of the locals' love for cigarettes by trading smokes for laundering a bag of dirty clothes or doing other unpopular chores.

G.I.s were always scavenging for alternatives to the boring army chow. "On Woodlark, we caught a parrot and cooked it for two days," Pug recalled. "Boiled it then fried it — still couldn't eat it. It was too tough!

"Then there was the time Bobby Jones and them got the wise idea to take one of them rubber rafts and go fishing (in the ocean)," he recalled. "When they got out there — of course they had their rifles with them — one of them crocks came up there. One of them shot it. It wasn't but a few minutes, four or five crocks came up there after 'em — where that blood drained. They bailed off that ole raft — the water was chest high — turned around, runnin' in that water for shore!"

Late in the evening of June 30 several ships became visible to lookouts on Woodlark. G Troop was deployed to repel an invasion, but it was soon evident the ships were the vanguard of the American occupation force from Townsville.

"This forty-five-day wonder lieutenant we had saw these three boats out there (off the bay)," Pug remembered. "Boy, they looked like battleships, but what they were, were our P.T. boats. Nobody would think you could sink a ship with a .30 caliber machine gun a thousand yards away. This ole lieutenant came a dancin', a runnin' up and down — got shook all to pieces. Runnin' up and down that beach out there: 'Where's your machine gun?'

"'It's in that box over there!' I kept it in that box so it wouldn't rust.

"'Get that thing out here! Set it up!' he yelled.

"'You want me to sink one of them battleships with that damn .30 caliber?'

"'GET THAT GUN OUT HERE!'

"I went off a singin', '*Take this letter to my mother far across the deep blue sea!*'"[4]

By late in the day of July 1, the remainder of the 112th Cavalry Regiment arrived, along with a naval construction battalion, an artillery battalion, and a Marine Defense Battalion — about 2600 men. Colonel Cunningham borrowed extra trucks at Townsville in order that every item of equipment could be loaded on a vehicle before it was moved into the L.S.T. (Landing Ship, Tank).

"We were supposed to take up position on the beach," C.W. reflected. "Them L.S.T.s looked so big, it looked like the end of the world! They came up there and throw'd that front end down and drove the stuff off. They had Caterpillars and everything —(It was a) a double-decker (and) unloaded in thirty minutes!"

The artillery battalion set up their guns facing the sea, the Marines assumed beach security, and the 112th moved to positions on the ridge running along the middle of the island. G Troop set up six-man pyramid tents and used the plentiful ground coral for floors and walkways. Bomb shelters covered with coconut logs were built and new gun positions were dug after the dense foliage was cleared. Roads were bulldozed out and the next day the Seabees began work on an airfield. Within three weeks the airfield would be ready to receive military transport aircraft (C-47s) and planes of the 67th Fighter Squadron.[5]

Even on the isolated island, Colonel Cunningham was a stickler for discipline. Men were expected to wear their khaki uniforms except when on work details where fatigues were customary.

Robert "Pickett" Wright (left) and fellow squad member Richard Riggs (author's collection; Wiggins family photograph).

As a distraction, Pickett Wright listened to the Japanese propaganda radio broadcasts almost every day. One day, he heard "Tokyo Rose" announce that the "men on Woodlark are given twenty-four hours to get off the island or your supplies will be cut off!" It proved to be an empty threat.[6]

On July 14, the new runway was ready to accommodate C-47s and the first planes touched down. One week later, the 5200 feet of runway was surfaced with ground coral. Guarding the airstrip and the new naval radar station on the ridge became the major responsibility of the cavalry. The regiment established an outpost line of resistance away from the main perimeter of barbed wire, bunkers and foxholes. The outposts were manned every night to prevent sabotage and insure early warning of an enemy attack.

Before going on guard duty, each detail was to go by the

canine corps (K-9 Corps) and take a German shepherd with them on patrol. The Army employed guard dogs, messenger dogs and scout dogs, but only scout dogs were trained to attack on command. The dogs were also trained not to bark so the position of his trainer would not be exposed.[7] Though the cavalrymen were able to take the animals on patrol, the dogs were trained not to have anything to do with anyone other than their immediate handler. They were not to feed or pet the dogs.

Pug laughed about the time he relieved C.W. on guard duty at the airstrip. "Once, ole C.W. was on guard duty with one of them police dogs. We went up there to relieve him. When that dog saw me, he took off toward me a draggin' ole C.W. on the seat of his pants along that gravel airstrip — holding on to that leash for dear life!"

The Woodlark invasion force did not receive a visit from the Japanese air force until the pre-dawn hours of July 27 when a single enemy plane dropped a bomb that exploded near a troop encampment. The explosion caused little damage, but for the next few days the whole island was on edgy alert and almost everyone made improvements on their crude bomb shelters.

The Navy air station sounded a false air raid alarm about dusk on Sunday, August 1. No enemy planes were sighted, so Pug and Legion Goodson continued to play musical instruments in their tent. A short time later, two Japanese planes dropped bombs, but the raid caused more excitement than damage. The only casualty in G Troop was a private from Pickett's squad who sustained an abrasion between his eyes when he and another trooper dived headlong for the narrow bomb shelter opening at the same time. Following a second air raid, the fighter squadron on Woodlark began daily patrols to intercept Japanese planes before they could create any mischief.

Except for the two air raids, duty on Woodlark was peaceful and monotonous. Outpost duty and routine details were the order of the day. Troopers had to improvise to fill idle time. Even on a primitive Pacific island, they were able to set up a distillery operation.

Pug remembered "It was on Woodlark where we found a copper pot and stole wheat mash and sugar from the kitchen. It took about two weeks to drip through." The architect of the operation was a trooper from Alabama. "He told me his first job was guarding a still," Pug said. "He was to shoot to kill!"

C.W. observed the results of the platoon's moonshine operation first-hand:

"Once, me and two other guys went down on the north side of the island to guard one of the trails coming up from the ocean. They had one of those jugs of that 'white lightnin'. I knew what they were gonna do. I had one of those dogs with me — I just tied that dog up and went to sleep. The next morning, they were passed out. I kicked 'em, but they wouldn't wake up. I went on back — just left 'em. They came in late in the evening."

Napping while on guard duty seemed to be commonplace while the regiment was in non-combat areas. First platoon had a deal worked out with the G Troop clerk to alert them by field telephone if an inspection was imminent. One night the clerk called the squad on guard duty and whispered that the Captain was on his way to the troop area.

A trooper who had a tough reputation was rustled from his hammock and sent out to man the sentry post. Moments after he was in position the captain and a sergeant walked up.

"Halt, who goes there?" challenged the sentry.

Captain Leonard identified himself and the sergeant, but the armed guard demanded the password. Taken aback, Leonard stammered then admitted he had forgotten it. When he attempted to advance, the PFC ordered his Captain to halt and reiterated that they couldn't pass without the password.

Leonard knew that the guard who had been with the troop since it left the States recognized him in the bright moonlight. But as the Captain took another step, he heard the click of the safety release on the sentry's M-1. The Captain told his companion to order the trooper blocking his path to put the rifle away. By this time, the chuckling by the rest of the squad from the bushes gave their prank away and the guard's squad leader ordered him to allow the visitors to pass. The irate captain was too embarrassed to linger and shortly departed. The squad never heard anything else about the affair.[8]

Machine Gun Platoon, Thanksgiving Day, 1943; Fellow squad members (front row, right to left) C.W. Wiggins, Pug Wright, Dewey Johnson, Malcom Tarlton. Standing, at far right, is Forrest Ritter (author's collection; Wiggins family photograph).

To occupy the restless troopers, Army special services provided them with musical instruments. Pug and Pickett put their previous musical experience to use. "Pug and Pickett helped keep up our morale with their music," a fellow trooper noted. "Pug's wit and humor was always good for a lift."[9]

"We built us a makeshift stage down there in the jungle on Woodlark," Pug stated. "Me and Pickett couldn't play worth a hoot, but we was all they had."

Along with the Wright brothers on guitars, Legion Goodson played the fiddle and fellow Texan R.C. Willingham provided the vocals. Pickett, Orvil Weddel, and Mudcat Patterson performed a burlesque skit in which they stripped off their clothes and donned grass skirts from the Red Cross souvenir shop to mimic tropical hula girls.

"Ole Gary Cooper came to Woodlark and they performed on our stage," Pug said. Along with Cooper, the USO troupe included Una Merkel, Phyllis Brooks, and "some Irish tenor. Merkel and Brooks were comediennes. They didn't have much of a show. Gary Cooper came out and done that deal, Lou Gehrig (the farewell speech from the movie *Pride of the Yankees*)." Cooper and Merkel always concluded their show by singing "Pistol Packin' Mama!"

"We also had a recreation tent there with tables in it," Pug added. "And we was sittin' around there that night and that tent flap came up and here they (Merkel and Brooks) came in. They came in where we were gamblin'— playin' cards. Those officers sure didn't want them women with us!"

The troop was given the day off on Thanksgiving 1943. Someone had the idea to assemble each platoon for a group photograph. The thirty six men of Machine Gun Platoon, G Troop, gathered for a memorable portrait much in the manner of an athletic team or class picture. Afterwards, pictures were taken of individual squads and gun crews. A few weeks later, the photograph of Machine Gun Platoon appeared in the *Abilene Reporter-News*.

Pug acknowledged that also was the day Sergeant R.D. Jones found the machine gunners' still and destroyed it. It didn't really matter, for two days later the whole regiment was loaded into trucks for the short trip to the harbor. L.S.T.s were waiting to take them to another unknown destination.

After dark on the first of December, the transports arrived at Goodenough Island, just off the southeast coast of New Guinea. ("We pronounced it Good-e-nuff," Pug added.) Approximately twenty-five miles long and twenty miles wide, Goodnough was an island of mountains and jungles with plenty of space for training. Clear rivers and pools provided places for laundering clothing and skinny dipping. The more adventurous types would dive from cliff outcroppings into the pool of water a hundred or so feet below.

Pug recalled that bananas were plentiful on the island. "We brought in bananas from the hills and hung them on the tent pole. Two or three would ripen every day. The first ones back (from training exercises) in the evening got the ripe ones."

The men of the 112th cleared their new troop areas of kunai grass, a tough narrow blade grass that could grow taller than the men cutting it, set up tents, and began a two-week course in jungle warfare tactics and amphibious operations. The troopers were also introduced to several new weapons, the Thompson machine gun, Browning Automatic rifles (BAR), flame throwers, and a modified M-1 with a grenade launcher attached. However, they received little training on any of these weapons. Each squad received one "Tommy Gun" and one BAR with which each man was allowed to squeeze off only twenty rounds.[10] The Wrights, C.W. and the rest of the regiment's enlisted men suspected something big was in store for their immediate future.

A major change in the 112th's command structure had been made when the regiment arrived at Woodlark. On July 1, 1943, the former executive officer, Lieutenant Colonel Alexander M. Miller, replaced Julian Cunningham as regimental commander when the latter was promoted to brigadier general in command of the Woodlark task force. Lloyd Leonard was promoted to major in Second Squadron headquarters and Captain Jack Howell, the 2nd Platoon's lieutenant back at Fort Clark, became the new leader of G Troop.

The mild-mannered Lieutenant Colonel Miller was a fourth-generation West Point graduate and a former English professor at the Military Academy. He arrived at Fort Clark a week after Pearl Harbor with his widowed mother. Though well liked, his mild-mannered demeanor led to the perception that he was weak and indecisive. In reality, Cunningham still dominated the decision-making process, often by passing the regimental commander to communicate directly with the squadron commanders.[11]

There was also a great deal of change among non-commissioned officers. John Coppinger and Jack Taylor were transferred and a new batch evolved from the ranks. C.W.'s good friend Sergeant Ray Czerniejewski was transferred to a rifle platoon. Pickett Wright would go into his first combat as a squad leader in First Platoon.

"They gave ole' Pickett all the eight balls, because he was the only one that would take 'em," his brother surmised.

The "big plan" for the 112th was Operation "Dexterity," designed to take control of western New Britain. Though there were over 100,000 enemy soldiers garrisoned at Rabaul on the eastern coast, it would be difficult for the Japanese to move troops overland and reinforce their stronghold at Cape Glouchester on the northwestern tip of the island. What the brass had in store for the cavalry regiment was a forced amphibious landing on New Britain,[12] seventy-five miles southeast of Cape Glouchester. The 148th Field Artillery[13] was attached to General Cunningham's Director Task Force while

112th Cavalry disembarkation, Dock #2, Goodenough Island (U.S. Army photograph; courtesy of the Texas Military Forces Museum).

the 158th Infantry would remain in reserve at Goodenough. The plan was for the cavalry to strike at the Arawe peninsula, creating the impression that the main attack was there. The Japanese would then be fooled into diverting many of their men at Cape Glouchester southward through the jungle toward Arawe. The 1st Marine Division would assault Cape Glouchester ten days later.

The harbor at the boot-shaped Arawe peninsula (renamed Cape Merkus after the Japanese occupied the Australian mandate in 1942) had once been a regular port of call for the ships of the Burns-Philip South Seas Company.[14] The most suitable beaches for landings were at the sole of the boot on the west coast and near the native village of Umtingalu just east of the peninsula. Aside from the limited number of beaches, the coastline was composed of stone cliffs, as high as two hundred feet in some places, interspersed with low ground that was covered by a mangrove swamp. The Japanese had moved in a few hundred soldiers who set up coast defenses on the mainland and on Pilelo, the largest of a cluster of islands about the foot of the peninsula.[14]

Alligators lined up in preparation for launching and loading, Goodenough Island, December 14, 1943 (U.S. Army photograph courtesy of the Texas Military Forces Museum).

Reefs line the coastline near Arawe, but the 112th Regiment was provided with thirty-nine amphibian tractors that could negotiate the shallow reefs they were expected to encounter. These amphibians, called "Alligators," after their original use for work in the swamps, were actually lightly armored personnel carriers that could hold about twenty armed men. They had propellers to push them through deep water at about four knots then the caterpillar tracks could move the amtrac across the reef and up onto dry beach. Armed with a .30 caliber machine gun and piloted by a Marine, the tractors could be used to carry men and supplies several miles inland.

The Army's plans included a diversionary landing at the beach near Umtingalu, slightly less than a mile east of the Arawe peninsula's base. An hour before the main invasion was to take place, Troop A had the unenviable task of making a pre-dawn assault to block the Japanese escape route to the east. While at Goodenough Island Troop A practiced landings in rubber rafts and carried a Texas flag they planned to place on New Britain soil after reaching the shore. If they did not catch the Japanese by surprise, their rubber rafts would be sitting ducks for the enemy on shore.

Pug mentioned an incident that supposedly occurred just prior to the invasion: "On Good-e-nuff, they caught this captain from an infantry outfit with a radio sending the plans of our invasion. They shot him the next morning — Came around to each troop asking for volunteers for a firing squad. Then they changed the plans."

Until evidence surfaces to support this story it has to be dismissed as army scuttlebutt, but Pug was right on the money in the assertion, "That was the stupidest plan. We all were supposed to land there where A Troop went in."[16]

C.W. became angry when he talked about A Troop's ill-fated mission: "A P.T. boat took a patrol and went in there a few days before where A Troop went in. That captain wouldn't even let 'em get on their rafts — Said it was too dangerous! A couple of G troopers were with that bunch."[17]

Troop B was assigned the task of destroying the Japanese communications station on Pilelo Island. Their mission also entailed the use of rubber rafts about the same time as A Troop's assault. Because the B troopers accomplished their mission with minimal casualties, it became only a footnote in the history of the assault on Arawe.

Before D-Day, the regiment participated in a full-dress rehearsal, including the use of landing craft in simulated combat conditions. General Douglas MacArthur, Allied commander of military forces in the Southwest Pacific Theater, showed up on December 13 to see the men off — or to "inspire us!" the machine gunners joked. The General was still trying to live down the nickname "Dugout Doug" from the days on Corregidor Island, Philippines, when he remained safely in his concrete bunker while his command on Bataan endured constant Japanese attacks.

The G troopers boarded their respective Alligators for the short voyage to the waiting transports. Then the troop-laden amtracs proceeded in single file past the generals and newsreel cameras. G Troop went first in the parade since their Alligators were to be the first group of amtracs loaded and the last ones off the transport.

The Alligators drove down the bank into the sea where their propellers took over, pushing the craft through the water, throwing up a trailing white spray. They headed toward the L.S.D. *Carter Hall*, anchored about a mile off the coast. The amphibians moved through the large door in the bow of the L.S.D. (Landing Ship, Dock) and clanked along the metal floor to their

Second Squadron commander Lieutenant Colonel Clyde Grant (second from left) reviewing final plans for invasion en route to New Britain. To his right are Marine First Lieutenant H.F. Harmon (operations officer for Alligator transports) and Colonel A.M. Miller (commander 112th Cavalry Regiment) (U.S. Army; courtesy National Archives photo SC-184081).

assigned position. Once they were all aboard, the landing ramp was raised behind them. About midnight, the three troop ships got underway, heading north. At Buna, Papua New Guinea, the transports rendezvoused with a Navy fleet of seven cruisers and several sub-chasers. P.T. boats went along to patrol the flanks of the convoy.

The trip was uneventful, but the men were more somber than on previous voyages. The troopers spent most of their time cleaning and checking weapons, or in silent reflection and prayer.

The men of G Troop would go into battle well armed. One trooper remarked that he went on his first patrol on New Britain armed with an "M-1 rifle with about fifteen clips of ammo ... our M1911 Colt .45 with 21 rounds of ammo. We had at least three frag(ment) grenades which were hung on and about our person in desultory fashion. We had one bayonet, one machete and most of us had a non–GI hunting knife. Then, in our pack, we each carried three rounds of 60-mm mortar, and in our left hand we each carried a can of machine gun ammo."[18]

A few minutes before 3 A.M., December 15, the lookouts sighted the southern coast of New Britain. The men of G Troop would soon face their baptism of fire!

5

New Britain

The men of G Troop were roused from their restless slumber well before daylight the morning of December 15, 1943. The South Pacific sky was slightly overcast, but a bright moon silhouetted the outline of the low hills of Cape Merkus, New Britain, barely visible five miles away. After a breakfast consisting mostly of beans or chili con carne, the anxious troopers gathered weapons and packs together to await the order to board their respective Alligators in the bowels of the *Carter Hall.* The locks were opened, the L.S.D.'s bay flooded, and the amphibious landing craft were soon afloat. A little before five A.M., the troop-laden Alligators fired up their motors, shattering the silence with a sound similar to a force of big airplanes. The doors of the bay were opened and the assault craft moved into the sea.

In about ten minutes they were underway, circling the mother ship and waiting the order to move toward the beach. G Troop was to make up the second wave of assault vehicles, while E and F troops were to lead the attack in ten armored amphibious tanks called "Buffalos." One and a half hours were allowed for the amtracs to make it to shore, so the landing itself was to take place in the early morning daylight. The Buffalos and Alligators proceeded in several columns and the trailing white lines of spray gave the illusion that the crafts were connected. As the amphibious crafts bobbed their way toward shore, the transport ships turned and headed out to sea. For a few moments, the troopers felt they were all alone, but they couldn't see the cruisers and destroyers lurking in the darkness. There was some grumbling about being left without support, but mostly the men had to deal with their apprehension about the impending battle.

The Wrights, C.W. Wiggins and the other enlisted men had not been told what they would be up against (or even if there would be any Japanese resistance) when they reached the beach. The riflemen had affixed bayonets

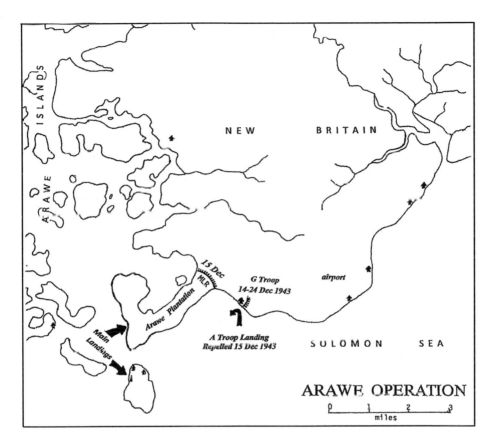

"Arawe Operation" (drawn by the author).

to their M-1 rifles because they were instructed to gouge enemy bodies to ensure they were not "playing possum."[1]

The sound of gunfire from the coast dispelled any illusion of another walk on the beach as at Woodlark. Over to the right, masses of red tracer bullets from the shore traveled out to sea in a low trajectory and ricocheted into the sky in mid-flight. Apparently, A Troop had not caught the enemy by surprise (Appendix B).

Within 100 yards from shore, twelve of A Troop's fifteen rubber rafts were sunk and sixteen troopers were killed. On board the fleet flagship USS *Conyngham* General Cunningham was incensed that Admiral Daniel Barbey would not order the ship's captain to commence firing at the shore-based Japanese guns that were ripping the rubber boat troop apart. After more than twenty minutes, the destroyer *Shaw* finally opened fire and silenced the enemy's guns at Umtingalu with one salvo.[2] More than three hours after the initial assault, a Navy sub chaser moved in to pick up survivors, but Loraine's Pooch Cranfill was not among them. His body was never recovered.

As the horizon began to glow with red first light, the seven Navy warships began their bombardment of the Arawe peninsula. It began with a yellow flash, a red tracer shell, followed by a white one on a low trajectory heading toward shore.

Within seconds, there was a whole line of white flashes that dwarfed the effect of the sun on the horizon. Big shells hit the beach and bounced before striking again. Bright explosions and eruptions of debris indicated direct hits and a fog of black smoke drifted toward the approaching amphibious force. Rockets fired from craft called DUKWs added to the dramatic effect.[3]

Shortly after seven, American strafing planes swooped down, one by one, their heavy machine guns peppering the beaches and continuing a trail of bullets through the trees up the peninsula. One Japanese airplane flew over, but departed quickly when every American ship concentrated their fire on it.

As Pickett's amphibian bobbed toward the beach, he noticed that one of his men was hanging over the side of the craft. "Bullets were flyin' over us and he was hangin' out, feedin' the fishes," Wright recalled. "I hollered at him, 'Get your head down!' He just yelled back, 'I don't care!'"

When the cavalrymen got close enough, they saw the damage the bombardment had wreaked. C.W. observed that "there wasn't a coconut tree left intact on the place, but the Japs were still there!"

C.W. and Pug did not have time to worry about what would happen when they reached the beach because their amphibian tractor stalled and was beginning to take on water.

"That ole Alligator we were on sprung a leak and we had to get off!" C.W. recalled. "Didn't think about it at the time, but I never could have swam that far (to the shore). I got on another Alligator with the tripod; Tucker got on another; and the ammunition bearer on another one. We didn't find each other until about noon! Those Alligators just drove up on the beach, lowered the ramp and we got off."

Most of the resistance had been neutralized by the bombardment and the first wave of the main assault had secured the boot of the peninsula when G Troop landed. "You couldn't believe all the equipment they unloaded on that beach," C.W. marveled. Within an hour of the first wave, the beach became cluttered with all types of supplies and equipment.

Pug Wright and his machine gun crew transferred from their floundering Alligator to a Higgins boat, but it was overcrowded and they wound up on another Alligator:

"About eight o'clock that morning, I waded out of that boat. The last one we got on didn't get to the beach so I had to bail off of it. Ole Mudcat

Arawe, New Britain 24 January 1944. This Signal Corps photograph was taken from about twenty yards behind what had been the main line of Japanese resistance. Troop A attempted to land just below the hill at the bottom left of the picture. The primary landings took place across the peninsula at the top left corner. (U.S. Army photograph; courtesy National Archives photo SC-360699).

was shorter than I was and the water was up to his chin, he on his tip toes. I bailed out with the machine gun, he had the tripod, Dewey Johnson had the ammunition, and we had to wade on in."

Pickett's Alligator reached the beach as scheduled and the machine's treads pulled it over the rocks and out of the water. The squad members jumped to the ground and moved into the coconut plantation toward the day's objective. Troop E cornered twenty or so Japanese in caves burrowed into the cliffs, killed several and moved on.

At mid-morning, a wave of Japanese Zeros flew in from Rabaul and strafed the peninsula. Troopers dived behind what was left of the coconut tree trunks as bullets plowed up the ground nearby, but little damage was done to the growing beachhead. Enemy bombs threw up harmless giant geysers of water when they landed offshore.

Pickett fired his rifle at the planes, but with no effect. Then American P-38 Lightnings and P-47 Thunderbolts flew in and engaged the Japanese planes. Pickett paused to watch the dogfight in the sky directly above him:

"My squad and I were right on the beach," he noted. "Those planes came across right at tree top level. A P-38 was fastest thing they had. He was in front of this Zero and a P-47 was behind the Zero. That P-38 darted out from in front of that Zero and that P-47 blowed that sucker all to pieces!"

Pug went on a personal mission before he left the beach. "The medics had gotten some of their stuff off and a five gallon can of alcohol was sitting there," he recalled. "I picked it up and carried it to the top of the hill. The gunfire was getting rough so I stuck it under some vines. We drove all the way to the end of that three mile long peninsula and then we dug in. When there was a break, I went back and got that alcohol. We got grapefruit juice from the kitchen and we drank it with the alcohol!"

The island's planters had fled some time earlier so the once neat rows of coconut trees were overladen with an invasive vine that presented an aggra-

Members of the 112 Cavalry Regiment advancing through the Arawe plantation, 16 January 1944 (U.S. Army; courtesy National Archives photo SC-219699).

vating obstacle for the troopers to navigate. Past the plantation was a valley covered in kunai grass.

The men of Second Squadron advanced three miles up the peninsula against only minor opposition. At approximately 14:30 the squadron achieved the objective of the peninsula's base and began to fortify their position (main line of resistance). Excluding A Troop, the regiment suffered only five killed and four wounded in action on D-Day.[4]

That night, "we formed a circle and set up OPs (outposts) about twenty-five yards away for our lookouts," C.W. remembered. "Me and Mudcat went out there on one shift. On the way back in, we met our relief and we were talkin' to them. One of 'em threw a gun in my belly and nearly killed me! I was too scared to say anything at first, but later had some tough words for him."

"The next night, that same guy killed Elmer Wilson," C.W. lamented. "Wilson told 'em he had to go to the bathroom, but he shot him anyway. That guy that shot him was never the same after that."

The morning following the invasion, E and F Troops dug in at the base of the Arawe peninsula. G Troop was ordered to hike about a mile down the coastline and occupy the native village of Umtingalu, the original objective of A Troop. Under the temporary command of Lieutenant Joseph Jefferies, 1st Platoon was ordered to advance along a bluff above the shoreline that ranged from seventy-five to a hundred feet in height.

Umtingalu turned out to be only four or five abandoned native huts nestled amidst a grove of coconut trees. There were no Japanese around and the enemy's anti-aircraft battery there had been abandoned. Troop G dug in on a high ridge that sloped sharply to the beach. A narrow trail, encased by a dense canopy of foliage, led down the slope to the shore. Pug recalled that his crew almost lost their machine gun there:

"That ole machine gun we took into combat — we drug it all over Louisiana — we could take that machine gun, blindfold ourselves and put it back together. We had played with it so much and drug it on those horses, the bolt just flopped around. Then we went on that mission where those rubber boats went off there and didn't make it. We had to go up the island around the edge to complete their mission. We were going around the edge of this bluff, just above the water — I guess eight or ten feet deep there. The Japanese air force started strafing us, strafing down the bank. Mudcat dropped that machine gun down in the water, that salt water. So we kept fishing and diving in there until we got it. That night we got on top of that bluff and dug in. The next morning, I started to clear that gun and I couldn't even pull the bolt back! That salt water had frozen it.[33]

Pug also recalled, "That was the same night we took the canisters out of gas cans and we filled them up with fruit, apples or anything. We dug holes just deep enough to lay your head off the back so you could see. Quesada had that (canister) under his head for a pillow. He reached up to get an apple out of it and the Jap position opened up with a machine gun and shot that can all to pieces right under his head!"

More likely the canister was hit by friendly fire for the night's darkness was frequently punctuated by the gunfire from nervous and trigger, happy cavalrymen. When a trooper from the first squad on guard duty stood up to urinate he was mistaken for an enemy infiltrator by a sergeant of Machine Gun Platoon. The machine gunner tossed a grenade in the direction of the "intruder" but fortunately the explosion caused no injuries.[5]

Although the Japanese resistance was light to this point, General Cunningham kept the majority of the regiment in their entrenchments at the base of the Arawe Peninsula. A system of trenches and camouflaged dugouts, fronted by barbed wire, became the cavalrymen's homes for the next few weeks. The troopers quickly learned that individual foxholes were not as practical as were those with space for three men that allowed one of them to be on alert at all times.

Numerous L.C.T.s continued to arrive at the beachhead, bringing tons of equipment, supplies and support troops. Between the initial landings and December 27, the Japanese air force flew numerous sorties against the entrenched GIs and the American beachhead usually in the morning hours. Japanese pilots were nicknamed "Washing Machine Charlies" because of the out of sync engine noise made by the attacking Zeros.

"Washing Machine Charlie would come every night," Pickett said. "(Those planes) sounded like a Maytag Washin' Machine!— blew a guy's head off in the chow line. That's the only one he ever got! After we got some anti-aircraft, he didn't come back."

Once the generals decided the Arawe beachhead was secure, the men of G Troop received a famous visitor. Motion picture actor John Wayne, in the area with a USO tour, had been hanging around Finschhafen, N.G., begging the high command to let him visit a combat zone. Wayne had just finished filming *The Fighting Seabees* and by the end of the war he would be recognized as the personification of the American fighting man in the Pacific.[6]

The troop was dug in on the ridge above Umtingalu when Pickett first saw John Wayne: "Wayne came up and talked to us behind those barbed wire entanglements. He put on a little show, had Major Grant's pants on — they were way too little. He told us he had the major's pants on then he pulled a brassiere out of the back pocket."

Pug added that "Wayne had Grant's shirt on. Grant was a big guy, but it wouldn't button. He had a Negro boy with him that beat on the tom-toms.

Wayne was raisin' cane to us about the mosquitoes — malaria, you know. He had a cup of our alcohol and grapefruit juice (home brew). He spent the night over there with us."

Wayne also wanted to go on a patrol with the 112th, but Grant would not allow it.[7] C.W. was not impressed; "He (Wayne) was going to whip 'em all (the Japanese)! But he was way behind the lines."

Soon after the New Britain landings, the introduction to combat exposed troopers that would be undependable in a fight. One of the first casualties of "combat fatigue" was G Troop's chief moonshiner.

"Ole Henry White, corporal, tried to get me to go stay in the hole with him after he flipped his lid," Pug recalled. "'Naw', I said. 'I'll go out yonder on the outpost and sit with those Japs, (but) I'm not sharin' no hole with a crazy guy!'

"They went down there and tried to calm him down and he'd take a dang machine gun and clip them tree tops off with it; shoot at you!"

Wiggins also talked about it: "He was in his hole clutching his rifle, eyes lookin' like a crazy idiot. (They) finally talked him out.[8]

Pug and C.W. remembered another G trooper that paid one of his buddies five pounds Australian to shoot him in the arm so he would be transferred back to the States.[9]

On the other hand, there was Forrest Ritter, a brawny, blond-haired nineteen year old from Alabama, who had joined the 112th as an overseas replacement and was assigned to Corporal Pickett Wright's squad in first platoon. Years later, Pug Wright remembered that Ritter's prowess with a rifle surfaced soon after the Arawe landings:

"They had Ritter carrin' bazooka ammunition there on New Britain. An E trooper got killed by a sniper behind some vines grown up on a coconut tree. Ritter made the remark, 'If I didn't have this ammunition, I'd go around there and get that guy!' And I told him, 'Throw it down!' You see, we were pinned down. And he crept around, inched around that bush with that old M1. One shot — Boom! — He came back just a grinnin'. 'I got 'em!'

"I told ole Pickett, 'That guy don't need to be carrin' ammunition. Let him use that gun!' So they made him ole Pickett's scout."

Forrest Ritter had little formal education, but he was a natural woodsman. Pug recalled that he often went shirtless in the jungle and was fearless in his dives from cliffs into pools or the ocean while they were on breaks in New Guinea.

"That Ritter was a sharpshooter. He'd carry that ole M-1 across his arms just like he was huntin' in Alabama," added Pug. "That's where he learned to shoot — squirrels. And he'd call his shots. When he shot a Jap, he'd call his shot! Tell Pickett just where he was shootin' 'em. Pickett checked him a time or two and he was right!"

Pickett acknowledged that Forrest Ritter saved his life soon after he became scout. "It was up around those caves. I was leadin' a patrol. This Jap was down behind this bank. He raised up and pointed some type of automatic weapon at me. Before he could fire, Ritter killed him!"

"Ritter filed his peep sight down" (on his rifle), Pickett remembered. "Our captain was gonna court-martial him. I went to Lieutenant Colonel Grant and he said if he can shoot better, he can saw it down all the way!"

Thus far, most of the Japanese soldiers encountered by the men of the 112th were corpses. For the most part, the fighting thus far had been against unseen snipers and infiltrators. Generally, American soldiers despised their unknown Asian enemy and neither side felt much compassion for the other. The Japanese soldier lived by the ancient Samari war code of "Bushido"—It was dishonorable to be captured rather than die killing the enemy. The Japanese propaganda machine had molded Nippon's soldiers into a fanatical and often suicidal frenzy. Americans were portrayed as devils who tortured their prisoners.

"The Japs didn't take any prisoners. We didn't either!" noted C.W., although he was talking about reality rather than a military mandate.

More than one G Trooper mentioned that prior to the Arawe Campaign they received orders not to take prisoners. No less authorities than regimental commander Colonel Alexander Miller and Lieutenant Colonel Philip Hooper said that no such order was ever given, verbally or written.[10]

The Americans' bitterness toward the Japanese paled before the Australians' hatred of their Oriental enemy. Working with the 112th on Woodlark and New Britain were members of the ANGAU (Australian, New Guinea, and Administrative Unit). Former civil servants, coconut planters, and traders, these Australian residents of the islands operated against the Japanese as coast watchers and guerillas. They enlisted the help of the local populations, which was not that difficult because the Japanese had treated the natives so badly.

Both C.W. and Pickett expressed admiration for these Australians' bravery and expertise, but acknowledged their animosity toward the enemy. Pickett related that "Right after we landed on New Britain that Australian ANGAU man wanted us to stay down so the Japs wouldn't see us and come on over so we could kill them."

The Japanese high command at Rabaul wasn't about to give up Southwestern New Britain without a fight. An additional battalion of Japanese troops was dispatched to Arawe, traveling by barge and marching overland. The leading elements would make contact with G Troop's forward outpost on Christmas Day.

The largest part of Troop G had returned to the Arawe Peninsula by Christmas Eve and only one platoon remained at Umtingalu to guard against a surprise attack. 1st Platoon set up at the top of the cliffs leading down to the beach from where any attack was expected to come. Troopers were scattered down the cliffs all the way to the sea to guard against a surprise attack.

Each night, a six man detail from the platoon was sent down to the beach to watch for enemy barges approaching from the sea. There had already been at least one false alarm. Corporal Wright was on outpost duty one evening when he heard two warning shots from one of the guard posts. He went down to investigate and found that a trooper had shot himself in the foot with his Colt .45.

"He said there were thousands of Japs out there, but we never found any," Pickett smiled. (Later) "Sergeant Thompson went to see him in the hospital at Finschhafen. Thompson said there weren't any Japs there! The guy got up and was gonna whip him!"

Before Corporal Pickett Wright led his five-man patrol to the beach below Umtingalu late on Christmas Eve, he was briefed about reports of Japanese barges moving along the coast. After an uneventful night, Pickett and Ritter began Christmas morning by checking out some of the caves in the cliffs that sloped to the beach. About the same time, a pair of army jeeps with an army chaplain and a detail of troopers took the road from the top of the ridge to the seashore where the bodies of some A Troopers had washed up on the beach. When the burial detail encountered a group of enemy soldiers, the jeeps made a rapid U-turn and accelerated back up the hill. The Japanese began shooting at the fleeing Americans.[11] A G Trooper recalled that when the jeeps passed his squad on the way to the top of the ridge, the regimental chaplain was sitting in the back seat of one of the jeeps waving a .45 automatic in the air and shouting, "Give 'em Hell. The Lord is with us!"

When he heard the gunfire, Pickett quickly scanned the jungle for its source and spotted a group of Japanese soldiers ascending the ridge, but out of range of his squad's rifles. The enemy had not seen Pickett, but neither had Lionel Carter and Red Wood, who were manning the point outpost a short distance away near some caves. They were looking the opposite direction oblivious to the enemy presence or Pickett, who was frantically waving his arms to attract his men's attention. When the pair turned around and spotted Pickett, they hastened over to join their fellow troopers.

Worried that they would be cut off from the rest of the troop, the cavalrymen made a rapid retreat down the trail toward the position on the ridge where their platoon should be waiting. Seemingly out of nowhere, they heard the sound of approaching aircraft. There was not time to discern whether the planes were friend or foe, for three American A20s, flying low and almost wing tip to wing tip, shot directly overhead. As they passed above the troopers, the planes opened fire with their machine guns, "the bullets striking the jungle less than fifty yards in front of us."

Carter wrote that "We dashed up the narrow, one person wide, steep trail leading up to the ridge, the thick foliage brushing our shoulders on both sides of our bodies, our guns held at ready, but knowing full well that if any one lurked on either side of the trail we would never get the chance to even fire."[12]

The men in the jeeps had alerted 1st platoon to the eminent threat and the leading element of the Japanese unit was greeted by the cavalry's Tommy Gun and B.A.R. Pickett and the men of his squad joined the rest of his platoon at the top of the ridge and they all beat it back to the safety of the main line of resistance at the base of the Arawe Peninsula.

It wouldn't be much of a Christmas for the individual soldier on Arawe. Pug bemoaned that their expected Christmas dinner did not materialize because "our plane dropped the turkeys on the Japs!"

C.W. chimed in: "I don't know anything about any turkeys. I spent Christmas in a foxhole and for dinner had salmon patties, dehydrated eggs and tomatoes!"

Christmas night, the newly arrived battalion of Japanese soldiers from the 81st Infantry Regiment under command of Major Masamitsu Komori launched an assault against the 112th's right flank. The attack was repulsed and the following morning, G Troop was ordered to set up a reserve line behind the main American positions. The enemy attacked during the day and night on the twenty-eighth and twenty-ninth of December. The fruitless assaults cost the Japanese much of their battalion's manpower, but they were reinforced by a second battalion late in the afternoon of December 29. The Japanese then entrenched in shallow foxholes concealed by heavy brush some 600 yards to the east, between the Americans and the pre-war airfield. The Japanese were outnumbered and frequently moved their machine guns so the American artillery and mortars could not zero in on their positions.

C.W. was sitting on his gun position "shootin' the bull" with some other troopers when the Americans' 148th Field Artillery began shelling the Japanese with their 105-millimeter howitzers:

"We were watchin' those rounds go over our heads. Just as they hollered, 'SHORT ROUND,' that thing went off. That short round hit right in the middle of us. I can't believe nobody got killed. I felt this burning on my back; there was blood on my back!

" 'I've been hit!'

" 'Oh, no you haven't,' they said.

"A piece of shrapnel about the size of a pin head had hit me in the back. It burned a little bit (and) the medic put a piece of tape over it. It's still in there."

Upon learning of the eminent arrival of an undetermined number of Japanese reinforcements, General Cunningham overestimated the enemy's strength and asked the 6th Army commander, General Krueger, for the reserve units still at Goodenough Island. The Second Battalion, 158th Infantry, was dispatched and the first company of reinforcements arrived at Cape Merkus three days later.

In an effort to break the stalemate during the final week of 1943, the 112th launched small probing units against the entrenched Japanese with little success. On New Year's Day, Troop B was ordered to attack the entrenched enemy positions blocking the route to Umtingalu. Following an American artillery barrage that did as much damage to the attacking force as the Japanese, B Troop was forced to withdraw in the face of the enemy's mortars and machine gun fire. B Troop suffered casualties of three dead and fifteen wounded.

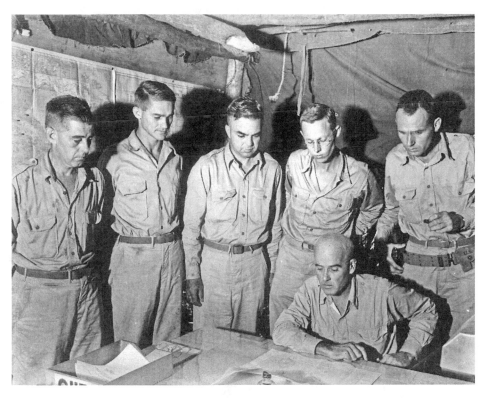

Caption: General Cunningham, seated, and staff at Arawe, New Britain, 6 February 1944. Standing, left to right: unidentified, Lieutenant Colonel Clyde Grant, Major D. M. McMains, Colonel A. M. Miller, Lieutenant Colonel P. L. Hooper (courtesy of the Texas Military Forces Museum; U.S. Army photograph).

On January 4, 1944, it came G Troop's turn to move out past the barbed wire into no man's land. It was still dark when the troopers moved through their barbed wire entanglements and spread out into a skirmish line—first platoon on the right, second on the left and third in the center. Machine Gun Platoon was spread out about twenty yards behind the rest of the troop. In order not to lose the element of surprise, there would be no artillery barrage to soften up the enemy's positions before the men moved out.

"The 'surprise' element, it was later learned, was immediately eliminated when, after forming a line of skirmishers and waiting for the command to advance, every smoker in the attacking force had to light a cigarette to steady his nerves," wrote Lionel Carter. "This would happen just before every attack and one Japanese lieutenant commented on it in a diary found on his body: 'The Americans give away their positions by smoking cigarettes just prior to an attack. Are they so brave or are they just foolish?'"[13]

"We moved out at four A.M.," Pug remembered. "G Troop crawled out in grass about two feet high in a coconut field. Machine Gun (Platoon) was to follow and if anyone was hit, a machine gunner was to replace him. The troop was under sniper fire when Captain Howell ordered a charge. When our guys raised up they were mowed down."

The first burst of enemy fire lasted less than a minute then abruptly stopped. G Troop called for mortar support, but it appeared to have little effect on the entrenched enemy. The machine gunners were ordered to crawl up and join the main part of the troop before the advance was renewed. The Americans were again met with a withering blanket of machine gun fire from the unseen Japanese.

C.W. remembered that "when the Japs opened up on us, Tucker got shot in the helmet and the bullet went around and down the back. It didn't amount to much, but he was bleedin' like a stuck hog—bleedin' out the back of his helmet. I told him to get out of there and he ran out.

"We were given the order to pull back," he explained. "On my way back, I ran up on that younger Olei boy. He was shot in the leg, in the thigh. I drug him out by the arm; (then) somehow I got him up on my shoulders and brought him back to our lines. I can't remember, but I guess the ammo bearer brought my gun back."

While C.W. was struggling to get a much larger Ruldoph Olei to safety, Pug was busy dodging bullets as he later explained:

"I crawled out with Corporal (Vernon) Voyles in front of me where I could touch his foot. He stopped when that machine gun fire cut off the tops of the grass right in front of us. I told him, 'Let's move up.' He didn't move. I shook his foot, but he still didn't move. I crawled up beside him; he had been hit by one bullet right between the eyes. I heard a groan off to my right.

I twisted like a cutworm and crawled over to a coconut tree. It couldn't stop a .22 bullet, but I felt safe. I moved over to where I had heard the groan. It was (Corporal) Henry White. A sniper had shot him in the back and it had gone through the heart and out through the chest. He was killed instantly."

Again the Japanese abruptly ceased their fire. William McDonnell of 3rd Platoon wrote that during the lull, "From the enemy line, in high pitched perfect English, a voice enjoined us, 'Americans, come on up and fight.' Somehow this had a rather hair-raising effect, until from the squad to my right came the reply of a deep voiced Chicagoan, who advised our would-be adversary where he could go."[14]

Meantime, Pug had taken cover behind a ridge where it was safe from enemy machine gun fire. He recalled, "Already there was the littlest guy in the army. He said everybody was dead! We had always been trained that if you went off the firing line you would go before a firing squad. I heard a BAR firing so I knew we were still engaged. I saw some litter bearers and sent Spider out with them. Then I lit a cigarette and stayed behind my ledge until the BAR stopped. When I felt the action had been broken off, I started back to our lines. I met an E Troop sergeant about half way back to the barbed wire. 'Is there anybody else?' he asked. 'I don't know,' I said. 'Don't go through the barbed wire,' he said, 'but through the zigzag gap.' "

Pug had made his way back through the gap in the barbed wire when he encountered an officer from 2nd Squadron headquarters:

"I saw this ole major a sittin' on a coconut stump; 'How rough is it out there, Wright?'

"I said, 'Go out and see for yourself!' and kept on goin'.

"Some others began to fall in behind me until there were about seven or eight of us. We came up on a group of officers, sitting in a circle — all the wheels, Cunningham, Hooper. One of them said something to me and I went right into the middle of 'em, not knowing if I was in trouble for leaving the line. Then Ole Cunningham said, 'Don't stop here; they've got a hot meal for you.' Boy, we ran back to that kitchen."

Pickett's squad did not suffer casualties during the day's fighting, but that did not mean the action was not hot and heavy in his sector. "Ole Captain Howell was runnin' from one place to another, jumpin' those bullets, when he got shot in the belt buckle," he noted. "(James) Vire and (Ed) Corley were on each side of my squad. They stood up with BARs on those machine guns while we pulled back. Platoon leader (Babe) Meeks told Vire, 'When we get back to Abilene, I'll buy you a steak!'

"(Later) we were up there huntin' souvenirs. Corley stepped on a bobby trap and got killed."

The casualties suffered by Troop G that day were high considering the number of men engaged — 4 dead, 21 wounded.[15]

Cunningham's army grew to 4750 men following the arrival of the battalion from the 158th Infantry Regiment, but the Americans would remain bogged down on the Arawe Peninsula for another twelve days.

Pug, C.W. and the others went about strengthening their machine gun positions. "Ole C.W. had a good gun position," Pug remarked. "They had those coconut logs with dirt piled up on 'em. It looked like two tons of coconut hulls out in front they stayed there so long."

The enemy was also busy, digging tunnels between their foxholes in order to more easily move their machine guns and men around. Openings to these holes were disguised so well an American patrol could easily walk up on one without realizing it was there.

C.W. "Bull" Wiggins posing with the Japanese officer's sword Forrest Ritter found on the New Britain battlefield (author's collection; Wiggins family photograph).

Japanese snipers took shots at the entrenched Americans and tried to play on their nerves by baiting them to come out in the open. Soon after the failed January 4 attacks, C.W. and the other G troopers heard a plea from the no man's land between theirs and the Japanese position: "I'm Vernon; come and get me!" No one fell for the ruse. The enemy had removed the dog tags from the body of Vernon Voyles and tried to entice some of his friends to "rescue" their fallen buddy.

An overseas replacement in G Troop remembered, "We spent every night in the foxholes. The holes were always full of ants, centipedes, long gray worms, rats or land crabs. It was a question of whether to jump in and get eaten or stay out and get bombed."[16]

General Cunningham convinced General Krueger at 6th Army headquarters that armor was needed to dislodge the Japanese and break the stalemate. On the morning of January 16, Marine tanks, followed by infantry, were ready to assault the enemy positions. Troop G waited in reserve.

The offensive opened with the arrival of a group of heavy bombers that dropped eighty-seven tons of ordnance on the Japanese positions. Once the bombers were done the American artillery began a twenty minute bombardment.[17]

"They brought in a few tanks," C.W. remarked. "Two bogged down and had to be blown up — weren't fit for where we were. After an air strike, the tanks cleared 'em out."

However, the U.S. Army newspaper *Yank* was far more dramatic, reporting that the tanks raced through scattering Japanese "like a pack of gigantic Doberman pinschers."[18]

The next day, B Troop mopped up and the enemy withdrew past the airdrome. All that was left for G Troop was to help clear the battlefield of underbrush and establish a new line of resistance. It was recorded in the regimental diary that 139 Japanese were killed during the attack. The next day the bulldozers moved in to destroy the enemy's breastworks and foxholes.

"After that raid," C.W. commented, "We gathered those dead Japanese up, dug a hole, and a bulldozer pushed 'em in."

One former cavalryman admitted that he and another trooper collected the silver fillings and crowns from the teeth of Japanese corpses to sell at a later date. When the G-trooper's buddy was later killed, the surviving soldier decided the pouch of silver was bad luck and threw his booty away.[19]

The Japanese offered little resistance thereafter and by mid–February the starving remnants of the once strong force was ordered to withdraw to the northeast. For all practical purposes, the campaign was over, although patrols were still hazardous because Japanese stragglers lingered in the area. A diary was found on the body of a Japanese officer and his words were translated, printed and made available for the American soldiers to read.[20]

Once the enemy withdrew, a ten-man patrol was organized to reconnoiter a prize objective of the campaign, the pre-war airfield. Lieutenant Rip Williams had become ill and was evacuated a day following the invasion, which left the 1st Platoon without an officer. When the ten-man combat patrol was picked to scout the airport, a brand new replacement lieutenant was sent along. The non-coms for the trek would be Sergeant Harold Paulsen and Corporal Pickett Wright.

The lieutenant "with new fatigues and his shiny new carbine slung over his shoulder" led the patrol past the main line of resistance and through the barbwire entanglements. But once the men disappeared into the jungle, Sergeant Paulsen stopped the patrol and reportedly stated, "Now, Lieutenant,

I'll take over this patrol. You go back in the middle of the patrol and when we get back to this same spot on the way back, you can lead us in!" The rookie officer seemed surprised but did has Paulsen instructed.[21]

Without difficulty, the Americans reached G Troop's old positions overlooking Umtingalu that had been abandoned on Christmas Eve. Fortunately the village was deserted and they continued on the trail toward the airport.

Because of reported Japanese activity past Umtingalu, Paulsen and Pickett turned off the trail and had gone about a hundred yards into the jungle when they discovered only one other man had followed them. The third man, Lionel Carter, was sent after the rest of the patrol, but when he didn't return, the two non-coms had to go in search of their men. When Carter showed up, he claimed that he had encountered a sole Japanese soldier who ran off into the jungle.

The going was arduous as the troopers pushed their way through brush and low tree limbs. After a nervous march through dense jungle, the patrol reached the "airport" which was little more than a field overgrown with kunai grass and short trees. Instead of venturing into the open area of the field, Paulsen and Pickett split the patrol into small groups to explore the jungle around the field. After the scouts encountered no enemy other than mosquitoes and ants, the patrol moved up the native trail at a rapid pace back to the regiment.

The lieutenant lead the patrol for the final fifty yards or so to the main line of resistance, but his experience was unnerving. "This is ridiculous," he had told the other men. "Sending ten men out alone on a patrol like this. Why we could all be killed! I'll never go on another patrol." And he didn't. His request for a transfer was granted.[22] The overgrown airfield was never cleared nor fixed up for American war planes.

Pickett stated that he would rather be on patrol in the jungle than waiting in the trenches. "I never lost a man on patrol — until the last one," he said. "My squad was always in front, and me and Ritter always alternated at the head of my squad."

This record is remarkable due to the inherent danger of patrols, because the regiment suffered a majority of its casualties in New Guinea during that type of operation in the jungle. It was especially dangerous for the point man, not only because he was a sitting duck for ambush, but also for lethal concealed explosive devices.

The Japanese were adept at setting up camouflaged wire trip explosives and hidden pits lined with bamboo stakes. Pug remarked that "A Jap lying on his face was not dead. Once, there was this Jap leaning against a booby trap. When they moved him, an explosion hit three men, one died!"

Pug Wright bragged about telling his mother he would take care of his younger brother as long as they were in the army. So he and Mudcat Patterson usually volunteered to go on patrols with Pickett's squad. While on patrol, Pug armed himself with a .45 caliber Thompson sub-machine gun. Popularized by the Chicago gangsters of the twenties and thirties, the "Tommy Gun" had a limited range and wasn't very accurate, but it was light and could be brought into firing position much quicker than the clumsier M-1 rifle or twenty-pound BAR.

"Pickett and Ritter would take the front," Pug remembered, "and he put me on the tail with a Tommy Gun — all day through them jungles and having to look back over my shoulder."

Patrols from the 112th ventured farther and farther away from the Arawe beachhead into the jungle's interior until they finally crossed the island and linked up with the Marines on the other side. There is some contention about which was the first Army patrol to link up with the U.S. Marines in mid–February 1944.

It had been only about six weeks since Ray Czerniejewski received a battlefield commission[23] when he was assigned the mission to link up a G Troop patrol with a Marine patrol at the divide of the island. A day behind him was a larger group under Major D.M. McMains, consisting of men from the 2nd Squadron, two ANGAU men, four native police and thirty or so native bearers. The McMains patrol proceeded up the primitive Pulie River in barges before striking out overland.

"The only officer in our patrol across New Britain was Czerniejewski," Pug Wright emphatically declared. "We had a lieutenant, an ANGAU man, and we had a platoon with one squad of machine gun. Pickett put me on the tail end with a Tommy Gun."

"The sister of that ANGAU man on that New Britain patrol had been killed by the Japs," Pickett explained, "Those Australians, they'd take those natives, go in those Jap camps, cut their communications. They did all kinds of damage over there!"

It was early in the rainy season and the Army patrol had to traverse rivers with water up to their shoulders. They negotiated rugged ridges, mangrove swamps and passed through several native villages. After darkness enveloped the jungle, the birds began their chatter. As long as the men cleared their path or rustled the brush, the jungle was silent, but when they stopped for any length of time, the air came alive with the voices of the many varieties of birds. At night, there was always a fear the enemy would surprise them in camp as Ritter and Pickett had once surprised a group of unlucky sleeping Japanese.

One night during the patrol, their ANGAU man surrounded the G troopers with his ten native policemen then moved into the GIs' camp. "We didn't even know they were there!" Pickett recalled. "All of a sudden that jungle got real quiet then they were in on us in a second."

The cavalry patrol was supposed to meet the Marines on the divide, but there was no sign of them. So the G troop patrol continued on through uncharted jungle to the northeast side of the island where they finally reached the Marines' base at Rein Bay. The McMains patrol was still plodding through the jungle, but the newspapers all gave the larger unit credit for being the first Americans to cross the width of New Britain.[24]

"I don't know, (but) it took us about ten or twelve days to cross that island," Pug recalled. "Pickett and Ritter went down there to that Marine quartermaster to get rations. By now Czerniejewski had a long beard. He went down to Marine headquarters and delivered his papers. And they invited him to supper — all of 'em sittin' around with their bars on. None of our guys wore officer's bars. On the supper menu they had rum to pour over the salad. Ole Czerniejewski picked up that rum and poured a glass full! We stayed there a couple of days and took a ship back around the island, back around to Arawe."

Life for the GIs on New Britain settled into a boring daily routine: patrols, outpost guard duty and details. As on Woodlark, natives from the numerous coastal villages became part of the troopers' daily lives. The cavalrymen moved from their foxholes into tents, a chapel was built, they washed their fatigues, and a makeshift barber chair was set up. By now, the troopers' uniforms were a matter of convenience and availability. Photographs of G Troopers in New Britain display various combinations of olive drab fatigues or whatever was practical.

Doyle Tucker returned to his machine gun squad after missing about a month because of his neck wound. The third man in C.W.'s crew now was Clyde Summers, an Oklahoman who had been with the troop since 1940.

During any lull from combat, someone in the troop always seemed to have one of those box cameras and on Arawe it was no exception. Although it was a violation to take personal photographs in a combat area plenty of pictures were made of the men at work or at leisure. They posed with captured enemy flags, holding bottled rice saki, and almost everyone had his picture taken with a Japanese officer's gold samurai sword picked up by 1st Platoon scout Forrest Ritter.

Mail call was always anxiously awaited. "When we'd get letters from home, everybody read 'em," Pug noted. His teenage sisters, Girldene and Dorothy, began to correspond with some of the unmarried G troopers. Photographs of girlfriends and lady pen pals were cherished and widely circulated.

"That ole gal I was writing to was down in Navasota," Pug explained. "And the only time that I ever saw her was when we came from Louisiana (the 1941 Louisiana Maneuvers). I was on a truck and she came up beside that truck — a whole bunch of them girls and boys out there — when we came through there. She wanted my name and my address. And I gave it to her. So she wrote me the whole time I was overseas and she sent four layer cakes. (After the war) I went to see her. Her dad was a justice of the peace and lived on a farm.

"I wrote another gal who joined the WACs and made sergeant. And I was still a PFC."

General Cunningham's Alamo force moved along the south coast of New Britain as far as Gasmata, about 75 miles east of Arawe. However, it was not the Allied command's intention to attack the strong Japanese base at Rabaul. Instead, GHQ had decided to cut Rabaul off and let it die — starve 'em out.[25]

According to Edward J. Drea, Chief, Research and Analysis Division, U.S. Army Center for Military History, the 112th Cavalry Regiment suffered 474 battle casualties during their operations on New Britain: 118 killed, 352 wounded and 4 missing. The regiment arrived there on December 15 with 1,728 troops and, though it received some replacements in January, the unit's strength was only about 1,100 men when the 112th left New Britain the first week of June.[26]

6

Australian Interlude

The pearl for American soldiers on furlough in the South Pacific was the eastern coast of Australia, especially the metropolitan cities of Sidney and Melbourne. In the former British colony, the GIs found a people whose appearance, language and culture resembled their own. Although the inlands of the continent were sparsely inhabited, along the 1750-mile eastern coast visiting soldiers found modern cities, much like those in the United States. An extensive railway system made travel between cities and towns easily accessible.

Early in the war, Australians welcomed the stream of American soldiers as saviors and some of the northern communities, like Townsville, became armed camps. There was some friction with civilians and jealousy from the lower paid Aussie troops, but the Americans were generally warmly received. With most of the able-bodied Australian males in the military, eligible females greatly outnumbered men among the local population.

As their position on New Britain became more secure that April, the 112th Cavalry began to give leave to a certain percentage of men from each troop. Armed with a ten-dollar raise for combat pay and anxious for their first female company in over a year, the troopers made their way to Australia by whatever means available.

The regiment also began the process of selecting troopers for rotation back to the States in March of 1944 and one officer and twenty enlisted men returned to the States that May. Pickett Wright had hoped to be selected for rotation, but another NCO was picked instead.

"Then Czerniejewski picked me to go to Australia with him," Pickett recalled. "First, we went to Melbourne, stayed a week there and then we went to Sidney. I was with two guys from the signal corps — I teamed up with them. I stayed two weeks in Sidney. I had a good lookin' girl. She was a secretary in the shipyards. She was wantin' me to desert the army and go to the mountains where they couldn't find us!"

Sidney was Australia's largest city with a population of about one and a half million people. It also was well south of the war zone so there was less of a military presence than in Brisbane or Townsville. From the vast harbor, one could see the city and suburbs covering the surrounding hills. Forty miles west of Sidney were the Blue Mountains with some of the most spectacular scenery on the continent. With its nightclubs and cabarets, Sidney boasted a livelier night life than the other Australian cities.

Pug Wright also took a vacation in Australia, but his leave followed a less regulation course than his brother's:

"Captain Howell let Pickett go. That split two brothers contrary to army orders. So they were hinting around that he was gonna let the rest of us go, but that L.C.M. was leaving that dock. We were down there, so we boarded it. There was five of us, one corporal and four privates."

The five G Troopers made it to Finschhafen, New Guinea, where they were put on extra duty, "shovelin' mud," Pug said. "We went over there to the airport and there's a guy out of the 112th over there, a sergeant. And he told us to have our bags packed and be ready at daylight the next morning. He sent a truck for us and they flew us to (Port) Moresby and took us to an M.P. camp. There, the next morning, we woke up to find four of us from G Troop on K.P., so we went down to that kitchen and got into a fight!

"Harvey Thompson went down to the gate sergeant and asked, 'What would you do if we walked out of this place?'

"'I'd mark you a.w.o.l.!' was the reply.

"'What'd you do with our papers?'

"And he said, 'I'll send them to your outfit.'

"That's all I wanted to know."

The next morning, the wayward cavalrymen found themselves assigned to kitchen police again. Upon receiving clean uniforms and a fresh supply of cigarettes, they picked up their dilly bags and walked out.

"That ole sergeant hollered 'Halt!' We just waved at him and kept on walking," Pug remembered. "We went over to the airport and laid down on those ole Red Cross benches in the snack bar and ate doughnuts. One guy chickened out and went back to the M.P. outfit and turned himself in."

The cavalrymen told the base dispatcher they would stay there until he could get them a flight to Australia. "He came up and said he had three seats," continued Pug. "But we didn't want three to go and leave one. So we flipped heads or tails to see who would go. Me and Stig won."

Pug and Stig arrived in Townsville, Australia, at about four o'clock in the morning and reported to the staging area for troops coming on or off the front line. A first sergeant from the 32nd Infantry Division arranged railway tickets for them on the coast railroad.

"We got on that train about nine o'clock and every station it went through they had to stop for tea. We got to Gladstone, Australia, a town on the east coast about the size of Childress. We asked the engineer, 'If we bail off this train, can we get back on it some other time with these same tickets?'

"He said, 'You sure can. It's a pretty good little town.'

"'Got any places to stay?'

"He said, 'You go up this street two blocks and there's a hotel. There'll be a light in the back of that hotel. That's my wife — she cooks there. Go in the back way and she'll fix you up with a room.' "

So the two troopers got off the train at Gladstone and sought out the railroad man's wife who found rooms for the servicemen. The time Pug spent in Gladstone was a pleasant and refreshing experience. Most of the town's shops were along one short street, its small houses of brick and wood scattered over the surrounding bluffs. Warehouses and a few factories were located along the railroad and waterfront.

"We found out later, the mayor of the town owned that hotel and he had six daughters," Pug noted. "There was a bar right down under the stairwell where we came down and two of them girls worked in that bar. And down the street one block was a Greek-American who had a modern cafe with an American jukebox."

The locals were friendly and Pug cultivated new friendships. One new girlfriend became pen pals with his sister Girldene, and Pug's Aussie female friend continued to write him after the war.

"We stayed there twelve days and went back and got on that train," he recalled. "They had gotten the word out, because when we got to Brisbane, the M.P.s got us."

The troublesome cavalrymen were put in a railway car with three sailors. The sailors had brought three large grocery sacks full of liquor onto the train and they shared it with their new Army buddies and any women who wanted to join them.

"That ole train had an isle on one side and the compartments had walls between them," Pug continued. "We kept runnin' back and forth to the diner where we stole all the cake.

"Before we got to Sidney, it was getting pretty rugged. They pushed us out of the diner. There was two M.P.s and a civilian law. They pushed us up to our car and locked the door behind us. When we got to our car, Stig turned around and hit that door, broke the glass out and cut his hand up. They took money out of his pocket to pay for all the damages — him and the sailors."

In the meantime, Harvey Thompson had made his way to Sidney where he and another trooper rented a basement flat with ground level windows that became a gathering place for G Troopers there on leave for "fun and frolic, booze and bull." One night "there was a young lady there who was a contortionist," Thompson recalled. "She could put her legs behind her head, roll around on the floor like a ball.

"It was an amazing exhibition and we were enthralled and near trance-like when she suddenly yelled that there was a peeping tom at the window. Well, you know Pug—rough hewn but ever the southern gentleman. He jumped up and ran outside with the lady to get that 'blankety blank' peeping tom. Shortly, we heard a loud yell, after which Pug and the lady came back in. Sure enough, she said, they got outside, saw a guy standing there. Pug, the defender of all womanhood, rushed up and slugged the guy! Unfortunately, the 'guy' was an iron statue and Pug fractured his hand!"[1]

Years later at a reunion in Abilene, Pug said Harvey Thompson was the "leader" of the G Troopers assembled in Sidney." After Pug's death, Thompson wrote, "Of course, Pug never followed anyone in his life, he was definitely an original, one of a kind and his leaving us was our loss, not his."[2]

While the war in the Southwest Pacific Theater entered somewhat of a quiet period, dramatic events were unfolding in the war against Germany. On June 1 the 36th Infantry Division broke through the Germans' 'Caesar Line' that had isolated a large American army in the Anzio beachhead. The Texas Division surged all the way to the outskirts of Rome where the "T" Patchers paused to reorganize before entering the city of almost two million people. Before daylight on June 5 the 36th Infantry was formed into a convoy of tanks and trucks to become the first American division to enter the Holy City. Along the moonlit streets the soldiers could hear the people at the windows of the tall buildings clapping their hands for the liberators. After daybreak the Americans crossed the Tiber River and drove past the Vatican.

Sergeant Edgar Wright was piloting a two and a half ton truck hauling his Medical Battalion's cooks. However, Ed missed a turn and entered the Vatican. "This gate was open so I drove in and made a big circle," he remembered. "I stopped and asked this nun a question, but she didn't even look at me. I drove right back out the way I came in and caught up with the convoy."

The division set up north of Rome and Ed made several trips into Rome. "I carried a load of men to that St. Peter's Church. Pope Pius made a speech to them. I waited outside by my truck, then took 'em back. I was in front of that church several times. St. Peter's is a beautiful sight."[3]

The 36th's fame lasted only a few hours, for a day after the Texas Division liberated Rome, the Allies launched the invasion of France over the beaches of Normandy. Pickett's twin brother Aubort Wright had only to wait six weeks to be thrown into the war with George S. Patton's Third Army. The 204th Artillery Battalion experienced its initiation in combat during the battle for St. Lô, France, that July.

"Every night during the war," remembered Pug's sister, "Papa disappeared for about seven minutes. Mama said she didn't know where his place was, but he was praying for the boys overseas."[4]

During the war, Childress, Texas, was a hub-bub of activity, especially with the new Army airfield nearby.[5] Because of the base and the absence of most all of the local young men because of the war, jobs were plentiful.

"There were always a lot of people at our house," noted Girldene. "Those training planes from the base would fly over. They would dive at us. One almost hit that wind charger and the wires. We would just wave — because they were boys!"

The girls' mother finally had enough. She went into the house and emerged with a .22 rifle. "I'll fix that gentleman," she exclaimed. "He's not divin' around here and tear down that wind charger."

Then there was the time the Wrights were driving down a Childress county road — Pa and Ma in the front, their three teenage daughters in the back. Things were fine until the planes from the base flew by. "Me and Dorothy were just wavin' at them from the back seat. Those planes flew right alongside and we kept on wavin'. The planes went up there and came right back at the front of our car and barely missed us. Ma and Pa kept getting madder. 'Get that number; I'm gonna turn them in!' he said. We just sat there quietly."[6]

The lives of the civilians in the United States were significantly altered by laws passed in 1942 and 1943 to free up food, fuel and other materials for the war effort. These new laws called for rationing, or limiting the amounts of goods people could buy. By 1943, rationed items included gasoline, fuel oil, tires, sugar, coffee, dairy products and canned foods. Each tiny ration stamp was good for about a month and was worth a specified number of points. To buy something rationed, a person needed enough stamps to supply the required points. When all a family's stamps were used up, they had to wait until the next month to get more. Gasoline rationing was particularly a hardship as drivers were limited to as little as three gallons a month.

New automobiles were unavailable for purchase during the war, and the tires people had to use on their older model cars were so bad that once Pug's brother Butch was changing a flat tire on the family car when another tire on the opposite side blew out.

Pug and Pickett were still in Australia on June 4 when C.W. Wiggins and the rest of 2nd Squadron, 112th Regiment, sailed from the harbor at Gasmata,

New Britain, to Finschhafen, New Guinea, aboard a fleet of L.C.T.s. C.W. had turned down a leave to Australia so that another man could go and thought he was in for a rest at Finschhafen. When he got there, C.W. found the same ole mud, bugs and misery that had plagued him in New Britain. The only difference was there were no Japanese.

The regiment's bivouac was in freshly plowed earth that the bulldozers scraped out of the jungle. As it would happen almost every late afternoon, a downpour that first day turned the camp into a quagmire. Not only did the troopers' boots sink into the mud, the soaked soil was not even firm enough to hold the stakes for their tents.

"We went there for a break," Wiggins related. "Had to clean out underbrush and set up tents. The first day we had off, this guy came out and said, 'Bring your rifles and be ready to move out in two hours!'"

After only eighteen days of "rest and relaxation" the 112th Cavalry received new orders. Even Regimental Commander Colonel Alexander M. Miller did not know where they were going, though he expected it would involve combat. Early speculation focused on the long awaited return to the Philippines, but this did not turn out to be the case.

The 112th's redeployment was connected with the final operation in General MacArthur's New Guinea campaign. The Americans' plan was to bypass the Japanese stronghold at Wewak and capture the airfields at Aitape and Hollandia as a prelude to an invasion of the Philippine Islands. The presence of a strong American force in northern New Guinea would also cut off General Adachi Hatazo's 55,000 man army at Wewak from the Japanese 2nd Army in Eastern New Guinea.

The American Army's landings at Aitape, New Guniea, on April 22, 1944, caught the enemy by surprise and the Sixth Army quickly took control of the Tadji airdrome. It was theorized that the 18th Japanese Army at Wewak was now irrelevant. However, General Adachi realized he did not have the supplies to hold out for more than six months. Rather than let his army sit idle and eventually fall to starvation and disease, he made the decision to send 20,000 of the fittest soldiers against the Americans. Only weeks following the Americans' occupation of Aitape, soldiers from three Japanese infantry divisions began their trek through the jungle to attack the American Sixth Army almost one hundred miles to the northeast. Plagued by malaria, on half rations, and carrying supplies by hand, it took Adachi's men over a month to get into position for an attack.

The U.S. XI Corps had left the American 32nd Infantry Division, commanded by Major General William R. Gill, at Aitape to secure the airdrome and protect against any Japanese excursion from the West. The Americans knew the enemy was on the move because the Allies had broken the Japanese code and were able to read their radio transmissions. When forward elements of the Japanese 18th Army attacked outposts of the 32nd in early June, Gill reacted by establishing a new line of outposts along the Driniumor River.

The Sixth Army headquarters scrambled to find any available unit to reinforce Gill's division. The reason usually given for the 112th's redeployment after such a short break was that it was the only idle regiment with combat experience in the area. However, critics who maintained the little independent cavalry regiment always got the short end of the stick point out that the 33rd Infantry Division had arrived in Finschhafen on May 11 and had since been undergoing jungle training. The 33rd was not deployed until September when one of its regiments participated in the Wakde-Sarmi operation in western New Guinea.

When he finally rejoined the regiment in Finschhafen, Pug had to report to headquarters and turn his papers in.

"I went down there and pitched my papers down. Ole Colonel Miller said, 'Better get to your outfit; their moving out!'

"Hutchens and them hadn't come back yet!"

Pug's Australian shenanigans did not go unpunished. "I was on latrine duty several times when I got back," he admitted.

On June 26, 1944, the men of the 112th boarded L.C.I.s (Landing Craft, Infantry) with orders to sail from Finschhafen and reinforce the defenses along the Driniumor. The ships carrying the regiment would follow the coastline of New Guinea and reach the beach at Aitape in two days. When the 112th boarded the transports, fifty-one men, including Lieutenant Colonel Grant, were still on leave (most in Australia) and many did not return to their troop until August.[7] Among the absentee troopers was Pickett Wright, who was relaxing in an apartment at Sidney. Lieutenant Czerniejewski decided it was time they return to their outfit.

"Czerniejewski came by that morning and asked me if I was going back." Pickett said. "I said, 'I'm not goin' back. I got some money left. I got a home here. I don't have to go back!' So he went back.

"A week later, I went to Finschhafen and when I got there our outfit was up at Aitape. I guess I got back from Australia around the first of July. There lay ole Czerniejewski in knee deep mud; layin' on a cot, just as muddy as he could be. When I walked in, he started cussin'. He couldn't get a boat out so he had to stay there in that mud until they got a boat for him. And I caught the same boat he did and got back to the outfit the same time as ole Czerniejewski! We took a supply boat up along the coast and joined the regiment at Aitape."

7

New Guinea

The jungles of New Guinea are unforgiving, with their dense forest and accompanying tangle of vines and brush. Along with the intolerable hot and humid climate come mosquitoes, leeches and all types of insects. The air is stagnant and the forest is permeated with decaying vegetation that emits a sour, unpleasant odor. Dampness is everywhere. "Rainy" and "dry" seasons are relative terms as frequent downpours turn what native trails there are into quagmires or slippery paths. Add the desperate and lethal Japanese soldier to this setting and one gets some idea of what awaited Pug Wright, Bull Wiggins and the other men of G Troop.

On June 28, 1944, twelve L.C.I.s carrying the 112th Cavalry Regiment arrived at Aitape, New Guinea. It had a contingent of about 1450 officers and men,[1] some 150 of them in G Troop. The planners of the operation in the 32nd Infantry Division made a serious miscalculation in the assumption the cavalry regiment would be approximately the size of a three-thousand-man regular Army infantry regiment. In fact, the 112th Cavalry arrived in Aitape with only about 85 percent of its assigned strength. What the 112th did have over a regular infantry regiment was its greater number of light machine guns, an essential component for defensive warfare.[2]

A day after disembarking, the cavalrymen were ordered to occupy the southernmost position on the 32nd Division's Driniumor River defensive line. The 105-millimeter guns of the 148th Artillery were too large to move overland to the Driniumor so they were left behind at Aitape. The regimental band packed away their instruments and went into battle as litter bearers.

Early the morning of June 29, the men of the 112th departed the congested, well fortified Aitape beachhead and were transported by truck as far as the Nigia River. Fifty men at a time, the troopers were ferried across the river by an engineer ferryboat. With each man carrying three day's rations and thirty to forty pounds of equipment (native bearers transported supplies), the column trudged forward through a tropical rainstorm. Having to clear the dense foliage as they moved along, troopers slipped and slid in the deep mud of the narrow trail. Gradually, the condition of their path worsened and as more men tramped along, the muddier and slicker it got.

When some troopers discarded equipment along the trail, General Cunningham became infuriated. However, the regiment made their objective, missing only two stragglers who had fallen ill.[3]

The 1st Squadron set up a perimeter along an unnamed river designated on the map by the letter "X" (short for the military jargon "X-ray"). The 2nd Squadron bivouacked for the night east of the river and the next morning pushed ahead to the Driniumor. After two days of marching in intermittent rain and sleeping in soggy clothing, Troops E, F, and G reached their goal late in the evening on July 1.

The Driniumor flowed from the mountain range to the south through the foothills and entered the coastal plain near the small abandoned native village of Afua. The only landmark in the area, Afua was used to identify the 2nd Squadron's position on the river.

"Afua was only three grass shacks," Pug Wright explained. "In one of the huts was a hen and a rooster that we called the 'shell-shocked rooster of Afua!'"

About a hundred yards wide, including twenty yards of sand and gravel beach on either side, the Driniumor River was usually about knee deep. However, run-off from the frequent rains could swell it to a torrent that was virtually impossible to ford by men on foot. It was the fear of American patrols that a sudden downpour in the mountains might strand them on the opposite bank of the river.

G Troopers learned early on about the lethal potential of the river. One time, C.W. Wiggins was perched on a boulder watching the water rise from a sudden rainstorm in the mountains when Lieutenant Ray Czerniejewski playfully came up behind him.

"I pushed Bull in the Driniumor," Czerniejewski admitted. "It was about twenty feet deep — and he went to the bottom! He was thrashing around so I jumped in after him. He grabbed me around the neck and nearly drowned both of us!"[4]

Past the beach were huge hardwood trees, buttressed by jumbles of slime-covered roots and along the ground there thrived a maze of vines and tropical plants. Though substantial in appearance, many of the large trees were so rotten a moderate gust of wind would push them over, providing ready material for use as breastworks.

The cavalrymen spent their first full day on the line digging three-man foxholes on the west side of the river. Wire communications were laid to the 1st Squadron on River X, but these cables would often be cut by the Japanese and it would be dangerous business to repair them.

The machine gunners cleared kunai grass and river debris from their field of fire. An ideal position for the machine gun was where the gunners had a clear field of fire over a wide area. Also it was important to have two machine guns covering the same field in order to effect a crossfire, in which case, the guns' bullets would crisscross each other and cover a wider area.

Pug complained that "they tried to put my machine gun out on an island in the middle of the river. And I refused. I told ole Lieutenant Dowd, 'Hell No! That's suicide!' He finally agreed to let us dig in along that bank."

In place of rain, July 3 and 4 were hot and steamy. Body salt rapidly formed on the GIs' fatigues, especially in the arm pits. "By the end of the campaign, our clothes would stand up by themselves!" C.W. remarked. Weapons had to constantly be cleaned because of the moisture and humidity. The sun blistered exposed skin and anopheles mosquitoes joined other bugs in assaulting the troopers as they prepared shelters and foxholes.

The threat of Japanese ambushes made it too dangerous for rations and supplies to be brought in by bearers along the food train trails so arrangements were made for cargo planes to parachute large pallets of food and ammunition at designated coordinates. In order for the 2nd Squadron to be supplied from the air, a drop zone was cleared out on the nearby knoll that became known as "the native garden."

"When we knew that plane was comin' to make a drop, everybody headed out to that garden," Pug recalled. "When a ration box would hit the ground — them ole ten in ones — it would bounce. If you got the right numbers, you got the bacon 'n' eggs: canned bacon and eggs. It wasn't dehydrated. This one kid — he wasn't out of our troop — was chasin' one box and another hit the ground behind him and bounced, hit him in the shoulder and killed him![5] But that didn't keep the rest of us from chasin' 'em. We went back every day, every time that plane came over."

Patrols sent out from Afua reported signs of the approaching Japanese army as early as July 2 and evidence of the enemy's 18th Army increased as Japanese patrols began to probe the banks of the Driniumor. Pug recalled that C.W. was shoveling out a foxhole while the crew's ammo bearer manned their machine gun with his eyes fixed on the opposite bank.

"Suddenly, ole Summers hollered at Bull, 'There's five Japs over there!' C.W. told him, 'Shoot 'em!' He did! — That machine gun cut the tops out of them trees and the Japs run off. C.W. grabbed him by the leg and jerked him plum away from that gun. And ole Summers was twice as big as he was!"

One Japanese patrol wandered too close to the Americans' position and the G Troop bugler shot and killed one of them. The bugler anxiously gathered up the fallen enemy soldier's rifle and sabre to add to his collection of souvenirs that he planned to sell once he got home to the States.

Concern about the enemy's whereabouts compelled General Julian Cunningham to order platoon strength scouts into the jungle east of the Driniumor. Corporal Pickett Wright and Lieutenant Czerniejewski had recently returned from their furlough in Australia when 1st Platoon, G Troop, was selected for one of these missions. Czerniejewski would command the scout with Sergeant Harold Paulsen second in command. An artillery lieutenant, his radioman and a medic were assigned to go along while a Piper Cub aircraft was to make periodic radio contact.

Early in the afternoon of July 9, with Pickett Wright's squad in the lead, the patrol of twenty men drew rations for five days and crossed the river into the uncharted New Guinea jungle. Pickett and his scout, Forrest Ritter, alternated at the head of the column.

The platoon was soon short two men because a replacement trooper dropped out along the route and Czerniejewski assigned another man to take him back to the regiment's positions on the Driniumor. The going was arduous, as one ridge after another had to be climbed through dense forest. Often the troopers had to pull themselves upward by grasping limbs along the way. The men moved along in single file, clearing vines and overhanging branches from the trail, and it was imperative to keep their sweat blurred eyes on the man to their immediate front. Birds shrieked then quieted as the patrol rustled through the brush. Gnats, mosquitoes and the humidity added to the troopers' misery.

The 1st Platoon spent the night in the jungle and the next day at about noon they reached their goal of the Hareck River. The hand-cranked radio transmitter would not work and when the Piper Cub couldn't make contact it gave up and flew away. No sign of the Japanese was found and, after spending the night, the patrol started back toward the American lines. Before leaving for the Driniumor that morning, their remaining rations were buried because the platoon knew it would be back with G Troop in time for the next meal.[6]

A day earlier, July 10, the 2nd Squadron had been ordered to make a reconnaissance in force east of the river in an effort to frustrate the enemy's plan of attack. Meantime, the 1st Squadron would replace the 2nd at Afua. The three troops of 2nd Squadron forded the Driniumor and the long and winding column hacked its way through the jungle, so thick at times the sun was completely blocked from view. It took the squadron all day to travel a little more than a mile through trackless jungle. At sundown Lieutenant Colonel McMains ordered camp established on high ground at the base of the mountains. Pug, C.W. and the rest of the exhausted, sweaty GIs dug in and consumed a cold meal of K-rations. Shortly before midnight, the jungle blackness was shattered by the sound of artillery and small arms fire to the north in a sector manned by a company of the 128th Infantry Regiment. It was a tense situation as the cavalrymen anticipated an attack at any moment throughout the night. American artillery lobbed a few shells into the jungle on the east side of the river, but at that time there were apparently no Japanese units operating near the 112th's positions.

The next morning, 2nd Squadron took only one hour to traverse the same ground covered the previous day. One trooper said they retraced the ground of the previous day in a jog. When they arrived back at Afua, Pug learned that his brother and the 1st Platoon had not returned from their mission. The 2nd Squadron of the 112th was allowed a rain-soaked respite of only three hours before starting back to River X at 1500.

Though the initial Japanese attack was repulsed, the 32nd Division's commander in the field was concerned that he had no reserves to plug into gaps in his line of defense. Task Force commander Major General C.P. Hall reluctantly granted the request to fall back to River X.

The usually calm and happy-go-lucky Pug Wright lost control of his emotions for one of the few times. He and Orvil Weddel wanted to remain at Afua to await the 1st platoon's return. Captain Howell tried to assure Pug that he could not help his brother by staying behind, but the distraught elder Wright had to be put under guard and ordered back with his squad. One hour following the 2nd Squadron's departure, the area around Afua was decimated by an air strike and artillery barrage.

The march back to River X was perhaps the unit's hardest of the war. A history of the campaign recalled the squadron's hardships: "...a torrential downpour punished them all afternoon. The heavy trail and slippery going slowed the native bearers, who, in turn, retarded the column's progress. After dark ... litter bearers got lost in the black maze, requiring the column to halt until they could be found. After that, men caught hold of the belt or shoulder of the man in front of them and led each other in a procession of darkness. The men stumbled along, and when they slipped and fell over slippery roots or brush on the trail, it caused a chain reaction as several belt holders crashed together in the mud." [7]

"If you didn't step exactly in the bottom of a rut, you slipped into it and damn but your feet and ankles hurt," remembered trooper Ben Moody. "It was so dark on the trail we tried to maintain contact with the guy in front, but it was a constant slip, slide and cuss all night. I remember that two scout dogs somehow managed to get into a fight. Pitch black and cussin' and trying to separate two big dogs and all in that narrow mud strip called a trail." [8]

The ordeal was too much for some of the men. When two members of G Troop lay down beside the trail and began to sob, the unflappable Pug Wright decided it was time to lighten things up.

"They hollered, 'Bring the machine guns up!' I started wading that mud and got up there and everybody had hit the ground on the other side of the trail, so I started singing, "Take This Letter to My Mother." I went up through there and ole Captain Howell stepped out from behind a bush. He damn sure threatened to shoot me with a carbine if I didn't shut up!"

That put an end to any tomfoolery.

Living up to the moniker "Bull," C.W. marched all the way back to River X without complaint and a .30 caliber machine gun on his shoulders. The bugler was not as stalwart. Weighted down with his newly acquired Japanese rifle and saber, he fell back to the end of the column. C.W. chuckled when the straggler was told, "Keep up or get rid of that stuff!"[9]

Upon reaching River X less than an hour before midnight, the regiment dug in. While Troop G was at River X, C.W. and another man were assigned to walk up to a nearby drop zone and bring back whatever supplies had been parachuted in. When C.W. reached the air drop area, he encountered a large supply of weighty Government Issue bread.

"I put some on my back like cotton sacks; some in front — it nearly pulled me over. That bread must of weighed a ton! When I got back to where I had to cross that river, I sent word ahead, 'Go tell 'em to come get this durn stuff. I can't carry it any further!' "

Hampered by an afternoon downpour, the Czerniejewski patrol did not reach the Driniumor until dusk on the eleventh. Although there were no signs of the regiment they proceeded to cross the river.

A member of the patrol, Tony Frangella, remembered, "...as we were crossing the river to get to Afua there was some Australian planes, B20 Bombers flyin' over. As they flew over us we gave 'em the 'V' sign, wavin' to 'em, not knowing what the hell was going on behind the lines. When we got across the river to the Afua camp, we were surprised — nobody was there. There were rations all over with holes in the cans, Japanese footprints, you know, with that toe stickin' out on that footprint on their sandals or whatever they wore — and a lotta ammunition that had been dumped. We didn't know they had been pulled out or where they were."[10]

There was no evidence of a big battle, although Afua's grass huts and the 112th's defensive positions had been torn up by the artillery barrage.

"Our outposts, shelter halves were shot full of holes," recalled Pickett. "Me and Ritter crawled along the bank of that river. We heard 'em (the Japanese) jabbering; they were in our positions! They didn't see us because they were facing away from the river toward our lines. Me and Ritter hurried back and we got out of there."

After a conference, Czerniejewski decided to take the platoon up river to the base of the mountains then swing west until they found the American lines. When the radio still failed to function, it was dismantled and left behind. No enemy soldiers were encountered, but as the patrol moved back across the river another Allied plane flew over and, not expecting any Americans to still be in the area, strafed the unidentified soldiers. Fortunately, no one was hit and the platoon sought refuge on a small island in the river where they spent the night. Hunger began to set it since all their remaining rations had been buried prior to their return to Afua. The next morning, without the aid of even a map, they started for the mountains as planned.

On July 12, only one day after the 2nd Squadron reached their objective of River "X," General Cunningham was ordered to reoccupy the positions the 112th had earlier vacated on the west bank of the Driniumor. Amidst intermittent showers, Troop G arrived back there late in the afternoon and took up a position on the defense line's southernmost flank, downstream from the rest of the regiment. Just to the north was the 127th Infantry Regiment's 3rd Battalion, having been placed under the control of General Cunningham's

Tony Frangella, Afua 1944, Driniumor River in the background (author's collection).

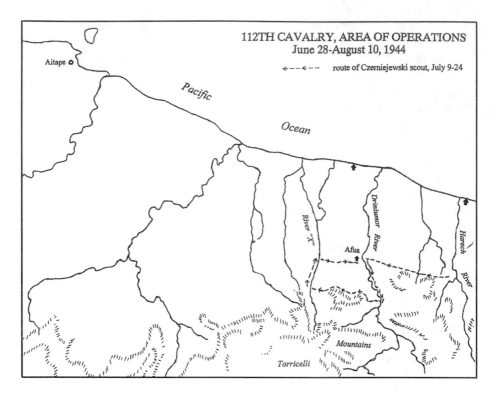

112th Cavalry, area of operations: June 28–August 10, 1944 (drawn by the author).

South Force. Cunningham ignored his superior's requests that he direct the South Force from a command post well behind the lines. The General's decision to remain on the Driniumor River with the cavalry further reinforced his standing among the men.

Pug was put on a detail assigned to bury the Japanese soldier their bugler had killed. Rigor mortis had set in so the body was stiff. In a seemingly odd twist, the troop received replacements from Aitape that day. The new men were from a canine platoon recently detached from the 44th Tank Battalion and were accompanied by their dogs. When the group of replacement soldiers walked up on the burial detail, a veteran trooper working alongside Pug sat the dead Japanese up and began slapping him, threatening aloud that the "prisoner" would never see Tokyo again unless he talked. The trooper then pulled his .45 and "killed" the prisoner as the startled new men looked on.

The cavalrymen's entrenchments were rubble as result of the air strike and artillery barrage. So the G troopers dug out new gun positions or occupied the craters from recent bombings. All work stopped once the sun disappeared behind the mountains to the west.

112th Cavalry command post, Afua, New Guinea, 9 August 1944 (U.S. Army; courtesy National Archives photo SC-287135).

C.W. noted, "It was so dark we stayed in our holes at night. You didn't dare leave your holes, even to go to the bathroom," your own men would shoot you! One man on each machine gun was always awake and on guard while the other two slept."

The night was pitch black and the only sounds were the rushing of the river and the Japanese on the other side. Occasionally, small arms fire could be heard off to the north. Pug could not help but worry about the fate of his younger brother and the missing patrol.

C.W. remarked that it was dangerous to even light a cigarette, because the enemy could spot the smallest flame. "Me and Tucker both smoked. We'd get in our hole, cover up with our ponchos and smoke. It would get pretty smoky under there!"

Often at night enemy infiltrators would sneak into the troop perimeter. "They'd crawl up and feel that loose dirt where you dug that hole and then crawl back," Pug explained. A Japanese soldier got close enough to throw a grenade into C.W.'s machine gun pit, but only the detonator exploded and no one was seriously hurt.[12] Alert troopers had to become adept at quickly diving out of their foxhole when a grenade suddenly came their way.

The Americans continuously sent out small patrols that plodded blindly through the jungle searching for the enemy. Once into the heavy jungle environment, no one knew when or where the silent Japanese soldier would be waiting in ambush. C.W. knew it was a scary and lethal business.

"When we went out on patrol," he said. "You were only supposed to go so far and then come back. Once, this ole lieutenant just kept on goin'. We got out there and you could smell them Japs." Finally, one of the disgruntled troopers muttered out of earshot of the lieutenant, "I'll just shoot the s.o.b. and then we'll all go back!"

As the campaign evolved into small unit close quarter combat conditions, the troop was on constant alert both day and night. The Japanese had only one artillery piece, but as dangerous as the threat of an enemy attack was the chance of being killed by an errant American artillery shell, Allied aircraft fire, or by a nervous trooper in the dark or bush.

On the particularly hot and clear night of July 15, the American artillery fired a routine volley into the jungle on the east side of the river. Riflemen were dispersed between G Troop's machine gun positions and Corporal Orvil Weddel was sharing the hole with C.W. and Doyle Tucker. Since Weddell was not a member of machine gun platoon it seemed unusual that he would be sharing a hole with Wiggins and Tucker. Orvil was friendly with several of the gunners, especially Pug Wright whose story telling meshed well with Weddell's comedy and practical jokes.

"Me, Tucker and Weddel were in the same foxhole," C.W. vividly recalled. "One man was to stand guard in the hole while the other two slept on shelter halves above ground on either side of the guard. The one inside the hole sat on our ammo boxes, about half of his body above ground level. When Weddel woke me up for my shift on guard, we traded places. Five or ten minutes later, one of our artillery rounds fell short. The explosion knocked me down into the hole, but I wasn't hurt. I got up and dusted myself off. I was arranging the boxes when Tucker, who was just a kid, jumped down into the hole. 'There's something wrong with Weddel!' he said. I touched Weddel's arm, but his body was already cold, a piece of shrapnel had pierced his heart. There was nothing I could do."

The constant stress of impending combat and the hostile jungle began to tell on the Americans. For all practical purposes, the regiment was left on the end of the Driniumor defense line to fend for itself against a much larger enemy force. Each man's chief motivation was that of self-preservation. Esprit de corps was sustained to a degree by the regard and respect they each held for their fellow troopers. The tension was greatest at night.

Lieutenant Colonel Philip Hooper (on the phone) and General Julian Cunningham in a crude HQ near the Driniumor River, Afua, N.G. (courtesy of the Texas Military Forces Museum; U.S. Army photograph).

"We had our position strung out along that river," Pug explained. "We'd tie them vines around our arms, run it to the next hole and he'd tie it around his arm (and so forth). When we got ready to change guard, we'd pull that vine. We all didn't have watches and if you didn't have a watch, sittin' up there on guard, thirty minutes seemed like five hours and you was waking the next guy up too early — and you was changing the guard about forty times a night!

"And them damn Japs — they'd crawl through there and get hung up in that vine and take it with them — Dang nearly pull you out of your hole!"

Two of Machine Gun Platoon's corporals were killed on New Britain and Pug's unit was still suffering a shortage of non-commissioned officers. Pug described how he received his promotion:

"Ole Howell called on one of those field phones and told me I was a corporal. I said, 'Naw, you're thinkin' about somebody else. I'm a machine gunner. I've lived a long time behind this thing and I'm stayin' behind it.'

"'Well, somebody's got to get them men something to eat!' he said.

"'Well, you don't have to worry about this squad. They'll get something to eat.' And he made me corporal over that squad. I stayed on the gun, because we were always shorthanded anyway and never did have a full squad."

The night of July 18–19, patrols from the 112th reported a large group of Japanese near the village of Kwamagnirk, directly between Afua and River X. Not only were there enemy forces in the cavalry's rear, it was likely that the 112th was surrounded by the Japanese army.

The missing 1st Platoon patrol commanded by Lieutenant Czerniejewski groped its way westward through the jungle for eight days, ever exposed to the frequent and sudden cloudbursts and assaulted by the steamy climate, hunger, and bugs. During one particularly rainy night the platoon spent in a "swamp," huge leeches latched onto several troopers' exposed skin and could be forced to release its hold only by the application of a lighted cigarette directly on the parasite.[13] The troopers' only nourishment came from the few bits of food they had on their persons or the unripe fruit found along their route.

"I would climb trees but could never identify where our artillery fire was coming from," Pickett recalled. "The gunfire sounded like we had taken back our positions on the Driniumor. We crossed a river (River 'X') and began searching for our lines. The first American I saw was a line stringer.

"I heard these guys talking; knew they were ours because they were speakin' English. Me and Ritter went over to this food trail track. I saw this guy bent over, stringing line — cable for telephone communications. I let him get between us and I walked up and pointed my gun right between his eyes. He was blond, tan, but he turned white! He gave me a cigarette, the first one I'd had in two weeks."

The lineman gave Pickett directions to the 112th's headquarters on River X. There the tired men received a hot meal and a welcome rest. One member of the patrol remembered that since they had no mess kits, "we formed a mess line with banana leaves, cardboard torn from cartons, or anything that would hold food."[14]

Only after chow were the troopers' wounds attended. Some of the men's shoe soles had worn away, leaving the bottoms of their feet a bloody pulp. Two of the veterans from Corporal Wright's squad went to the field hospital because of their injured feet and did not accompany the platoon when it returned to the Driniumor line. Pickett and Ray Czerniejewski were outraged by these men's absence because almost all the men in the platoon were suffering from the same condition.

Soldiers in New Guinea were frequently affected by the condition described as trench foot. Despite the constant wetness of troopers' feet, the imminent and constant threat of attack made it impracticable for them to remove their combat boots and allow the feet to dry. One G-Trooper suffering with that condition said that "whole wads of rotten skin would just come off when you took your socks off."[15]

After being outfitted with new clothes and equipment, the 1st Platoon prepared to return to their troop on the Driniumor River line. Though there was a large amount of traffic from River X to the Driniumor, the jungle was swarming with Japanese patrols, lurking in ambush along the trails. The Czerniejewski patrol was not the only reconnaissance force to be separated from its troop when the 2nd Squadron evacuated the Driniumor positions the morning of July 11. A missing E Troop patrol would link up with the 1st platoon along the trail.

The platoon had one day of rest. Then, with Wright's squad still in the lead, it started back toward the Driniumor on July 21. His BAR man was among the two men in his squad on sick call, so Pickett carried the heavy automatic rifle himself.

"We were going down the trail — a food train track," he recalled. "We were resting at a rise in the trail when four or five Japs came up at the foot of this little hill. I was sitting in the middle of the trail with that BAR. They hadn't seen us. I motioned for everyone to take cover. Ritter went behind a tree off the trail and another ole boy went off to the other side. When I gave the signal, the three of us opened fire. We got all but one of them, who escaped.

"I looked back and the rest of that platoon was bunched up about a hundred yards down the trail. It was just stupid for them to be bunched up like that. I told 'em if the three of us had been overrun, they would've been killed!

"Right before we got to the Driniumor is where Ritter got his silver star. When we came to this knoll I left the trail and went around to the other side. Ritter heard a noise in this high grass. This Jap raised up and started to turn his machine gun toward me. Ritter fired twice from the hip. When we rolled that Jap over, he had one bullet in his head and another in the chest."

Wright's squad spent one more night in the jungle before reaching an element of the 112th on the Driniumor line. The previous evening, Pickett was resting on a fallen tree when Ritter came over to him: "He told me, 'Bob, we're the oldest patrol leaders. The law of averages are bound to catch up with us!'

"That really bothered me because he never was afraid of nothing. I couldn't figure it out. It was his time to lead so I said that I'd lead the squad on in. Two hundred yards later he was dead!"

The First Platoon stopped to rest on the last ridge before reaching the Driniumor. They saw soldiers down below in a perimeter and assumed that they were part of their regiment's defensive line. Pickett and his men walked down the hill, crossed a small creek, and approached these American soldiers. None of the G Troop platoon were aware they were joining C Troop, which was encircled by the Japanese, under fire and cut off from the rest of the regiment. Furthermore, the C troopers thought the First Platoon was a relief force sent to rescue them.

"I was in front; Ritter was behind me," Pickett related. "When this ole lieutenant came out and extended his arm to shake hands, a round — from a Japanese mountain gun — hit at my right foot and turned me a flip. The shrapnel that hit my ankle glanced upward and hit Ritter right under his helmet. They said my rifle was blown up against a tree."

The wounded Pickett Wright was moved inside the C Troop perimeter. Ritter had been killed instantly. Rumor was that the First Platoon's scout had not been wearing a helmet, because he often wore a fatigue hat instead. But after that, more G troopers began wearing their helmets full time.

The First Platoon had no choice but to join Troop C in a desperate effort to keep the Japanese from infiltrating their positions. A history of the campaign explained the extreme nature of their efforts to defend the fifty-foot diameter perimeter:

"Japanese snipers had climbed nearby trees and fired down at anything that moved. Anyone standing up was a potential target, and the tension was enormous. Any movement was dangerous because Japanese infantrymen less than fifty meters way could fire into the tightly packed perimeter. Furthermore, a slough filled with old logs and other debris from previous flash floods ran into the perimeter. This slough provided the Japanese excellent cover to crawl closer and closer to Troop C's lines. All the cavalrymen could do was fight back, tend their wounded, and, under cover of darkness, bury their five dead. According to veterans of that fight, they really did not expect any relief...." [16]

Pickett remembered that he was "laid under a big tree. About sundown, you could hear that mountain gun fire — and then it would land!" [17]

Nighttime was particularly agonizing. It was pitch black and the only sounds were the rustling of leaves by nervous troopers or Japanese infiltrators. Occasionally, the quiet was shattered by the gunfire from a nervous trooper.

On the morning of the twenty-third, a Piper Cub scout plane flew over. The beleaguered troopers ignited a phosphorus grenade as a distress signal. The plane circled and dropped a note: "Stay put! Help coming!"

That afternoon, a relief attempt by Troop E was beaten off. And then, about mid-morning on the twenty-fourth, a fire fight broke out east of the C Troop perimeter. Suddenly, American riflemen burst out of the jungle and, firing as they ran, rushed through the perimeter, chasing the Japanese back across the river. It had taken a battalion of the 127th Infantry Regiment to break the siege. A much larger perimeter was established for the night. A heavy rain began about midnight and continued into the next morning. Shortly before noon, Pickett Wright was carried on a litter back to the G Troop area north of Afua.

He later reflected about his wounds: "On all those patrols I heard bullets whizzing by my head and never thought I would get hit. But when I did, it put the fear of God in me.

"Guys that had been wounded before and came back to the troop were never the same in combat as they were before. Now I knew why!"

8

River of Death

About mid-morning on July 25, the rain that had poured all night abated and an eerie mist rose from the steamy jungle ground. The missing 1st Platoon patrol made its way back to G Troop as four men carried Pickett Wright on a makeshift litter made of a GI blanket wrapped around two poles, his mangled foot swathed in bloody bandages. He had little time to spend with his brother and friends before being evacuated by native litter bearers down the river to the field hospital at Aitape.

The younger Wright brother was carried out by four natives along a path that paralleled the river. The trail wound through openings in the jungle and an occasional field of kunai grass. Occasionally, the Driniumor could be spotted through breaks in the foliage. Soldiers from the 32rd Infantry Division were dug in along the banks all the way to the sea.

Pickett remembered that "on the way, we passed Doyle Tucker, who was standin' on the bank, eatin' out of a can of beans. He smiled and waved.[1]

"Those natives carried me with four poles up on their shoulders. Right in front of me was four Fuzzy Wuzzies with a Jap. As soon as the shootin' started, they would disappear. Every time a plane came over, mine would set me down and run into the brush. The ones carrin' the Jap would just drop him!"

The sky was overcast and it rained off and on the next day. The only enemy activity came from the Japanese artillery piece which fired off a few rounds. The 112th sent out small units to look for the enemy on the twenty-seventh.

That day, Doyle Tucker was selected for a patrol east of the river. He left his soggy foxhole, picked out a Tommy Gun and moved out with the patrol into the jungle.

"They just came by and picked you for those patrols," C.W. Wiggins lamented. "You didn't have any choice."

A few hours later, word was received that two G troopers had been killed in a Japanese ambush. One of them was Doyle Tucker. C.W. had tried to counter the negative influence of some of the heavy drinkers on the youngster, but it didn't make any difference anymore. Tucker was only twenty-one years old.

That night a recent replacement trooper crawled out of his foxhole after dark to relieve himself. Leaving one's hole at night violated a cardinal rule of jungle warfare and gunfire from a fellow trooper's Thompson found the individual prodding through the darkness. The replacement suffered a dangerous leg wound and was taken to the field hospital at considerable peril to the men carrying him. As they approached each foxhole, the troopers called out their intention of passing by so they would not be shot. Following treatment to stabilize the fallen G Trooper who had lost a lot of blood, he was evacuated by native litter bearers to the coast. The bearer responsible for the crucial bottle of plasma was told that he was incorrectly holding the container upright whereas the blood would flow into the patient's arm only if the top was pointed downward. Apparently the native did not understand, for when Private Thomas Sullivan reached the beach he was dead.[2]

Thus far, the 112th Cavalry had been on the defensive. From July 13 to the end of the month, the regiment suffered 260 casualties, seventeen percent of its strength at the start of the campaign; and that figure did not include 426 men lost to disease

P.F.C. Doyle Tucker, Woodlark Island (author's collection; Wright family photograph).

and trenchfoot.[3] However, General Cunningham bowed to the desire of General Hall to commence offensive operations against the Japanese after he reorganized his shrinking forces by shortening the length of his line of defense. G Troop, which had occupied the regiment's most northernmost position along the river defense line, was placed in reserve on a ridge near headquarters and the drop zone. Cunningham would be ready to attack by the first of August but General Adachi beat him to the punch. Reinforced by two regiments of reinforcements from the 41st Division the Japanese managed to assemble a force of four thousand soldiers to concentrate against the cavalry's positions around Afua.[4]

On August 1, the now desperate Japanese launched a frenzied dawn attack against C Troop's sector at the southernmost section of the line. The enemy was almost accommodating to the cavalry by charging en masse, rank after rank into the Americans' machine guns. Artillery, mortar fire and the Americans' guns massacred the attackers, their dead left in piles outside C Troop's positions. Troop G was ordered to counterattack at 8:30 A.M., but all that was left were a few enemy stragglers. The large numbers of Japanese corpses were unsettling sights. For the rest of the campaign, a necessary but unpopular task was burial of the dead. It was an urgent task as freshly killed bodies began to decompose in a matter of a few hours in the damp climate.

The American forces always ceased military operations after dark and withdrew into their defensive positions. The Japanese took advantage of this tactic by conducting small unit harassing attacks during the night, but they were unable to pull off a successful nighttime assault involving large numbers of soldiers.

Pug Wright remembered that "they pulled us back over there around ole Cunningham and we dug in up on that ridge. I pulled my shoes off, the first time I'd had 'em off in thirty days. We thought we was in a rest camp and that night they attacked us!"

At about 3 A.M. the morning of August 2 an enemy patrol infiltrated the G Troop area at the edge of the drop zone and launched a hand grenade assault against the entrenched Americans. Though the enemy was repulsed, two G troopers were wounded in the Japanese attack. One of the wounded was Joe Bynum, who was placed on a litter made of wood and taken from the ridge in the direction of the field hospital. Captain William Davis, the squadron's medical officer, encountered the litter bearers along the trail and decided to examine the wounded man there by flashlight.[5] Lieutenant Ezra Meeks and T4 Leonard Parker were heading up the trail toward the noise of battle when they hesitated at the place where Bynum was being attended. Back on the ridge, mortar support was called for to discourage the enemy sniping.

"That was the night C.W. and Mitchell were way down on the end of the line," Pug continued. "They called down there on that lil' ole phone: 'Pug! They're blowin' us off the hill!' They had knocked a hole in our lines and I called them (the mortar platoon) and told 'em fifty yards to the right. Well, they pulled it to the right fifty yards. Then I told 'em 100 yards in. And one round went behind us."

The 60-mm mortar round that fell short exploded above the head of the medical officer treating Joe Bynum. Wounded was Leonard Parker, who confirmed that "the same shell killed Captain Davis, our medical officer, Corporal Van Sawyer of Loraine, and Private Luke Fowler."[6]

Meanwhile, the troop's machine gunners continued to feed ammunition into their overheated guns. Multi-colored tracer bullets that made up every fifth round buzzed through the darkness like a swarm of angry bees. American artillery shells landed all around them, tearing away the tree tops and throwing up geysers of water each time a round landed in the river. The artillery and mortar fire became so intense C.W.'s crew was on the verge of being driven from their position by their own Army. Pug manned his field phone and called off the barrage:

"And I called 'em and told 'em: 'Hold the fire of those mortars and lift the artillery! We'll fight it out with our damn machine guns!' That's what they done. They stopped the artillery off C.W. and Mitchell, and stopped them mortars."

Pug's machine gun crew was heavily involved in the firefight as well.

"Ole Mudcat (Patterson) sat out there with his feet down in that hole, smokin' that cigarette, firing that machine gun. Them mothers were right down under them tree roots and you couldn't get 'em with our machine guns.

"I was barefoot that night and I had to carry ammunition. That damn Tarleton hollering out there —'About out of ammunition!' I said, 'Why don't you tell the damn Japs that! Just keep hollerin'!'

"So I go down," Pug continued; "We had some ole dogs tied to a tree right down there at the foot of that little ole hill — and I was more afraid to go by them dogs after that ammunition than I was to stay up there on that line. But I made three trips down there carryin' that machine gun ammunition to them guns."

At daybreak, the cavalrymen discovered several helmets and rifles, two machine guns, a dead Japanese soldier, and "numerous trails of blood."[7]

"That ole 43rd Infantry captain come over there the next morning," Pug remembered. "We had gathered up twenty-eight helmets and three or four machine guns and one mortar and that captain came up to ole (Sergeant) Willie A. Sunday and said, 'What was ya'll shootin' at over here last night? Hogs!'

"Willie A. said, 'Well, they might have been hogs, but they's all carryin' machine guns in their mouths!'"

Caption: Scout dog "King," 26th quartermaster Dog Platoon, with handler, New Guinea 1944 (courtesy of the Texas Military Forces Museum; U.S. Army photograph).

Casualties among G Troopers continued to increase. On August 3, a G Troop patrol was attacked across the river and Sergeant Jim Wheeler of Abilene was killed. The next day another patrol, led by Lieutenant Robert O'Brient, was ambushed in the jungle.

G Troop was still off the line lounging and cleaning weapons when, early in the afternoon of August 4, Willard Keast of F Troop burst into their troop area and asked for volunteers to go on a rescue mission for Lieutenant O'Brient and four other men. He said they had been wounded and were still in the jungle. Headquarters would not assign a relief force, but told Keast he could ask the idle G Troop for help. O'Brient was from Roby, Texas, and had been an enlisted man in G Troop back at Fort Clark. It was not hard to find friends who would go after him.[8] Sergeant Tom Pat Glass of Abilene had a relatively safe job as unit clerk, but he was a good friend of O'Brient and received permission to go along.

Pickett's wounds had caused Pug to think about his own mortality. "I had quit volunteering for patrols after Pickett got wounded. I told Mudcat, 'Odds is against us, and I ain't even gonna do it!' Howell sent a runner back and told me, 'I'll volunteer for you!'

"Now you had to go if they took a combat platoon. So me and Mudcat went down there. Our machine gunners (his squad) had done volunteered as riflemen and I told them, 'Well, as far as I'm concerned, I'd rather have you on machine guns, but I will put riflemen on machine guns.' I wound up with (Bill) Hillison and (Jake) Whitten on Tarleton's gun with him."

A thirty-one man relief patrol under the command of Lieutenant Ray Czerniejewski was assembled. Unbeknown to them, O'Brient was already dead. One of the patrol's survivors made it back to the American lines despite a stomach wound and another was found by the Americans three days later.

Already wounded and weakened from dysentery, Private Keast led the way. The rescue patrol crossed the river, entered the jungle and walked right into another Japanese ambush. Pug found himself in his tightest spot of the war.

The ill-fated patrol worked their way along a ridge, crossed a ravine and entered "a flat, in a valley" near where the O'Brient patrol had been attacked. The foliage was so heavy enemy soldiers could easily be hidden in ambush. Suddenly, machine gun fire peppered the leading elements of the American patrol. Corporal Hillison was hit in the first salvo and tried to crawl away. He was killed by another machine burst.[9]

"A number of us started firing at the enemy positions," Keast remembered, "when I felt something like a bolt of lightning hit my right arm, knocking my gun out of commission, tearing my arm to shreds and lodging bullets in my shoulder. I was bleeding so profusely and, being sick to begin with I collapsed behind a tree. Soon the medics were dragging me from the area and giving me plasma there on a stretcher."[10]

It now seemed that the jungle in front and on both sides of the patrol was alive with enemy soldiers. Sergeant Tom Pat Glass took two bullets in the chest and one in the throat. Tarleton's machine gun was quickly knocked out of action.

"Tarleton was off to my right and I couldn't see his gun," Pug explained. "I don't know what happened, but he came runnin' out of the bushes — him and Whitten ... and ole Whitten had his finger shot off — it was hanging down. And Hillison had been his third man.

With the forward element of the patrol in disarray, Lieutenant Czerniejewski called for the men still on the trail to move up and began to organize a defense. With Tarleton's machine gun out of action, Ray sent Mac and the wounded Jake Whitten back to the Driniumor to report the patrol's predicament. They turned over their machine gun ammunition to Dewey Johnson and headed back down the jungle trail.

Japanese prisoners of war at command post, 112th Cavalry Regiment, Afua, 9 August 1944 (U.S. Army; courtesy National Archives photo SC-259683).

"I don't know how they got out because we was surrounded," Pug recollected. "They were behind us, beside us and in front of us. And Czerniejewski pulled us off in a big hole — 'Tarleton and them got out to get us help!' he said.

"Things was gettin' hot. Ole Mudcat was a hangin', standing in the bottom of that shell crater. He couldn't hardly shoot that machine gun so he was hangin' on the side of that bank with that gun. I kept on Czerniejewski to let us fight our way out, and he finally agreed."

The patrol initiated an orderly withdrawal, firing their weapons as they retreated. However, the enemy trailed them and stayed on the American's flanks.

"I saw a clean place," Pug said. "I told ole Mudcat, 'Set that tripod right there in that clean spot.'

"Ole Dewey Johnson was with us — he's carrying the ammunition. So he went to that clean spot. I was shootin' that machine gun and carrin' it. I set it on that tripod and them suckers must have had holes dug. I could see just the tops of them all around us on that ridge."

1st Platoon's Charles Hufstedler vividly remembered that day: "Lieutenant Czerniejewski ordered a withdrawal back over the top of the ridge and as he came by me he asked me to give covering fire (from behind a log) while the rest withdrew. I was firing as fast as I could when one Jap machine gun zeroed in on me, but just as it did, Pug Wright and Mudcat Patterson — who had set up their machine gun at the top of the ridge — opened up on the Jap gunner and his assistants. If Pug had not killed the Jap gunner when he did, I would not be here today. As it was, I was shot in the right hip, the stomach, intestines and chest."[11]

"We lost that tripod," Pug continued. "After that first time it was too much trouble. Mudcat would scoop it up, scoop the machine gun up from me and never stop firing. And when I would get to where he was I took it from him — I don't remember whether it was three or four boxes of 300 rounds per box — and when we got over this slope, down in that little creek bed, we had thirteen rounds. That's all we had. Me and him burned all up our arms."

By this time, Hoyt Bynum and a medic had managed to drag Hufstedler to safety. "That medic didn't want to carry Hufstedler back," Pug said. "Said he wouldn't make it! I pointed my machine gun at him and said that he WOULD!"

The survivors of the relief patrol hurriedly retraced the trail back to the Driniumor, leaving two dead troopers behind. Hillison and Glass were killed and Sergeant Harvey Thompson, and troopers Bill Duckworth, Ed Keast and Jake Whitten were wounded. Pug had beaten the odds and so did Hufstedler, who survived despite his serious wounds.

The Japanese launched their last big attack of the campaign a little after six in the morning of August 4. The fanatic banzai charge against the regiment's northern sector manned by B Troop was a complete failure. When it was over, the river was filled with 200 of the enemy's dead.

After that, the Japanese began their retreat back to Wewak, but G Troop had not suffered its final casualties. During a drive by the 2nd Squadron to harass the retreating Japanese army, the cavalry was ambushed by a group of Japanese. Ray Czerniejewski was waving orders when a bullet hit his hand, mangling three fingers. During the same firefight, Trooper Oskar Carlsrud of 2nd platoon suffered a fatal neck wound to become the eleventh G trooper to die in action since July 10.[12]

C.W. stated that "the Japs threw their guns in the river. We were sitting on the bank and the Japs crossed the river a few hundred yards downstream, but we didn't shoot because we had orders not to. Didn't think about it at the time, but they were pitiful — hungry, ragged, no equipment, disorganized. I don't know where they went. (They were) just wanderin' around in groups."

The Japanese 18th Army was finished as an effective fighting force and never again would be a threat in New Guinea. It was estimated that the enemy's 20th and 41st Divisions lost over 8,000 men, most of them killed in battle or dead from wounds and illness.[13]

The defense of the Driniumor line was the defining event in the history of the 112th Cavalry. On New Britain the regiment was able to repel numerous attacks and persevered due to their overwhelming advantage in resources. Though the cavalry suffered significant casualties at Arawe, there was never a chance that the regiment would be overrun. The battle along the Driniumor River was a different story. Against a much larger Japanese force, the 112th held its ground and inflicted large numbers of casualties on the enemy. If the troops of the 112th had been routed, the results would have been catastrophic. Instead, the former horse soldiers held the line and the victory was theirs.

Photograph of a woman taken from the body of a Japanese soldier by a G Troop burial detail (author's collection; Wright family photograph).

The 112th remained in its positions on the Driniumor for six more days, patrolling and burying the dead. They came to sense the humanity of their enemy when photographs of wives and children were found on many of the dead Japanese.

"One time, when we were burying dead Japs," Pug recalled, "one went into rigor mortis and sat up out of that grave just like he was alive. Ole C.W. put his foot on the Jap's chest and pushed him back into the hole and covered him up."

On August 10, 1944, the regiment finally received the order to return to Aitape. The troopers began the march down the Driniumor toward the sea where trucks would take them the rest of the way. On the march to the coast, the bugler and his trophies became bogged down in the middle of the river. A corporal ordered Wiggins to help him, but C.W. refused.

"If he'd get shut of that junk he could keep up!" he argued. "That was the only time I disobeyed an order."

Once at Aitape, the regiment pitched tents, replaced tattered clothing and missing equipment, and commenced a return to regular army routine. Instead of foxholes, the troopers now had the luxuries of pyramid tents, cots and mosquito netting. Pickett wasn't there. He had already been evacuated to the U.S. Army hospital in Finschhaven.

"We had just come off the Driniumor," Pug recalled; "They called a inspection and I was chief of section. I don't know where I was, but when I came back, them guys had their field gear laid out for inspection. I told them, 'Hell with that inspection!' We just came off the line up there for fifty days and half the guys' shirts was tore. Ole C.W. had all his laid out there and was laying down on his bunk — the tent's flies were opened up. And they even had mine (gear) laid out there, my pistol with a clip out of it layin' on the bed all shined.

"I said, 'What did ya'll do this for?'"

"'Well, if you don't stand inspection, they'll take your stripes — bust you,' one of them said.

I replied, 'I don't care, it don't worry me; just forget that inspection. Tell 'em to go to hell!

"They said, 'No, we cleaned up for you. If you're not our sergeant, we'll get somebody else —*sorrier* than you are!'

"So I picked the pistol up and I put that clip in it and let the bridge go home. It's got a latch on the side. You just flip that thing to load it. Naturally, your hammer's back — it's a regular .45 automatic. I pulled that trigger before I put it my holster and when I did, boy, it fired!— pointed right over ole C.W. It went right through that fly right up over him.

"'Good grief! You'll get somebody killed!' He never moved, he just kept layin' on that cot."

The cavalrymen soon discovered that the local native village across the river was having some sort of celebration and the sleepless soldiers remembered that "those natives played the drums and danced to the same tune all night long."

C.W. and one of the recent replacements, a "kid" named Bill Garbo (he often referred to the younger men as "kid"), crossed the Army's foot bridge made from steel matting to visit one of the native villages. They spent the day and took photographs of and with their new friends. As in previous relations with the natives the cavalrymen noted that there were no women about. The Americans speculated the native females were either hidden or evacuated because of the threat from the Japanese.

Photographs of C.W. taken at Aitape suggest the effects of the recent campaign. The fatigue showed on his face and despite the quinine, he had contracted malaria and like most of the troop had diarrhea. "He was so skinny he wouldn't make a shadow," Pug observed.

A particularly callous incident occurred while the regiment was recovering in camp at Aitape. Some of the men in G Troop suggested that a knife Forrest Ritter had taken off a dead Japanese officer be raffled off and the money sent to his parents. "It was an exceptionally ornate knife," wrote Lionel Carter, "made of silver and with the handle encrusted with jewels. The departed Japanese must have come from a well-to-do family." But on the day of the drawing, it was discovered that someone had stolen the knife from Ritter's barracks bag left with the supply sergeant for safe keeping. The troopers decided to send the money collected for the raffle tickets to Ritter's parents anyway.[14]

Each month, six men from each troop were to be sent back to the States under the Army's rotation program, whereby the veterans would gradually be replaced without compromising the integrity of the regiment as a fighting unit. Several troopers, including C.W., were due to be rotated as soon as transportation could be arranged. But after two weeks at Aitape, it was announced that the regiment was returning to their previous positions along the Driniumor River.

"It was a glum group that groped their way down that slippery jungle trail," wrote Lionel Carter in his memoirs; "...it must have been a strange and terrible experience for those who were untested in battle and encountering the jungle for the first time. One big difference this time was the absence of shooting and shelling, and another more horrible one was the countless skeletons laying half in and half out of the river along the Driniumor. Stripped of all flesh, they gleamed whitely in the mud of the river, bleached by the sun that seeped through the foliage and washed by the water that gurgled around them."[15]

Recovery of their dead buddies and tedious patrols were the order of the day. Some were recovered, but many were not. Among the latter number was Forrest Ritter who was hastily buried near where he fell. According to G troopers, an artillery shell had obliterated the marker on Ritter's grave as well as those of four C troopers interred nearby.

A veteran G trooper related his experience of recovering bodies when he and four other men were sent out with a member of the patrol that had suffered the death of one of its members. "We found three or four Japs and our guy. Because of the time after being shot, you can imagine what condition the body was in.... It was quite a chore getting him back because of the terrain and the guys got sick and I had to send back to the troop just to get some fresh people to help. I recall that because of the underbrush we had to use just two guys at a time to carry the stretcher. When we went up a hill the body fluid from the corpse ran onto the front of the trooper carrying the stretcher; when we came down a hill the body fluid ran onto the back of the trooper. The odor as you know was just terrible and we had it on our uniforms. I remember that when we got back to the troop area we were given new uniforms and we all washed in the Driniumor for at least an hour trying to get the smell off our bodies."[16]

Encounters with Japanese stragglers were rare and the monotony was worsened by the tropical climate. Pug was on a patrol that encountered a party of highland natives that had ventured down from the mountains. These aborigines were armed with spears and adorned with feathers. The Americans decided they were from one of New Guinea's tribes of cannibals.

Finally, word was received that a ship was available to transport the men due for rotation. No one from G Troop had been rotated back to the States since the Driniumor campaign began in June, so quite a few troopers left the regiment. One who had been scheduled for rotation, but would not return was Van Sawyer. The death of his friend since childhood had left C.W. the sole survivor among the three Loraine members of the 112th.

After adding the number of casualties of the recent campaign to the men returning to the States, "there weren't many Texans left in the regiment," observed C.W. Military historian Dr. Edward J. Drea wrote that in New Guinea the 112th Cavalry suffered 317 battle casualties or twenty-one percent of their authorized strength, probably 26 or 27 percent of their actual pre–Driniumor strength. Among those casualties were two recipients of the Medal of Honor.[17]

One who stayed behind was Pug Wright, who said his promotion made him "essential personnel." For those who did remain there were some rewards.

"We got a beer ration when we were pulled off the Driniumor," Pug remembered. "I like to got drowned. I was throwin' them cases off (the ship) and swimming back into the bank with 'em. I bailed off too early and barely made it."

And Pug attended his first USO show since the Gary Cooper troupe visited Woodlark.

"Bob Hope and Frances Langford — they came to Aitape. That's where ole Bob Hope said, 'Frances Langford thought she was the first white woman on that island. She hadn't walked ten feet when she looked down there and she saw Eleanor Roosevelt's tracks!'"

The biggest cheers were reserved for the tunes of Langford and a leggy brunette dancer. Some of the troopers had not seen a white woman since the two women accompanied Gary Cooper to Woodlark.

Though the 112th had functioned as a de facto regimental combat team for more than six months, it did not become a Regimental Combat Team

Aitape, New Guinea 1944; Standing: Frank Harbiewski, Malcolm Tarleton, Willie A. Sunday, unidentified, Alonzo "Pug" Wright. Sitting: Vic Remischewski, John Humyak, Dewey Johnson, Mudcat Patterson (author's collection; Wright family photograph).

(R.C.T.) in fact until October 1, 1944. The unit would be expanded to 2,008 personnel and would include the 148th Field Artillery Battalion and the 3296th Signal Services Platoon. Two new troops, designated Troop D and Troop H, would be added to the 112th Cavalry Regiment. Command structure would remain the same: Brigadier General Cunningham would be the commander of the R.C.T. and Colonel Alexander Miller continued as regimental commander.[18]

The cavalrymen spent the two months following the conclusion of the fighting along the Driniumor patrolling, integrating new recruits, and training. Without any advance warning, Colonel Miller was notified on the evening of October 31 that the 112th would be leaving Aitape the next day for an undisclosed destination.[19]

The regiment spent most of the following day packing and boarding the A.P.A. (attack transport) *U.S.S. Frederick Funston* in the harbor. The troopers were not allowed to carry extra unessential equipment and a pile of captured Japanese souvenirs accumulated on the beach. The 112th's troop ship departed at midnight and moved up the coast to Hollandia where it joined a Navy fleet assembled for the invasion of the Philippines.

Pug's next stop was at the island of Morotai. "I got off on Morotai with a detail. There wasn't nothing on that island. There was an air base — (just) a little bitty ole island up on the north end of New Guinea." The 112th R.C.T. tarried on Morotai for a week, hauling supplies, training and undergoing inspections.

While C.W. and several others were stuck at Finschhaven waiting for transportation back to the United States, Pug and the 112th R.C.T. were aboard a ship in the Philippine Sea, anticipating the first battle in General MacArthur's campaign to retake the Philippine Islands.

9

Leyte, P.I.

"When those two men came out to the farm and told us Pickett had been wounded, Mama went to pieces," Girldene Wright Wiggins recalled. "Because they had to sign for him I remember Mama said, 'We sent that boy over there to be killed!' But they really hadn't, because the war hadn't started yet and he was only supposed to be in the army one year."

Pickett's sister-in-law added, "Papa told her, 'Don't you cry!' Of course we didn't know how bad he was wounded. She asked me to go fishin' with her. We went down there and she cried her eyes out for two hours." [1]

Subsequent to Pickett Wright's transfer from Aitape to the Army Hospital at Finschhafen, New Guinea, doctors performed surgical procedures to close his ankle wound. In addition, he was suffering malaria and dengue fever, both often accompanied by delirium.

Pickett's right lower leg was encased in a bulky plaster of Paris cast that increased his misery because of the tropical heat. Wright and the other patients were lodged in large open air tents where nurses and doctors had trouble controlling the bored soldiers. Once, he was restricted to the ward after he ruined his cast in the omnipresent New Guinea mud.

"I spent the last three weeks or so there out of the cast," Pickett remembered. "The doctor told us to bathe in that salt water. I swam in the ocean — stayed all day. I went further out in the ocean until one day I saw this shark fin approaching. I hurried to this little pier off the beach and, after that, I stayed close to the shore."

"Pickett went a.w.o.l. on his crutches," Pug said. "He went twenty-five miles and when they found him, he was with another outfit!"

For Pug Wright, the invasion of Leyte would be different from previous landings, because many of his friends were gone: Bull Wiggins and Mudcat Patterson rotated back to the States; Orvil Weddel and Doyle Tucker dead; his brother wounded. Though he never acknowledged any bitterness, Pug had to be resentful because he was one of the few enlisted men from Fort Clark still with G Troop. The army decided that a cadre of non-commissioned officers was needed to transform the large number of new recruits into an effective combat unit. Pug Wright fell into that group of essential personnel due to his recent elevation to squad leader.

"There were only twenty-two of us left (in the troop that left the States in 1942) until we got replacements," Pug recalled. Herman Stokes and John Humyak were the only other men in Wright's squad that had sailed to Aitape the previous June. Replacements,

Alonzo "Pug" Wright (right) and fellow troopers posing with battlefield souvenirs (author's collection; Wright family photograph).

mostly youngsters like eighteen-year-old Vic Remischewski, had to be counted on to fill positions vacated by the veteran machine gunners. The Army had been deactivating units that had little value in jungle warfare and these transfers from the recently disbanded 815th Tank Destroyer Battalion had little or no infantry training.

One newcomer to the regiment from the 815th was a twenty-one-year-old draftee with a Harvard degree named Norman Mailer. "They were tough men," he said of the veterans in the 112th Cavalry. "Many had lost friends in the fighting, and some had lost their wives what with having spent their last two-and-a-half years in the Pacific.... They would sit on the deck honing their bayonets for hour after hour with a dull glaze over their eyes. They were cold, hard men....

"So, it wasn't that it was nasty, or mean as much as it was with many of them that they just had no interest in you. A lot of them had had their buddies go home, and they were still here. They wondered why they were still there. We were coming in, and it was just too much work to make friends."[2]

Roughly resembling a molar tooth, Leyte is the eighth largest island of the Philippines, but the high command felt it was strategically important because of its airfield and natural harbor at Tacloban. General MacArthur had not expected the Japanese to put up such a strong fight for Leyte, but the enemy rushed in reinforcements, tripling the size of its 21,000-man army there. The Americans also committed additional troops, which included the 112th.

A central range of mountains literally formed the backbone of the 115-mile-long island. The densely forested range was composed of numerous jagged ridges and deep ravines that gave the defending Japanese forces a distinct advantage. Once past the narrow chain of ridges that separate the Ormoc Valley from Carigara Bay, the valley extended southward about fifteen miles to Ormoc Bay. Through Ormoc Valley ran a narrow road, key to the plan for conquest of the island.

Soon after the American's initial landings, the Japanese chose the strategy to fight it out in the rugged mountainous terrain of the island and hold on to the coastal port of Ormoc in order to supply their efforts. The Americans quickly conquered eastern Leyte and secured the island's airfields. However, the campaign in the mountains would have to be conducted during the rainy season. The mud swamped army vehicles and forward units had to be resupplied by native bearers.

G Troop would also make the Leyte landing with a new commanding officer. Captain Joseph Jefferies, formerly a platoon lieutenant in Troop A, replaced Captain Howell. The battle for Leyte was well underway when the 112th Regimental Combat Team arrived there on November 14, 1944. The men were to descend on cargo nets into landing craft alongside the mother ship for the voyage to "White Beach" near Tacloban.

"Before we landed, the kamikazes (Japanese suicide planes) came into our convoy," recalled G Troop machine gunner Bill Garbo. "I remember while we were gathering on deck to go over the side and get down into the Higgins boats, the kamikazes were flying just slightly above the water and flying as straight for as many of the ships as they could....

"There was nothing we could do but watch. They were shooting the kamikaze and he was hit. His right wing just folded off. At that point, he just turned on his side, dipped in, and hit near our fantail ... and exploded. Of course we saw that and in a manner of minutes, we were going over the side, getting into the Higgins boats, going in, and landing."[3]

G Troop reached the beach without enemy opposition and assembled in a nearby coconut grove to await further orders. The troopers did not have time to set up tents, so they just unfolded cots and bedded down for the night. In order to escape the fighting inland, hundreds of Filipino civilians had assembled in refugee camps along the coast.

Pug recalled that after that first night he awoke to "these Filipino women just hollering all around, wantin' to wash our clothes. I told Stokes, 'Boy! This is what I've been lookin' for. Wantin' to wake up in heaven — women all around!'"

Amazingly, the machine gunners' moonshine still made its way to Leyte as Ira "Ike" DeJager explained in 1994. "I remember having a still and we packed it in the supply room weapons carrier when we went from the Driniumor River to Leyte. I never drank any of the stuff but understand it was good. He made it out of dried apricots and raisins and anything else he could get hold of."[4]

As always, it seemed the campaign was to be conducted in rainy weather and, though Leyte was still jungle topography, there was a significant difference from the other islands the cavalrymen had occupied since leaving New Caledonia. Most Filipinos were of Malaysian stock, but their language and religion dated back to the Spanish colonial period that ended only forty-five years earlier when the United States wrestled the islands from Spain. By American standards, the life style of the Filipinos on Leyte was well below poverty level. Most of the houses were made of bamboo with palm leaves on the roofs and sides, and tied with rattan. Many of the dwellings were raised on pilings to provide room for the family's pigs and chickens underneath.

For the entirety of the Philippine campaign, the 112th received assistance from Filipino para-military forces. The former guerillas, armed with a variety of firearms, bandoliers and knives, acted as guides and interpreters for the cavalrymen. The Filipinos were indispensible as allies and were ruthless as guerilla fighters against the Japanese.[5]

On the day following their arrival, the 112th R.C.T. was attached to the 1st Cavalry Division.[6] Their initial assignment was to assume beach defenses along Carigara Bay off the northern coast and mop up any Japanese resistance in the Mount Minoro area.

Pug Wright's machine gun squad and G Troop remained in 2nd squadron of the R.C.T., commanded by Lieutenant Colonel McMains. The squadron bivouacked at Barugo and was assigned the task of manning the beach defenses at the coastal city of Carigara. The G troopers ran small unit missions in their few days on the island and, though one man was wounded by a short mortar round, they saw no combat. Malaria disabled far more of the veterans than enemy bullets.

Malaria attacks its victim every few weeks with icy chills, dizziness and shakes that rapidly saps its victim's strength. In World War II, the army didn't consider that disease severe enough to transfer the infected soldier back to the States, so men were returned to the front lines when the symptoms abated.

The third week in November, McMains' squadron was ordered to assume positions along the southeastern slope of Mount Minoro in preparation for an attack against Japanese positions on the heights.

"They told us to pack out that morning," Pug recalled. "We got about half way up. We had ole Jefferies as troop commander then and his dog robber put his tent up there. And so I asked them guys (the replacements)—I said, 'You ever shot a machine gun?'—They came out of a armored car outfit or something."

One of the newcomers announced, "Oh, Yeah! We've shot machine guns."

Pug wanted to keep at least one veteran on each gun and told the spokesman for the replacements, "O.K., I'll put you as assistant gunner."

"So, I told him—this character—to pick that machine gun up. Instead of pulling the belt out of there, he picked it up and pulled the trigger. He shot three or four holes right up over ole Jefferies head in his tent. He came out and was chewing me out."

The irate captain screamed, "Don't you teach them men nothing?"

Wright responded, "I don't even know that son 'a bitch's name!'

"He (the replacement) was the one we left in the jungle—pulled out and left him," Pug acknowledged. "He had that tripod to the machine gun. We took his ammunition and left him a .45 pistol."

Rain fell on G Troop during most of the march from the coast to Mount Minoro. The going was arduous, over slippery jungle trails that were frequently intersected by waist deep streams. The cavalrymen's progress up muddy trails and steep slopes was made more difficult due to the weight of the metal boxes of machine gun ammunition and the guns themselves. The hills were covered with dense jungle vegetation and the constant rain turned the approaches to the mountain range into quagmires. About a mile west of Mount Minoro, the troop arrived at a key objective, a Japanese-held hill that controlled the way to a trail that ran along razorback ridge for the length of the mountain range. The enemy had fortified the ridge with foxholes, trenches and palm log covered shelters. Clouds hovered about the ridge's peak and visibility was limited to only a few yards.

G Troop's advance was halted when Pug's rookie machine gunner caught up with the squad.

"Just at dark we went up and dug in at the foot of a hill," Pug continued. "We was fixin' to bayonet charge that hill (and) I looked down the trail and there came that son of a bitch. It had been six days and then he came up. He jumped in a foxhole up at that crossroad—that roadblock. The supply sergeant jumped in on top of him and a tree burst killed that supply sergeant, hit him in the back. That was Woody's hole. (Walter) Wood had dug it because he was there beside the supplies. I don't know what that guy's name was yet. He was a good combat soldier after that."

The assault on the Japanese positions was initiated by the 1st Squadron on November 24. G Troop fell into a position to the left of Troop B and Troop A set up on the other flank. After a barrage from the large guns of the American artillery from the plain below the mountains, B Troop assailed the heights (called "Baker Hill") and was repulsed three times with significant casualties. The assault was to be renewed the next day with G Troop taking the place of B Troop as the lead unit.

G Troop established its perimeter for the night and, as at the Driniumor, there was the threat of Japanese soldiers crawling through the darkness up to the American entrenchments. Pug had to warn his nervous rookies to be on constant alert for the arrival of an enemy hand grenade. In addition to the miserable conditions, Pug was suffering from a disabling attack of malaria.

"We spent the night on a steep slope wrapped in our ponchos with heavy rain pelting us all night long," remembered Bill Garbo. "We just slept, perspired, and we were totally soaked. When morning came, the rain let up, and we prepared to move up and take the hill."[7]

By this time Pug was seriously ill with a fever. "We only had one bayonet charge," he said with regret. "I didn't go up that hill—I sent Stokes. I always felt bad about that!"

The next morning, G Troop prepared for their attack amid a heavy fog on the slopes. Just after noon, the American Army ordered a massive barrage of heavy artillery and mortars designed to neutralize the Japanese resistance.

"Without warning we were in the midst of that rearing, ripping, ear-shattering nightmare that is the artillery barrage," wrote G Trooper William McDonnell. "The orange-red bursts and ensuing smoke and fire were all around us. Somehow it was difficult, upon watching, to comprehend the deadliness of the display. In another of those dreamlike sequences, we somehow spurted and slithered forward and out of the field of fire."[8]

After an artillery bombardment of about thirty minutes in duration, G Troop moved up the slopes of the ridge. The shell-shocked Japanese defenders that escaped the barrage unscathed put up only a half-hearted resistance. In just over an hour G Troop secured enemy positions that had repulsed repeated attacks for three days—and without the death of a single man.[9]

"That's when I had malaria," Pug stated, "and I went to the hospital from there. I was in that field hospital for two weeks and as soon as they got me back they took my pack and my guns, everything but my pistol. And that Kilroy gave me a handful of codeine, Atabrine and aspirin. I'd go as far as I could and then I'd take a handful of codeine. Then I'd go a little further.

"They called G Troop for security guards around Cunningham's head-quarters," he continued. "My first sergeant sent me down there. R.D. (Jones) was the one that detailed me."

With that Friar Tuck fringe of hair around the base of his skull plate, Brigadier General Julian Cunningham had the appearance of a kindly grand-father and often his commands were designated by the code name "Baldy Force." Despite his looks, Cunningham was a strict disciplinarian from the Army's old school. During the days when he oversaw the regiment's training back at Fort Clark, Cunningham would slap a riding crop against his boot while lecturing one of the cavalrymen. After being named regimental commander in November 1941, he was given the credit for transforming the 112th from a lax National Guard outfit into a combat ready unit. As a battlefield commander, Cunningham was sometimes too cautious for his superiors, but he was not one to be impetuous with his men's lives.

Pug gave his commanding general credit: "Ole Big Foot would carry his pack and the ole man would wade that mud waist deep just like everybody else."

"Big Foot" was fellow Texan Rufus Thomas, who had entered the regiment about the same time as the Wright brothers in 1941. Back at Fort Clark, Thomas used his huge hands as the troop horseshoer.

"After we got overseas," Pug said, "Thomas, the biggest guy in G Troop, was General Cunningham's bodyguard. Alton A. Vaughn, the smallest, was jeep driver for the general. They stayed all the way, (until) Big Foot finally got wounded."

Apparently, Pug's service with headquarters ended before December 19, for on that day the General was wounded in the leg after he went to the front to more closely monitor the activities of the 1st Squadron. Cunningham was evacuated to an aid station of the 32nd Division from where he was returned to Leyte Valley to recuperate.[10]

"I stayed with them (Cunningham), I don't know how long, and then they moved us into Tacloban — down there at MacArthur's headquarters. We was guard at Leyte for MacArthur!"

After the battle of Baker Ridge, the 112th pushed to within a mile and a half of the strategic objective of the Ormoc Highway on November 30.[11] There it was relieved and went into bivouac at a town called Jaro. Shortly after Christmas, G Troop was selected for a special assignment.

When General MacArthur asked for a cavalry security guard for his head-quarters at Tacloban, the numbers of the regiments under control of the 1st Cavalry Division were supposedly put in a hat and the 112th Cavalry Regiment was selected to provide a troop for that assignment. General Cunningham referred the matter to his 2nd Squadron commander, Lieutenant Colonel

McMains, who selected Troop G. Just after Christmas, 1944, G Troop was transferred to MacArthur's headquarters.[12]

Located on the northeast coast, Tacloban was Leyte's capitol and largest city. With a population of 31,000, Tacloban was poor like the rest of the island. There were a few Spanish villas, but most of its structures were nipa huts and shanties with open sewers.

General MacArthur's headquarters was the largest residence in the city and it had been used by the Japanese as an officers' club after the original owner was killed. Temporary buildings were put up nearby for the rest of the GHQ staff and an elevated catwalk was installed between the buildings. Pug and the other security guards would often see the General on the veranda of the two story stucco house. MacArthur would pace back and forth along the porch, usually smoking his trademark pipe, sometimes accompanied by aides, sometimes alone.

Pug and his fellow G Troopers did not stay at Tacloban very long, for on the night of January 3–4, 1945, General MacArthur's headquarters was loaded aboard ships in Tacloban Bay in preparation for the invasion of the main island of the Philippines. G Troop's LST fell into line as the convoy sailed out of Leyte Gulf and through the Surigao Strait. The ships ran without lights, but they passed close enough to see the lights on the islands of Mindinao and Negros.

*   *   *

While Pug was preparing to embark on his fifth amphibious landing of the war, C.W. and fellow G troopers Mudcat Patterson and Thurman Procter were aboard a ship in the Pacific Ocean en route back to the United States. This time the trip across the ocean took only fourteen days instead of the twenty-two it had taken the USS *Grant* two and a half years earlier. During this voyage, there was no zigzagging and no convoy to wait on.

"The ship I came back on had a bunch of women," C.W. mused. "The ones that weren't pregnant had

C.W. Wiggins in 1945 (author's collection).

babies. They (even) had a baby show!—(There were) Red Cross nurses, W.A.C.s.

"I was countin' on seein' that Golden Gate Bridge," he said. "But we landed at San Pedro. (This was January 13, 1945.) We walked right off that gangplank, right onto a train. It took us to a post nearby. (I) had on those ole faded khakis — had never been washed in hot water. (They) wouldn't even let us go to town. We stayed there two or three days then took the train to Fort Bliss. I got new uniforms there and then went on a thirty-day furlough.

"All of us were scared,' he admitted. "(But) I had never doubted that I would make it back home!"

* * *

Pickett beat C.W. back to the States by almost a month, returning home to Childress on furlough in mid — December. He was able to spend only three

Robert "Pickett" Wright (second from the left), war bond drive—1945 (photograph provided by the Robert "Pickett" Wright family).

days at the farm, because the fever and chills of malaria returned. His sister remembered that "he had a high temperature and was talking out of his head. You could tell he was talking about the war!"

Mr. Wright drove his son to the Childress Army Air Field hospital and Pickett was shortly transferred to McClosky Army Hospital in Temple, Texas. When the malaria attack subsided and he was ready to return to duty, Pickett was assigned to participate in a government-sponsored war bond drive in Oklahoma. Many of the other spokesmen on the tour were officers who had not been overseas, so Pickett's war record was enviable.

"We gave talks throughout Oklahoma on that war bond drive, two shows daily," he recalled. "I guess we hit every major town in Oklahoma. I was on that war show up in Muskogee when that pilot who was in that air battle when we made our beach landing (on Arawe) came backstage. He said he was the pilot in that dogfight.

"On Memorial Day, we honored the war dead in Tulsa on a hill out there. The next day, the newspaper had a long article wrote on each of us. The paper estimated 6000 people were out there."

Another attack of malaria landed Pickett back in McClosky Hospital where he incurred the ire of a by-the-book officer for not doing daily calisthenics with the rest of the patients. As a combat veteran he had no use for army routine and regulations that served no purpose. The vengeful officer made sure Pickett received an unpopular assignment, as he explained:

"I found myself going to McLean, Texas, at a German p.o.w. camp. I was there about two weeks — I didn't like that place so I told that captain; I said, 'Either you get me another place to go or I'm going on my own!' About a week later I was put on a train and shipped to Lubbock (Texas).[13] I was there about a month (at Lubbock Army Air Field). They classified me as sergeant of the guard — the title was — guarding German prisoners. I had eighteen men under me."

Pickett and his men were responsible for guarding the German prisoners on base and when they were taken to nearby farms for work detail. He recalled that the Germans did little work except when they were being closely watched. However, the prisoners posed little or no threat of escaping, because the war in Europe was over and they too were biding time, waiting to be sent home.

Another disabling attack of tropical fever landed him in the hospital once again. While a patient at a Lubbock hospital, Pickett received a visit from Jessie Robertson, a member of his old squad from G Troop. Accompanying Robertson was a pair of sisters. The eldest, Mary Leigh Pride, came to visit her boyfriend, a military policeman stationed at the base there. Pickett was more interested in the younger sister, a slender brunette named Jean

Pride. Bob was immediately attracted to her and began to cultivate a romance. The relationship with Jean helped him in another way, too. Once, while involved in a soldiers vs. civilians disturbance at the *Busy Bee Cafe* in Lubbock, Pickett was nabbed by the military police. Fortunately, one of the MPs was the boyfriend of Jean's sister and Pickett was released.

Still, Pickett was not enthusiastic about the regular army routine and regulations. He got into trouble for leaving the base while on duty and for allowing his men to get drunk while in their billets. Perhaps the last straw came the night his captain checked the guard then searched out Pickett: "There was only one man on guard and he was so drunk he didn't even know his name!" the irate captain exclaimed.

Pickett remembered, "That ole captain told me, 'You deserve a court martial, but your discharge is coming due. I'm gonna recommend they send you to the Hereford prison camp[14] with orders that you don't get out of that camp until discharged!'

"I stayed there about a week. I didn't get out of that camp either, because everywhere I'd go there's somebody watchin' me. I didn't guard any prisoners and I didn't have any duty. The only thing I got to do there was to go to my barracks and to the mess hall. I stayed there until I got my discharge."

10

Luzon, P.I.

Although Leyte was the decisive battle for the Philippines, the conquest of Luzon would be the costliest. After Leyte, the Japanese Navy was disabled, the enemy's supply lines crippled, retreat impossible. What the Japanese still did have was the fanatical will to fight and die for their Emperor and country. So began the bloodiest campaign of the Pacific War. On Luzon, the U.S. Army would suffer 37,870 casualties, 8,310 of them killed in action.[1]

During the American's voyage from Tacloban, the slow-moving Navy convoy was harassed by kamikaze suicide planes and the enemy's midget submarines. The suicide planes sank an escort carrier and managed to hit twenty-one other ships in the Task Force. The American's crowded troop transports traveled three days behind the warships whose job it was to bombard the beaches at the designated invasion point — Lingayen Bay. The place of invasion was about halfway up Luzon's west coast and 110 miles north of Manila.

A bombardment by the big guns of the Navy ships had not been necessary because the Japanese had already withdrawn to the mountains. Before daylight on their third day at sea, the huge American armada entered Lingayen Harbor. On January 9, 1945, 68,000 men of General Walter Krueger's 6th Army swarmed ashore.

That afternoon the L.S.T. carrying G Troop of the 112th Cavalry Regiment moved into a landing position on the beach. As it was late in the day, the unloading would not commence until the following morning so the L.S.T. backed off to a position in the middle of the bay in order to avoid saboteurs or Japanese suicide boats. That night the American ships were subjected to shelling from large guns hidden behind the hills to the northeast. "An hour or so before dawn we were treated to a mind-boggling sight," recalled G Trooper William McDonnell, "as a stupendous fusillade of anti-aircraft fire descended into the heavens in search of an unseen flight of enemy aircraft."[2]

"The ships there used napalm when we went into Lingayen," Pug Wright said of the American shelling of the enemy in the hills. "That sky was full of fire — phosphorus!"

At about two in the afternoon General MacArthur arrived at San Fabian, a few miles west of Lingayen. The Seabees bulldozed a little pier for his boat to dock, but MacArthur ordered it bypassed in order to make a dramatic wade to shore as he had done at Leyte. A crowd of Filipinos cheered when he reached the beach.

"He got off a battleship. We were on an L.C.T.," Pug remembered. "The first thing off our ship was MacArthur's toilet and the reason for that was it was the last thing loaded. You couldn't get the trucks off! We walked up the street and them little Filipino kids — hundreds of 'em — just flocked around him (MacArthur). He'd pat 'em on the head."

The general's cavalry security force marched to the nearby village of Dagupan, where MacArthur's first GHQ was established. "And he went up to the end (of the unpaved street)," Wright remembered, "up close to a church there — the church grounds. There was a building built way up high. I guess it was two story. That was his house and that's where he stayed."

G Troop set up tents nearby and stood guard around MacArthur's headquarters and other homes that housed his staff. While at Dagupan, the enlisted men were on guard two hours, were off four hours, back on guard duty for two, and so on. The duty ranged from standing at attention by the door of a building to manning a fortified position on the outskirts of the perimeter.

One of G Troop's toughest tasks was supervision of the hordes of Filipinos who came from the countryside to see the returning general. A great deal of activity also centered around a warrant officer named Hogan from headquarters who was busy grilling the security guard, trying to find out who stole the General's oranges!

Unlike the topography of the jungles of New Britain and New Guinea, Luzon had roads, stretches of open country, cleared fields and terraced mountainsides. The American plan was to strike out southward from the Lingayen beachhead toward the primary objective — Manila. The roads along the way were cluttered with soldiers and military vehicles moving south and Filipino refugees fleeing in the opposite direction.

Pug recalled with horror the time the truck in which he was riding was strafed by an enemy aircraft: "We had always been on foot before. I never felt so helpless — no place to hide!"

The troopers passed through Spanish towns reminiscent of ones they had visited near the Texas–Mexico border. Many of the towns had no visible damage caused by the war. There were still plenty of the nipa-palm huts, but also there were the plazas, ancient adobe, stone Catholic churches, and even substantial masonry municipal buildings. The villagers spoke Spanish and broken English.

On January 25, General MacArthur moved his headquarters to Hacienda Luisita, near Tarlac. He felt Krueger was moving the Army along too slowly and picked Tarlac because it was well south of 6th Army headquarters.

MacArthur's headquarters, which included G Troop, set up on the grounds of a country club near town. The cavalry troop set up HQ at the golf course's club house.

"It had a golf course, swimming pool and nearby ran a narrow gauge railroad that serviced the local sugar mill," Pug noted. "We started drinkin' that alcohol from them sugar mills. We'd fill up vinegar jugs — got 'em from the kitchen — with alcohol. We'd use lighter fluid then we drank it or used it to *treat* wounds."

Pug recalled that "The Army had all the teletype machines in a school building — row after row, and running all the time. We'd walk guard around that and we'd run patrols."

The 1st Cavalry Division was still seventy miles from Manila on February 1 when General MacArthur ordered its commander to make a dash for the country's capital. A flying column of that division reached the city at dusk three days later. Although the Japanese army had evacuated Manila for the mountains, the fanatical Nipponese Naval commander remained in the city with 20,000 men, mostly sailors, determined to contest it from house to house.

Greater Manila included 110 square miles and over a million inhabitants. Before the war, the capital city was a modern city of both businesses, elaborate government buildings, schools and parks. It was a city of century old churches and residential districts of thatched huts. Though paved, many of the streets were narrow, little more than alleys. The city proper was intersected by the Pasig River, which flowed into Manila Bay. An extensive port area lined the bay and ran for over a mile on both sides of the river.

North of the river was the business district and south of the Pasig, near the river's mouth, lay the old Spanish city, Intramuros. The old city's outer walls were up to forty feet thick at the bottom and in places the stone walls reached a height of twenty feet. Prior to the Japanese invasion, MacArthur's residence was in an air-conditioned penthouse in the modern Manila Hotel, just off the bay and southwest of Intramuros.

Under pressure from the American 6th Army, the Japanese Manila Naval Defense force burned military supplies and facilities, blew up the six bridges across the Pasig, and withdrew into Intramuros. Strong winds drove the flames into the numerous thatched roofs and much of northern Manila was soon on fire.

"They took all of North Manila without shelling," Pug remembered. "But when you'd start to take a building it would blow up in your face. They (the Japanese) had booby trapped everything. The 37th and that other division there refused to go past the river if MacArthur didn't shell it (Intramuros)."

Even when it became obvious the Japanese would contest Manila from house to house, General MacArthur persisted in banning air attacks, maintaining that bombing would kill civilians and alienate the population. Still, his generals pleaded with him for air and artillery support prior to an assault on the fortress. Pug Wright remembered walking guard one night outside MacArthur's headquarters at Tarlac.

"That was the night I was walking guard right in front of the door, and there's his execs, three or four majors and colonels, in there. I know the 37th Division general was there. And he said he wasn't going to cross that river without support. See, that was the only thing they had to cross on, the Jones Bridge — the Army put that in. So he gave 'em permission to shell the city and I mean the rest of it from there on was flattened. That Manila Hotel was a modern hotel — about thirty stories. I reckon they bombed it — cut it from one corner to the other, made a triangle out of it. That was the only thing left standin' in north Manila!"

Early in the morning of February 16, General MacArthur, accompanied by his aides and a security guard, set out to inspect the progress of the 38th Infantry Division on the Bataan Peninsula. Pug and the other men who accompanied the general vividly remembered this particular trip to the front.

The motor pool sent two jeeps out to pick up the G Troop security detail, Lieutenant Cole of 1st Platoon, and four enlisted men including Pug and Tony Frangella. They drove to MacArthur's headquarters where the detail cooled its heels until the general was ready to leave. Sergeant Frangella remembered that the general's driver was talking to someone over the radio and he told us "they were bombing, shelling the hell out of Iwo Jima."

When MacArthur emerged, "he had a flag and a .38 or .32 pistol in his right rear pocket," recalled Frangella. "It was chrome plated. I remember that distinctly."

The general rode in a Cadillac while the security detail followed in the two jeeps. When the trail became too arduous for the automobile, MacArthur switched to one of the jeeps.

"We had two jeeps — G troopers were in the second jeep, four guys, and they had MacArthur's dog robber (aide) and two more officers in his jeep with a driver," Pug noted. "His dog robber was a major!"

"After that patrol with MacArthur we quit callin' him 'Dugout Doug,'" remembered Pug. "We went out there where Wainwright surrendered and he went around and talked to them guys that was dug in up there. We stayed there a while then got into the jeeps and that s.o.b. headed right out — shells fallin' all around."

"Well, we got into that territory where the 38th Division was still fighting," Frangella continued. "The MPs and so forth, they kept tellin' us, 'Don't go forward; it's dangerous!' And we couldn't do nothin'—Just tell him and just kept goin' and followin' him.

"We finally came to a spot where the infantry evidently had a little showdown with some Japs and there were two Japs laying there, still warm. MacArthur got out of the jeep. Of course, we got out with him — We just circled him. He was lookin' at these dead Japs and in the February or March edition of *Life* magazine this picture's in there, and I thought, right next to him was our lieutenant.... We left that spot and we got up maybe another half a mile. What I think was, the infantry radioed ahead and told 'em to chop a tree down over the trail so MacArthur couldn't go any further! And right there he had to turn around and come back."[3]

The artillery bombardment of Intramuros began on February 17 and continued for seven days. The shelling finally breached the stone walls and on the twenty-third, American assault troops stormed the walled city. Vicious house to house fighting continued for almost ten days before Intramuros was secured. American and Japanese casualties were heavy, but Filipino losses among the civilian population were staggering. Estimates ranged as high as 100,000 killed by accidental gun fire, shelling by the artillery, fire, or murdered by the Japanese. Most of the survivors were homeless as Manila had been reduced to rubble.

On March 5, General MacArthur moved his headquarters to North Manila.

"We set up in the Taiwan Bank building," Pug recalled. "Put cots on the second floor. The kitchen and everything else was on the third floor. They had a 105-mm howitzer sitting in that lobby and it shot out that window right point blank into the Walled City."

In Manila, Wright met a young Filipino woman who was a lieutenant in the local guerrilla force. The top of her head barely reached a height even with the breast pocket of Pug's 5'11" frame. Once the Walled City was secured, she offered to show him around the city, which was in ruins.

"I found her up there livin' on a bunch of chuck houses that had been blown up," he said. "We went down through there (along the river) and snipers — stragglers — got to shootin' at us. I crawled then ran out of there. When I got back, I told ole Stokes and them, 'I think she tried to get me killed!'"

General MacArthur brought his wife and son to Manila after the city was secured and the MacArthurs moved into the Bacrach mansion a few miles north of the river. "He had a thirteen room, two or three story house," Pug said. "We had to baby-sit for 'Little Dugout' up there at that house."

Tony Frangella recalled that "Woody King was in charge of the detail that guarded his home. There were all influential homes around there. One home was almost destroyed — that's where we stayed. We pitched tents on the grounds. We had heard that the Japanese had stayed in there and when the Japs left, the natives tore hell out of the place. We guarded MacArthur's staff, and that's where I realized Mrs. MacArthur was there and Little Arthur and of course the president (President Manuel Quezon of the Philippines)."[4]

The 112th R.C.T., minus Troop G, landed at Lingayen Bay, Luzon, on January 27, 1945. After being attached to the 1st Cavalry Division on February 9, the 112th operated along the Army's flank, protecting the line of communications along the eastern edge of the central plains. General Cunningham, who had sufficiently recovered from his leg wound to resume command of the R.C.T., had been lobbying to have G Troop returned to the 112th and his request was finally granted in early March.

"Our last night in Manila was spent in a desperate attempt to absorb all the good memories we could," wrote one of the G Troopers. "In the morning, it was a badly hung over group of men who mounted up and moved into the boondocks."[5]

G Troop rejoined the regiment on an outpost line about fifteen miles east of Manila. "The outfit was east of Antipolo where that world's richest Catholic church was," Pug noted. "And we tore it down. They had shelled it, ruined it!"

By the time Pug rejoined the 112th, the regiment's mission had evolved into one of patrolling and outpost duty. The regiment was dispersed in small outposts in the foothills to guard the 6th Army's main supply line to Manila and keep an eye on the enemy operating in the mountains above. G Troopers manned was divided into six outposts with instructions to regularly radio headquarters (HQ) at the barrio of Marungko, where half the troop was held in reserve.[6]

Working closely with the American troops were thousands of Filipinos who had been operating as guerrillas against the Japanese since the fall of Bataan. Some had prior military experience; many were there to get the money the U.S. government was paying. The Army used the Filipinos in conjunction with their own forces, mainly to provide information and serve as scouts.

Pug was sent out in the field to "Number 8 outpost" with a squad of seven troopers and eight or ten Filipino guerrillas. His orders were to radio HQ every hour during the day and every thirty minutes at night. But every time the cavalrymen turned on their radio, the enemy picked up their signal and lobbed a few shells based on the coordinates of the radio transmission. His squad had to move its position so many times, Pug got to where he wouldn't call in. He told his men, "Forget that s.o.b.!"

"We found this little ole shack on a hill — had trees around it," he recalled. "The Filipinos would go out through the lines into the country and steal eggs or get chickens. We were livin' better 'n a hog up there. One day, someone spotted this horse, guy on a horse, comin' up the valley. I sent 'em down to see who it was. So they sneaked down there and saw that he was an American, a G.I. His horse had a wire bridle on and it was part of the cavalry the Japs had there early in the war."

The rider was a member of G Troop who had been sent by Staff Sergeant Woodrow King to find the missing squad. He had picked up the horse and bridle along his route and decided to return to his true calling as a cavalryman.

The messenger told Wright to call Sergeant King immediately. When Pug radioed Woody he was informed that Captain Jefferies "was gonna bust" every one of the missing cavalrymen.

The final instructions to Wright were, "You better call Jefferies, he's having a shit fit!"

Pug did as he was told and informed the troop's commander, "George, this is George 8. I have nothing for you; Do you have anything for me?" He then terminated the call because the Japanese were probably tracking his transmission.

"Ole Jefferies started in on what all he was gonna do," Pug remembered. "I just hung my receiver up. Then I turned it back on. He was calling the Colonel. 'I recommend Wright be busted! (He's) been gone ten or twelve days.' Colonel Grant said, 'Well, you fill out all the papers and when we get back, I'll act on them.'"

Pug's position as a section leader would soon not burden him any longer. The few men left in the regiment, who survived the fighting in New Britain and New Guinea and were then sent to the Philippines without a furlough, were near the breaking point. Some experienced emotional breakdowns, others just gave up, and some, like thirty-one-year-old Pug Wright, just tried to survive. The comradeship that was felt among G Troopers throughout the New Guinea campaign no longer existed for the few remaining horse soldiers because most all their friends from the days at Fort Clark were now gone.

Once Pug returned to troop headquarters, his assignments ranged from probing patrols to guard duty for supply trains sent to restock the troop's outposts. Reconnaissance patrols usually were made up of four men, an officer or an NCO, and a Filipino guide if available. A combat patrol was at least of platoon strength. While the regiment was operating against the Japanese in the foothills north of Antipolo, Pug went to the hospital for the second time since his arrival in the Philippines.

"We were up in the hills, dug in at a little ole village there — dug in around a garden," Pug recalled. "I don't know the name of it. (Lieutenant) Meeks was leader of the platoon when we went on patrol. We had them guerrillas with us. The Japs attacked us three or four times and we went up there and we tried to take a plantation house. I ran about two miles with that dog-gone machine gun. My feet were all blistered and hacked up.[7] That night they attacked us again."

The next day, Pug and a fellow G trooper who was wounded were sent to the hospital. Pug recalled that the wounded man "was standin' up, shootin' over a rice paddy with his pistol. And they throw'd a hand grenade in his hole. He couldn't get a hold of it and was wounded that night. Stokes and Humyak, a bunch of them, came up there with a pack train carryin' supplies. Meeks sent me out to the hospital. When they evacuated me, we made a makeshift litter (for the wounded man). On the way back, we got attacked. He bailed off that litter! Said, 'I'm not gonna die on that son 'a bitch — I'm gonna die running!'"

Pug was sent back to Tarlac City where the Army had turned a schoolhouse into a hospital. "A few days after that, Stokes got blowed off a hill up there and came to the hospital," Pug remembered. "There weren't many G troopers left on the line. There was twenty-six of us in that hospital at one time. Some of them had syphilis and gonorrhea, but they were in the hospital.

"They treated syphilis with penicillin — shoot you in the buttocks every four hours with that dang ole penicillin. When they first started usin' it, it was just like a wad of cotton and it took a big needle."[8]

One day, Pug, Stokes and a G Trooper who was there being treated for venereal disease were sitting on the banister at the front of the hospital when a group of new army nurses arrived.

"Fifteen or twenty new nurses got off a plane out there and they were comin' up that stair," Pug said. "Ole Stokes was standin' up. He didn't say nothing to them as they walked by. (Then) he just popped off to the guy with VD, 'How's your ass?' That nurse thought he was talkin' to her. He had a terrible lot of explaining to do!

"I was in the hospital there thirty days," he continued. "And they kicked me out. If you stayed thirty-two days, they had to evacuate you and this doctor came down there — he was a captain — (He) asked me, 'How's your feet?'

"I said, 'You're the doctor!' — of course I was everywhere then.

"He said, 'Where's your unit?'

"I said, They're up in the hills. I don't know where they are!'

"He says, 'I'm gonna give you some medicine to doctor your feet and you can go back to your unit.'

"And I says, 'Oh, Yeah! I can do that, because I still got buddies. They can keep them son a bitches pinned down while I pull the bandages off and doctor my feet!'"

G Troop was operating in the hills east of Manila, but Pug was not anxious to return to the front line just yet and he got his opportunity as he was leaving the Red Cross shack. A G.I. drove up in a jeep, hopped out and left the keys in the ignition. Pug told Vic Remischewski, another G Troop machine gunner who had been in the hospital with stomach trouble, "I'm gonna steal that jeep."

"And he says, 'Why?'

"I ain't going to the hills just yet."

The pair jumped into the Army jeep and headed for Manila. The two wayward troopers were able to find a hotel room, but the capitol city was in ruins and had little to offer its own people, much less house and feed visitors. The machine gunners' hotel accommodations consisted of two bamboo beds. Boiled eggs were the sole fare they had for breakfast and rice was the only thing served for dinner. Pug was dying for a cigarette and the only place to get them was from the Army.

"We went down to that casual outfit, where the MPs are. They gave us some cigarettes and of course some rations. (Then) we caught a truck and went to the 112th."

In early April, General Cunningham's "Baldy Force" (the 112th R.C.T. and the 169th R.C.T.) was assigned the task of defending an east-west line just north of Mount Oro, directly between the two sections of the Japanese Shimbu Army Group.

Pug recalled that the night he got back to the 112th's base camp northeast of Antipolo "they had a outdoor theater and one of them G.I. shows. There was about five or six hundred out there watchin' that show. Two Japs got in there among 'em, throwin' hand grenades and everybody was jumpin' up, tryin' to run. I got in a stampede in New Caledonia about like that — a bunch of people get stampeded and they can kill each other.

"And I told Remischewski: 'Lay down on the ground!' And he tried to get up twice and got kicked in the chin. I got up once and somebody kicked me right in the top of the head. We just flattened out on the ground during all this turmoil. It was dark, at night, you couldn't have no lights there and all you could see was that theater (screen). I skylighted that quartermaster comin' down through there with guns. Well, they didn't know how to fight. They'd shoot each other. And I told Remischewski, 'Stay right here until they get settled down. Them son of a gun's will shoot you!'

"So, next morning, we decided we better get out of there. It was thirty-seven miles from there to where G Troop was and they gave us a belt of ammunition, a carbine, rations, cigarettes and a pack. And we walked that thirty-seven miles and got back. G Troop had about a hundred men. They had a little ring built up on a hill. I don't know how long we was up there. (Then) we went to what they called Ipo Dam."

About seven miles east of Luzon's central plain, Ipo Dam lay on the winding Angat River in the Sierra Madre Mountains. The dam was crucial because it controlled Manila's main water supply, but a Japanese army of about 7,000 dominated it. The terrain in that area was particularly rugged and there were a number of caves among the jagged rocks of the mountainsides to give the enemy places to hide from American artillery and air attacks. The Japanese had spent months preparing their defenses in the deep caves and added tunnels from a main shaft to exits on the slopes.

The G troopers spent days climbing in the mountainous terrain to reach their designated command posts behind the enemy positions. There had not been any rain in weeks and the landscape was parched.

Pug stated that during the Ipo Dam operation, "We just put up an outpost behind their lines. We'd watch them guns come out of them mountains — big guns came out on railroad cars and they'd fire. Well, we'd watch that. When we heard it hit the ground and explode, we'd run an asmus on that gun position and radio it back to our artillery. They had, I guess, two miles of them 190mm artillery pieces just lined up, wheel to wheel, blasting them mountains — plus all day long aircraft bombing them, trying to blast them all out."

Bombs and artillery shells barely damaged the caves, but a heavy concentration would keep the enemy below ground. The rainy season began in mid–May and three days of heavy downpours grounded the American warplanes until the weather cleared on the sixteenth. Over the next two days nearly 680 American airplanes bombarded the caves with 113,000 gallons of napalm, the largest use of the incendiary agent during the Pacific war. Each fire bomb obliterated an area 70 by 150 feet and would send up a column of smoke over a mile high. The infantry moved in to clear out the Japanese defenders, cave by cave. Within a week, the enemy resistance crumbled and the survivors melted away deeper into the mountains to the east. The rest of the campaign consisted of rooting out and mopping up the remnants of the starving and disease-ridden Shimbu Group army.

The Japanese had long since exhausted their food supplies and the mountains were stripped of what crops there were. Most of the enemy soldiers were eating roots, grass and tree bark, but some were so desperate they resorted to eating human flesh. The Imperial Japanese Army had issued directives with instructions how to prepare human meat for consumption. However, they discouraged the practice of cannibalism on their fallen comrades. Pug experienced firsthand the desperate plight of the enemy:

He recalled that while on patrol in the mountains, "We saw a small group of Japs around a fire on a small hill. We fired on 'em and they ran off. There were two dead Japs there and they had cut off a piece of one of 'em's thigh."

By the first week in June, the 112th R.C.T. was still operating in the Sierra Madres Mountains when Pug was notified he was to be rotated back to the States:

"They called the remainder of the original guys that went over. They called us out for rotation! There was 154 men in G Troop when we went over (seas) and when they pulled us all out, there was twelve of us. And they was fixin' to charge that hill the next morning. And so I told 'em, 'We'll walk guard tonight. You sleep.' So we did and the next morning at daylight — at six o'clock — they charged that hill and we went back.

Sadness veiled his face when Pug recalled the death of Vic Remischewski right before the veterans were transferred out. "He was just walkin' around in the area where they was dug in and one rifle shot got him. Some sniper shot him from way off."

"We (the departing cavalrymen) were pulled back to Antipolo," he continued. "We stayed there. We signed up for a plane or a ship, but on a plane, you got out quicker, but they'd fly you down to New Guinea somewhere and you'd wait down there. It took over a month to get on a ship, (so) me, Stokes and Humyak started kicking rations out of those planes."

Kicking out supply pallets that parachuted to the ground was dangerous work. A man could easily lose his balance or get tangled up in the parachute line and be pulled out of the doorless C47 airplane. The attraction of this duty was getting to see territory it had taken weeks to fight their way across.

The Army even had the audacity to ask Pug to sign a waiver to remain in the Philippines; "I told 'em, ole MacArthur's aide or whoever he was, 'Those sons o' bitches are goin' through China I expect!'"

Pug waited over a month to catch a ship back home and when he did, the "rusty tub" took thirty-four days to get back to the States. Pug was anxious to get home as soon as possible, but "there were 110 cases of malaria on board and they tried to quarantine us in Hawaii. I got back to the States the day they dropped the A-Bomb!"—August 6, 1945.

Pug Wright received his discharge from the United States Army at Fort Bliss, Texas, eight days later. His brother Ed beat him home by three weeks. The 36th Infantry was in northwestern Austria when the war in Europe officially ended on May 8, 1945 — V-E Day (Victory in Europe Day). Because he was among those who had the highest number of points, Ed was on his way home four days later. Aubort was the last of the Wright brothers to return to the States, serving with the Allies' occupation forces through October.

*   *   *

After Pug and the other veterans departed, the men of the 112th R.C.T. continued to battle the beleaguered Japanese for another two months. During June the 112th conducted operations designed to root out the remaining Japanese units in the foothills and mountains east of Antipolo. More G Troopers were killed and maimed.[9]

The final fatalities suffered by the regiment were on June 21, 1945, near Santa Inez, Luzon.[10] G Troop was making a sweep through an enemy held area when the point platoon encountered machine gun fire from an enemy ambuscade as they were crossing a dry river bed. Several G troopers were hit by Japanese machine gun fire and the Americans scrambled for whatever cover they could find.

Sergeant Anthony Frangella was among several men that volunteered for a patrol to extricate the besieged platoon on the river. PFC John Sexton was forward of the others in the relief patrol when he was badly wounded by burst of machine gun fire. When Frangella saw the seriously wounded Sexton in the river bed, he left his position of cover and made his way to the fallen comrade. As Tony began to drag Sexton away from line fire, the enemy machine guns concentrated their fire on the two men and the wounded trooper was hit again. For bringing his fellow trooper to safety, Sergeant Frangella received the Silver Star Medal for "courageous conduct on the field of battle in keeping with the highest traditions of our armed forces."[11]

The Americans pinned down in the river bed were unable to move without drawing gunfire from the well positioned Japanese and the officer in charge of the platoon seemed indecisive about what to do. After spending the good part of the day behind meager cover in the tropical heat, it became obvious that the platoon had to escape their predicament before it got dark.

When the First Sergeant passed the word then blew the whistle to move out, Bill Garbo removed the weight of his pack. He later wrote, "Since I was at the edge of the river where the trail went into the trees, it was natural for me to hold back until some of the troopers from the front got out, then I carried Sergeant Anderson (who had a leg wound) piggyback and ran down the riverbed; the snipers were breaking rocks all around us. When I reached the medics by the edge of the river, I put Anderson down for treatment (and) there was my buddy from Kentucky (Sexton). They indicated he was too far gone when I asked about his condition. I felt his wrist and got a faint pulse and began shouting, 'Do something! Do something for him' and I just held his arm and looked at him. He was dying."

After Garbo rejoined the platoon on a ridge above the river he saw an American running away from several Japanese soldiers who were shooting at him. In the early part of the ambush, that trooper had hit the dirt and remained motionless through the afternoon. He was left behind when the rest of the platoon pulled out at dusk. "He said that he could hear the Japs laughing and moving around," wrote Garbo. "He remained still while they came over and kicked the bodies over. When they got to him, he jumped up, threw his B.A.R. into the chest of the nearest Jap.... Then he threw two hand grenades at them and ran out."[12] The maneuver caught the Japanese by surprise and the trooper was able to outdistance the enemy soldiers to safety. In addition to Sexton, G Troopers PFC Earl Colee and PFC Lewis Krantz were killed that day and five other troopers were wounded. They were the final fatalities suffered by G Troop during combat.

The Luzon campaign came to an official end on June 30 and the 112th returned to its staging area at Antipolo. The 112th Regimental Combat Team left Luzon for Japan in late August, 1945. On the morning of September 2, the unit was aboard one of the 260 Allied warships in Tokyo Bay to observe the official surrender of the Japanese on the USS *Missouri*. The next day, G Troop and the rest of the regiment landed on Japanese soil and for the next four and a half months served in the Army of Occupation. The 112th Regimental Combat Team was deactivated in Japan on January 26, 1946.

Epilogue

C.W. Wiggins spent a furlough at home after returning to the States in January 1945. Upon the conclusion of his leave, Seeb was sent to a medical facility in Hot Springs, Arkansas, to recuperate from a variety of tropical maladies. Located at the gateway to the Ouachita Mountains, this picturesque resort city was famous for its forty-seven thermal baths, purported to have healing properties. During World War II, an Army-Navy Hospital was located there, and the military had use of two of the city's hotels.

Following two weeks of therapy, C.W. was offered the opportunity to remain at Hot Springs and work in the kitchen. He accepted rather than take a chance on a less attractive assignment. Of course this was a glamour job compared to what he had experienced the previous year.

"I stayed at the Arlington Hotel for four months," he smiled. "I even had maid service."

While at Hot Springs, C.W. began to correspond with Girldene Wright, whose address he had obtained from her brother Pug. They exchanged photographs and began a long distance relationship.

"C.W. sent me pictures of him and Pug," Girldene recalled. "Mama told me to write him a thank you note. Then he sent me a letter. Me and a couple of my friends began talking about going to Hot Springs. Mama said, 'Forget that. He might be an outlaw!'"

C.W. was mustered out of the Army at Fort Sam Houston (San Antonio, Texas) on June 29, 1945. He borrowed his parents' automobile and, on Girldene's birthday, July 4, drove to Childress for his first visit to the Wright farm.

Many of the single G troopers knew that Pickett and Pug had three unmarried younger sisters back home. Several ex-troopers visited the Childress farm with romance on their mind leading one of the Wright girls to remark that "We had our choice of about ten, but there were a couple Pickett wouldn't allow us to be alone with!"

Pickett Wright had already returned home, soon to marry Jean Pride, the Plains, Texas, girl he met while in the hospital in Lubbock. His ankle had healed sufficiently enough for him to play a few baseball games in the semi-pro Red River League. He stayed in Childress for a while, but eventually settled in Denver City, Texas, where he founded a successful appliance store and air conditioning business. Fishing was always one of Pickett's favorite pastimes and in his later years, Bob purchased a place on the shore of Possum Kingdom Lake then turned the family business over to his son.

Jean Pride and Robert "Pickett" Wright, 1944 (author's collection; Wright family photograph).

Soldiers returning from the war had already lost four years, so there was not much time or the desire for long engagements. C.W. made frequent trips to Childress and a short courtship culminated with his marriage to Girldene Wright on December 23, 1945. There was one prenuptial condition — that she never refer to him as "Bull." He took Girldene back to the farmhouse down the road from where his parents lived and resumed the vocation that had been interrupted in 1941.

There wasn't much money to be made raising a few animals and farming the dry land around Loraine. C.W. took advantage of the G.I. Bill and went to night school in Colorado City. Of course he was more interested in the $100 monthly government stipend than attending classes on agriculture, a profession he had practiced most of his life. That was a lot of money in the early 1950s. Late in 1955, C.W. moved to the fertile, irrigated farmland of the South Plains near Morton, Texas, and became a successful cotton grower.

Pug Wright was discharged at Fort Bliss on August 14, 1945, and returned to Childress. One thing he didn't want to do was return to the farm. Anyway, his brother Ed was already in the process of taking over the family farm from their father. Pug tried to make some money in western music and in radio, but that was going nowhere so one day he stomped into the Army recruitment office and re-enlisted.

Pug enjoyed his time in the Army more than Pickett and C.W. But this time it was different. He had the option of returning to the 112th R.C.T., but he turned that down because that unit was still in Japan. The post-war Army was one of strict regulations, boring routine, and none of his old friends were there. Pug was the last of the Wright boys to settle down and raise a family. He married Edna Mae Mills on July 22, 1949.

The former jungle fighters proceeded with their post-war careers and the raising of families. There wasn't time to dwell on the war, though the effects of wounds, disease and haunting memories were always with them. They tried to put thoughts about the war behind them. But they never did, nor could they. Nothing in life could ever approach the Pacific War experience in their minds.

Although not physically wounded like Pickett, Pug and C.W. also suffered from the lingering malaria and mental scars. C.W. did not speak of the war for many years and only through renewed associations with old army buddies at reunions did he begin to open up at all. A house fire destroyed most of his memorabilia from the war, though the medals remained as a reminder. As time went by, his memories of the time with the cavalry grew dearer.

The years passed and the United States became embroiled in new wars. The veterans' children grew up during the time of another jungle war. Pug was the only one of the three to have a son who served in South Vietnam.

Eventually, Pug and C.W. drove back to the Rio Grande country, but Fort Clark had changed. The old wooden barracks were gone, and all but one of the stables had been torn down. Most of the stone buildings remained — the guard house, commissary, NCO club, theater and stone barracks — though many had fallen into ill repair.

The Secretary of War had declared Fort Clark surplus in 1945. Kinney County did not want it, so the post and grounds were sold for salvage then the fort was stripped of anything of value. Fortunately, someone saw Fort Clark's potential as a guest ranch. In 1971, it was sold to a private recreational community.[1]

The old fort survives today. The stone barracks now provide guest rooms, headquarters is an office, the officers' club is a restaurant, the guard house became a museum, and the manicured parade grounds are now par three golf courses.

As they grew older, the nightmares became a hazy memory and the former cavalrymen began to yearn for the nostalgia and comradeship from their days in the army. Former soldiers assert that there was no relationship like the bond men form with fellow soldiers in the life and death struggle of combat. After that first battle, most petty differences melted away. Unlike the time they spent together earlier in the States, a special relationship developed between men caught in desperate conditions.

Lionel Carter's newsletter, *The Reunion Review*, kept the connection with war buddies alive with correspondence from former troopers, historical notes and the editor's memoirs of his experiences in the 112th Cavalry. But there were also the death notices, and with every issue, the ranks of the old regiment dwindled with the publication of each obituary.[2]

The 112th Cavalry Association held an annual reunion in Dallas, but G Troopers often held their own gatherings. Jack Howell helped organize the 112th Cavalry's West Texas Chapter reunion in Lubbock, Texas, near C.W.'s home, but he attended sporadically because not many men from G Troop came to those meetings.

Pug, his wife Edna Mae, C.W., Girldene, Pickett and the Coppingers flew to Joliet, Illinois, for the Midwest Chapter reunion of September 1979. Mainly attended by former G troopers in the Illinois area, the Texans were able to reminiscence with friends they had not seen since leaving the shores of New Guinea thirty-five years earlier.

The crowning jewels for the ex-troopers were the G Troop reunions of 1985 and 1989 at the three-story Embassy Suites in Abilene, Texas. These special events were held on the second floor hospitality room and patio that overlooked a garden atrium and restaurant.

A majority of the surviving G troopers who had been at Fort Clark attended at least one of the two reunions. Even many ex-troopers from the 112th's Midwest Chapter made the trip

C.W. Wiggins and Ray Czerniejewski, Abilene, Texas, 1989. Ray passed away on November 2, 1992, at the age of seventy-five (photograph by the author).

down and a number of former Abilene troopers attended, including the reunions' organizers and hosts John Coppinger, Jack Taylor, Dallas Currier, John Davis and Colonel Clyde Grant. The final event at each of the three-day affairs was a memorial service that concluded with the reading of names of the troopers who had been killed in combat or had since passed away. After the 1989 fete, the hosts expressed the regret that there probably would not be another Abilene reunion because of the advanced ages of its organizers. There were other reunions, in Dallas, Illinois, and Mississippi, but they lacked the uniqueness of the Abilene gatherings for the G troopers. With each succeeding year, the ranks of the 112th Cavalry veterans grew thinner.

Pug Wright cherished the reunions and his face brightened as he reminisced about his experiences with the cavalry. There were few left alive who could boast that they had sat in the saddle for the United States Cavalry. He treasured the memories and the lifelong friendships it fostered. On July 30, 1991, death forever silenced Pug's stories of the war and the cavalry.

Alonzo "Pug" Wright, Amarillo, Texas, 1988. (photograph by the author).

His death led the rarely emotional C.W. Wiggins to reveal his feelings about the men he served with during the war. "I knew Pug like a brother — and all the rest of them."

After Pug's death, a fellow G trooper, Lionel Carter, wrote to the family: "He was a good and brave soldier, the kind you would pick for a foxhole buddy. With his calm acceptance of any situation and his almost complete distain of any type of danger, he, without threatening or cajoling, set an example that calmed and reassured those around him regardless of the seriousness of the situation. Just as fear will spread like wildfire, calmness and acceptance of the situation will calm a group so as to meet any life-threatening situation with the courage to overcome and survive. That was the gift that Pug Wright gave us."[3]

C.W. "Bull" Wiggins passed away in March 2002 and Robert "Pickett" Wright died in April 2007. Nearly all of the G troopers of the 112th Cavalry Regiment have left us, but with this volume and others, their memories of those days with the cavalry will become frozen in time. It is the hope that this account will remind the generations of the future what these men endured and keep their spirit alive for descendants and others to experience.

Appendix A. 112th Cavalry Troopers on Active Duty July 20, 1942

*Appendix A is a roster of the members of the 112th Cavalry who were transported from San Francisco to New Caldonia, an island in the Southwestern Pacific, in July 1942. * Means a member of the Texas National Guard before the 112th Cavalry Regiment was nationalized. † Means the individual was originally designated to go overseas with the 112th Cavalry Regiment on the USS Grant but his name was marked through prior to departure. ‡ Means a person added as a replacement for an individual who was marked off the passenger list.*

Troop A, 112th Cavalry Regiment — USS *Grant* (USS *Republic*, AP-33) Passenger List July 20, 1942

Captain
Wright, Edward Jr.
1st Lieutenant
Fenley, Thomas A.
Jefferies, Joseph H.
2nd Lieutenant
Anderson, Harold M.
Batts, Joseph Jr.
First Sergeant
Smith, Jack*
Staff Sergeant
Horner, William A.*
McCurley, George J.
Spann, Felix W.
Sergeant
Akers, Oakley M.*
Baggott, Floyd R.*
Crisp, Johnny P.*

Davis, William C.*
Hill, Fitzhugh P.*
Hughes, Wurlington W.*
Rowe, William H.*
Ulrick, Edward B.*
Corporal
Beverage, Harry L.
Cross, Charles I.*
Davis, Jessie H.
Day, Joseph S.
Hall, Robert L.
Jackson, Roy C.*
Jones, William B.*
Kilgrea, Byron G.†
McMillon, James T.*
Nardi, Frank J.
Rose, Ralph M.*
Sligar, James W.

Veroni, Joe J.
Tech 5
Anderson, Edward, Jr.
Davis, Horace P.
Gill, George V.*
Holloway, Robert J.*
Jones, Elbert F.*
Mason, Frank L.
Nelson, Delbert P.*
Nicotori, Joseph A.
Private First Class
Adams, Louis C.
Allen, William E. Jr.
Arms, Charles
Baca, Charles L.
Bailey, Harvey H.
Baker, Audrey M.*
Bell, Charles E.*

Bird, John H.
Booher, W. W.*
Brabham, Charles C.*
Breland, L.B.
Broadway, Miles L.
Clanton, Roy L.*
Claridge, Rupert R., III
Cox, Donnie
Cranfill, Williard J.
Davis, Alex R.
DeFoo, C.H.*
Durkee, Frank E., Jr.*
Green, Johnny E.*
Griffith, Loyd E.*
Horton, Eugene R.*
Jenest, Homer C.
Kelley, Ernest L., Jr.*
Knight, Jay P.*
Kuczynski, Raymond F.
Lee, Johnnie J.*
Levine, David
Makowsky, Daniel J.
Martin, Homer R.*
Massey, Henry W.*
Mazur, Joseph R.
McCord, Arthur R.*
McMinnich, Elmer L.*
Michello, Charles W.
Miller, Harold W.
Novak, Sylvester R.
Place, Edward W.
Reinmiller, John
Restic, Warren L.
Reynolds, Theodore M.
Rowley, Richard L.
Russell, Clifford R.*
Sanders, Jodie J.*†
Sharp, Wallace C.*

Smith, Forest D.*
Troutner, Bryce L.
Willingham, Charles H.*
Yazinski, Leo H.
Zeller, Arthur V.
Ziegler, Harry G., Jr.

Private
Abramovich, George L.
Anderson, Clarence W.*
Armstrong, Robert C.
Arnold, James L.
Baggett, Horace G.
Baker, Victor G.
Barron, Juan E.
Bauman, Delbert*
Bevillo, Garney J.*
Bochs, Gerhardt J.
Doty, Archie*
Easman, Elbie R.C.
Elam, Billie T.
Forester, Joseph J.
Foster, James D.*
Gafford, Johnny H.*
Gautschi, Roy E.
Gresham, William C.*
Guy, Wesley L.*
Hanna, Ivah E.
Harris, Alvis W.*
Harvey, Joseph G.
Hassler, Vestle T.
Hilliker, Everett R.
Hollandbeck, Ralph M.
Howard, Alton M.*
Hudson, Lloyd F.*
Hudson, William E.
Hufstetler, Roy D.
Hurlbut, Edwin W.
Johnson, James C.*

Kegley, Sidney B.
Klobucar, George A.
Knight, Dewey P.*
Lattimore, Miller*
Mahoric, Paul
Martin, Ellis E.*
Mathis, A.T.*
Mayfield, Edgar O.*
McCutcheon, William R.*
McKenzie, Mack Z.
McMullen, Frances E.
McWhorter, Truman E.*
Merchant, Charles W.
Molesky, Joseph P.
Mollencop, Paul F.
Rackler, Grover N.
Rodriquez, Fabian T.*
Ronzi, Eugene J.
Shumaker, James R.
Sloboda, Joseph F.
Spodeck, Walter S.
Thibodeaux, Silas
Tomak, Michael C.
Varina, Charles W.
Wathen, John L.
Wells, Earl F.
White, Billie F.*
Wofford, Woodrow F.*
Wyatt, James H.*
Yorks, Julian
Zimmerman, Ralph
Saglser, Calvin O.‡
Franklin, Frank D.‡
Garrison, George T.‡

(Printed in Reunion Review,
*May 1990, No. 63, pp. 919–
920.)*

Troop B, 112th Cavalry Regiment — USS *Grant*
Passenger List, July 20, 1942

Captain
Laird, William J.
1st Lieutenant
Monnlo, Frank
Thomas, George C.
2nd Lieutenant
Mockenfuss, Walter B.
Moland, Harmon L.
First Sergeant
Browning, James M.*
Staff Sergeant

Burnard, Norvin T.*
Thornton, Jack*
Woodard, Walter B.*
Staff Sergeant
Brashear, George E.
Bryant, Howard N.*
Campbell, David W.*
Centrello, Angelo
Johnston, Charles R.*
Patton, Thomas J.*
Reed, Douglas B.*

Stuart, Garrett R.*†
Tech 4
Cantrell, George T.*
Farris, J. B.
Henninton, T.C.
Wier, T.G.*
Corporal
Bogan, Sidney T.
Brown, Charles
Daines, Roy W.
Goldman, Lindsey S.*

Hanvey, James E.*
Rigsby, Claude R.*
Roberts, Earl L.*
Sharp, Vernon E.*
Tampone, Vincent D.
Vaughn, Billy J.*
Vigne, Johnny W.*
Wilkinson, Harry*
Youngblood, Fred E.*

Tech 5
Donihoo, J.U.*
Meazell, Smith A.*
Mounger, Earl T.*

Private First Class
Akin, James D.*
Beaupre, Cecil E.*
Belfast, Frank
Belica, Joseph L.
Blackwell, Rudolph J.
Bononno, Carmen M.
Carrillo, Richard
Carroll, Lee E.
Caughey, Raymon
Copus, Hank
Cox, Elbert
Creech, Edward
Davis, Frank N.
Davis, Orville W.
Dearfield, James
Delawder, Earl F.
Diaz, Jose M.
Dobbins, William B.
Dougherty, Robert M.
Driggs, Richard E.
Durso, Nicholas P.
Elkins, Garvey, Jr.
Ellis, John
Foote, James C.
Garrett, Henry A.
Gerza, Charles P.
Gibson, Raymond A.
Gonzales, Santos
Gray, Troy M.
Hanlin, Maurice O.
Harlin, John E.

Heikkila, Reino A.
Hutchinsson, Homer E.
Knight, Walter G.*
Lorance, Lee R.*
Morgan, James R.*
Morrah, James H.*
Mullen, Paul A.*
Perkins, Perry I.*
Phennel, Earl T.*
Roffman, Carroll M.*
Schottine, Thomas L.†
Springer, James T.*
Stakes, H.W.*
Sutton, Roy E.*
Tarrer, Jimmie W.*
West, Clovis L.*
Wilkins, James D.*
Whetstine, Robert O.*
Youngblood, Jack C.*

Private
Artice, Kenneth N.*
Aubrey, Ephriam T.
Becker, Martin H.
Blackburn, Lawson
Blanton, Robert H.*
Bloedorn, Arnold G.
Bloomberg, Natham
Bonnet, Albert E.
Brincefield, Early J.
Brooks, Paul E.
Brown, William A.
Bruno, Francis F.
Burt, Charles R.
Callaway, Ollie L.
Callis, Clyde H.
Campos, Natividad
Carpenter, Ashton R.
Carrozze, Nick
Cates, Wilson
Chandler, Aaron S.
Chaney, Faris H.*
Chapman, Delbert C.
Charlton, Burl P.
Collins, Daniel F.
Cordaro, Leonard G

Couey, Guy J.
D'Angelo, Guido A.
Demjen, Louis, Jr.
Dillow, Hibert W.
Dooner, Thomas F.
Duffy, Warren R.
Flint, Edward J., Jr.
Flood, Leo E.
Fuller, Wesley H.
Gonzales, Billy G.
Hamilton, William E.,
   Jr.*
Hanvey, Everett M.*
Hayden, Lavelle C.
Komarzec, Walter A.
Lewis, Thomas E.*
Luna, Pete F.*
Mathias, Harold K.
McCoy, Mat A.
McDonald, Charles M.
Medina, Cruz P.
Miller, George W.
Miller, Lloyd A.
Mixon, Eddie L.
Murphy, Charles F.*
Neal, Charles W.
Pena, Lamberto D.
Presnall, Clyde
Ramsey, Harry
Reigle, Leroy
Renfro, John W.*
Richardson, Charles E.
Shaw, Russell C.
Shelton, Glenwood R.*
Speight, Samuel A., Jr.*
Teague, Leo*
Van Zandt, Howard J.
Vega, Carlos
Yagle, James
Richholtz, Charles N.‡
Hamm, Earl D.‡

(Printed in Reunion Review, *May 1990, No. 63, pp. 920–921.)*

Troop C, 112th Cavalry Regiment — USS *Grant*
Passenger List, July 20, 1942

Captain
Hunnicutt, Sam L.
1st Lieutenant
Brewton, William S.
Tipton, Quentin R.
2nd Lieutenant
Pearce, Arthur R.
Rowkand, Preston R.
Phillips, Eillie C.*
Staff Sergeant
Driggers, Tommie E.*
Higgins, Noel S.
Murray, J.D.*
Sergeant
Bryner, Wendell S.*
Donals, William A.*
Markham, Charles D.*
Nichols, James A.*
Petrie, Richard M.*
Strahan, Jack J.*
Tilson, Jack A.*
Wickless, Lester L.*
Tech 4
Galloupe, J.W.*
Holiday, Lynton H.*
Thompson, Leslie N.
Berry, Edgar L., Jr.*
Cannaday, Lonnie S.*
Carter, Woodrow*
Creed, Gene
Dennie, Harry C.*
Grau, George J.*
Griggs, Harvey*
Krassow, Frederick W.
McDermott, Travis P.*
Phillips, Jerome B., Jr.*
Priest, Joseph E.*
Smith, George H.*
Smith, Guy N.*
Allen, Truett D.
Crumpton, Vancarl*
Darby, James O.*
Ector, Arthur J.*
Graham, James A.*
Harman, Richard*
Private First Class
Abshere, Herman O.*
Adair, Charles V.*
Akin, Walter E.*
Beasley, Charles G.*
Brady, Irby H.
Brice, Jim E.*

Caudle, A.J.*
Coulter, Phillip R.*
Frye, Rex E.
Gailowski, August F.
Giacomo, Leomard J.
Gill, William R.
Grady, Donald F.
Grimes, Johnnie B.
Hare, James
Harris, Joseph W.
Hass, Robert L.
Hicks, Luther J.*
Higginbotham,
    Deamond W.*
Hile, John E.
Hill, Livie B.
Huey, Matt F.
Huffman, Duane
Hutton, Dudley G.*
Johnson, Ernest
Jolly, William D.*
Keener, Gaines F.*
Kessler, Clarence E.
Key, Harold J.*
Klussman, Raymond*
Klussman, Walter*
Konkel, William H.
Korsberg, Carl L.
Kubin, Victor E.
Kuchinski, Raymond E.
Lampe, Willie*
Lanning, William R.
Marcinko, John T.
Norwood, Chester E.*
Roso, C.C.*
Schulz, Alvin H.*
Stephens, Troy L.*
Stinson, Charles R.*
Stinson, Pete V.*
Striplin, Edward B.*
Teel, O.C.*
Turner, Dewie C.*
Private
Beasley, Ralph H.*
Brandenburg, Sam P.*
Carl, Robert H.
Carpenter, Walter H.*
DeGregio, Paul A.
Diez, Lawrence F.
Edwards, Raymond M.
Eiler, Leonard E.
Fischer, Martin E.*

Genthe, Roger V.
Gerecke, Edgar D.
Gonzales, Gregorio R.*
Gordon, Frank M.
Grim, Hurman W.
Grubar, Stanley
Guissanic, Thomas F.,
    Jr.
Harless, Dewey D.
Harmon, James P.
Harris, Charles R.
Harvell, Carlton G.
Hiebert, Abraham F.*
Hodquist, George D.
Hoft, Paul J., Jr.
Holt, Roscoe G.
Howes, Harry W.
Ivy, James H.
Jefferson, Bert H.
Jenkinson, James R.
Johnson, Richard C.
Johnson, Roy G.
Joiner, J.B.
Jolley, William L.
Jones, Jewell C.*
Jones, Jodie R.
Jones, Thomas F.
Kimbler, John W.
Klym, George
Koch, Evan
Kukla, Casimer C.
Kurish, Andrew J.
Lampman, Darrell D.
Libow, Fred
Lowe, James O.*
Martinez, Claude L.
Matamoras, Rodolfo
Mathony, Francis J.
McCarthy, Kenneth C.
McKay, Thomas C.
Miller, Ell.*
Miller, Howard J.
Nunn, Clayton T.*
Palliser, Harvey
Palmer, Walter
Priest, William V.*
Prost, Ernest L.
Rondon, Lubin*
Schaffner, Milton
Simpson, Delma
Spota, Edward J.
Stoffer, Charles W.

Swords, Leonard R.
Thompson, John D.*
Warren, Rufus R.*

Wilhite, Rudy

(Printed in Reunion Review,

May 1990, No. 64, pp. 937–938.)

Troop E, 112th Cavalry Regiment — USS *Grant* Passenger List, July 20, 1942

1st Lieutenant
Crume, Woodrow W.
Hughes, Hugh P.
Shaw, William B., Jr.
2nd Lieutenant
Appledorn, Harry J.
Hovey, Wendell R.
First Sergeant
Southard, Harold D.*
Staff Sergeant
Kirk, Eugene V.*
Wedgeworth, Clyde N.*
Sergeant
Carder, Lloyd P.*
Elder, Harry E.*
Fulton, Edwin C., Jr.*
Leonard, Harry L.*
Lubbering, Harry J.
Mezga, Joseph C.
Musso, Ross J.*
Phillips, James L.*
Tech 4
Gilman, Claud L.*
Lanier, Clyde C.*
Patterson, Jack*
Rushing, Ollie C.*
Stegent, Johnie M.*
Stokes, Ben J.
Corporal
Anderson, Riley R.*
Douglas, George B.*
Hancock, Hollis H.*
Haney, Curtis L.*
Hawkins, Walter L.C., Jr.*
Killen, Vernon T.*
Kurz, Frank J.*
Loughlin, Lorenzo D., Jr.*
Nance, Thomas W.*
Palmquist, Clark L.
Teague, James E.*
Wallace, William K.*
Whitman, Vernon J.
Tech 5
Clark, James D.*
Killen, Jake C.*

Ross, Lawrence J.
Whitman, Vernon J.
Private First Class
Barrett, William E.*
Broughton, Elbert
Casford, Ray A.*
Cisler, Elmer J.
Garison, Harvey R., Jr.*
Garlington, Lynn A.*
Heverly, Paul M.
Holbrook, Clarence S.
Hudspath, Allen V.*
Hughes, William O.
Jones, Walter E.*
Kent, Edgar L.*
Kent, Oscar B.*
Kingsley, Clarence S.*
Lopes, Paul
Lutkus, Charles A.
Lyon, Jesse W.
Macksoud, Nicholas J.*
Martin, Carl D.*
Marquez, Ricardo R.
Martinez, Avelardo
McCain, William A.
McClanahan, Jack J.
Megee, Ernest A.
Mogus, Anthony J.
Monroe, John A.
Nagg, Steve
Newsom, Forest
Novak, Peter
Parris, Loy B.*
Pearson, Kenneth K.
Pennington, John W.
Pickett, Eddie E.*
Potter, Lloyd W.
Price, Edward J.
Provincio, Carlos A.
Quillin, L.J.
Quinn, Claud F.
Quintana, Ismael
Reeves, Robert E.
Reos, Mike G.
Reyes, Victor
Ross, George H.
Salas, Frank

Schladitz, Henery H.
Sickmiller, Kenneth T.
Silverman, Harold
Stokes, Ollie L.
Stuchlik, Jerry F.*
Twardowski, Willie*
Urban, Vernon W.*
Vance, Wilbur A.*
Wade, R.T.*
Ward, Ezra D.
Wheat, Thurmon*
Young, Calvin B.*
Private
Atkins, Charles W.*
Barrios, Rafael
Battenfield, Aubrey A.*
Blanton, Horace E.*
Boyle, Julius B.*
Brown, Otis L.*
Burgay, Radford*
Cason, Paul R.*
Childs, Charles E.*
Clark, Payl D.*
Cox, Revis
de la Garza, Carlos B.
Dimas, Francisco R.
Duesterhoft, Herbert*
Elliott, Edward
Fagon, George A., Jr.*
Farley, Charles M.*
Ferguson, Raymond*
Flentge, Albert A.*
Harper, James D.
Kenjura, Edward*
Kerr, Dewey W.
Lee, Rudolph M.*
Lemin, Joseph*
Lujan, Juan O., Jr.
McCullum, Edward J.
Miller, Donald L.
Mitton, Ralph C.
Moreno, Angle H.
Newsome, William T.*
Norton, Charles C.
Palmer, Herbert D.*
Parker, Ernest C.
Phillips, William H.

Pittman, Luther W.
Prebilski, Bernard A.*
Radziwon, Walter
Rageth, Loyal L.
Ramey, J.W.*
Ray, Clyde A.
Reno, Charles W.
Rico, Jose
Riojas, Susano R.

Roberts, Perry C.*
Robertson, Ernest T.
Rodriguez, Ramon
Rohel, Herman J.
Sanchez, Charlie
Smith, William M.
Stephenson, James G., Jr.*
Stone, George W.*

Wasson, Albert L.*
White, Charles H.*
Whitley, George W.
Zientek, Joe I.*
Zientek, John J.*

(Printed in Reunion Review, May 1990, No. 64, pp. 938–939.)

Troop F, 112th Cavalry Regiment — USS *Grant* Passenger List, July 20, 1942

Captain
Hood, Manley E.
1st Lieutenant
Hare, Almon R.
Van Riper, Warren H.
2nd Lieutenant
Labadie, George V., Jr.
Washburn, Wendell M.
First Sergeant
Toliver, Charlie B.*
Staff Sergeant
Armentrout, Norman G.
Norman, Forrest S.*
Warren, Houston G.*
Sergeant
Barron, Joe A.*
Campbell, George H.*
Fielder, Floyd F.*
McNew, Ben J., Jr.*
Smith, Fred*
Sneed, Dale, Jr.*
Taylor, Ben F.*
Yancy, Charles M.*
Tech 4
Corbitt, James B.*
Holguin, Salvador
Lynn, Arthur J.
Willis, Wilbert*
Corporal
Adams, Verlin D.
Brown, Hyson E.*
Carroll, Milton H.*
Hale, Lloyd W.
Herbert George W.*
Hill, William R.*
Land, James B.*
Lee, Clifford H.*
Moring, Wilson C.
Peace, Jacob*
Smith, William W.

Tipton, Guy E., Jr.*
Wedgeworth, Everett L.*
Tech 5
Chadwick, John B.*
Gradick, Ben*
Moody, Benjamin P.*
Ross, Hubert E.*
Scudder, George*
Wallace, James E.
Private First Class
Bradford, Chancy M.
Brown, Ellery C., Jr.*
Brown, Jesse I.
Caldwell, Thomas F.*
Carter, Price E.*
Dixon, George M.
Duncan, Raymon E.
Feagin, Albert S.*
Fernandez, Roberto
Fields, John P.*
Granberry, George P.*
Harris, Jesse C.*
Harris, Tommie B.*
Holstead, Louis M.
Howard, Woodrow P.*
Johnson, Jack A.
Kennard, Rather C.*
Lee, Herbert J.*
Leegoria, Miquel
Long, Allen G.
Low, Roy J.
McCleeny, James T.*
McCollough, Cecil
McKeever, Roland T.*
McNeal, John A.*
Maxfield, Lloyd R.
Metcalf, R.A.*
Meurer, Alex
Monastero, Joseph
Muncus, Hubert J.*

Murphy, J.B.*
Nelson, William C.
Ostrowski, Edward W.
Ostrowski, Walter J.
Santa Cruz, Alfonzo
Spurlock, Clifford C.*
Stansbury, W.C.*
Stephenson, George H.
Stockstill, Jack A.*
Stumpf, Willard M.
Templeton, Pat*
Thompson, Wylie E.*
Triana, Frank
Waddill, John D.
Walker, David L.
Wallace, Jack W.*
Wallace, Stanley J.
Walley, Doan
Warshaw, Isaiah
Wheeler, Oren B., Jr.
Woodard, J. W. Reed
Wylie, Benjamin F. Jr.
Private
Adare, Clifford W.*
Anderson, Lloyd W.
Anerton, Robert O.
Barton, John C.
Bentley, Archie R.*
Bergren, Walter R.
Bilczewski, Mitchell S.
Blackwell, William H.
Bornemann, Elmond F.*
Bradshaw, Marvin C.*
Brady, Gaston C.*
Brown, William B.
Caldwell, Jim L.*
Clark, Newman W.*
Dercoli, Joseph P.
Gaddis, Tommie
Giron, Santiago

Hullett, Erwin T.*
Jenkins, Tommy B.
Johnson, Guy L.*
Jones, Walter D.*
King, Richard H.*
Kirby, Charles M.*
Kurzawski, Raymond J.
Lester, Lewis H., Jr.
McGinnis, Charles B.
Mendoza, Artomic R.
Morton, Joe B.
Munoz, Domingo
Myers, Deward R.G.*
Orosco, Adan
Pettit, Robert B.†
Reese, Aubrey H.

Rivers, Bernardo
Roberts, Harold S.*
Rochelle, Claude M.
Rodgers, Emmitt
Rodriguez, ?
Roth, Harold L.
Sanchez, Felix T.*
Shannon, Robert*
Sitton, James E.*
Small, Grady
Sniegocki, Joseph B.
Stephens, Francis L.*
Stokes, Kenneth S.
Tolaro, Carl B.
Toth, Steve
Turner, Alfred T.

Turner, Ray B.*
Valerie, Felipe
Vannicola, Leonard R.
Wagner, Lewis J.
Welsch, William C.*
Wiles, Charles F.
Wilke, Claire M.
Williams, Abrey B.
Yates, Noble E.
Jaynes, Roy‡
Hillman, James R.‡

(Printed in Reunion Review, *Christmas, 1990, No. 65, pp. 964–965.)*

Troop G, 112th Cavalry Regiment — USS *Grant* Passenger List, July 20, 1942

Captain
Leonard, Lloyd L.
1st Lieutenant
Stallings, Jesse D.
Tucker, Joseph A.
2nd Lieutenant
MacIntire, Samuel C., III
Williams, Riford S.
First Sergeant
Currier, Dallas O.*
Staff Sergeant
Agnew, John B.*
Harris, Robert A.*
Isbell, Charley D.*
Sergeant
Agnew, William R.*
Beasley, Ernest D.*
Bell, James T.*
Coppinger, John P.*
Dorton, Lester F.*
Lewis, Therron E.*
Price, Ernest V.*
Taylor, Jack*
Tech 4th Grade
Bynum, Raymond H.*
Gannaway, R. Lee*
Newman, James K.*
Thomas, Rufus J.
Corporal
Beasley, Edward W.*
Czerniejewski, Raymond C.
Glass, Thomas P.*

Hood, Roscoe*
Johnson, Max
Meeks, Ezra H.*
O'Briant, Robert P.
Paulsen, Harold E.
Sunday, J. Ray*
Thompson, Harvey E.*
Wheeler, Jim F.*
Young, Harold D.
Zabloudil, Jake Jr.*
Tech 5th Grade
Daniel, Charles C.*
Ham, Ernest L.
Giles, Max*
Johnson, Chemist W.*
McKinney, Arvel
Private First Class
Bynum, Joe E.*
Cudd, Hugh E.*
Davis, John E.*
DeJager, Ira
Eason, Lloyd J.
Griffin, Guy W.*
Hillson, William E.
Hufstedler, Charles E.*
Humyak, John
Jagodzinski, Leonard
Johnson, Dewey M.
King, Woodrow W.
Kush, Howard
Lacey, Melvin J.
Lane, Ralph J., Jr.*
Maroney, James W.*

Matthews, Ralph T.
Mitchell, Silas V.
Moody, Sidney J.
Moseley, Sol Y.
Mucha, Fred H.
Olei, Rudolph A.*
Olei, Theodore*
Parker, Robert H.*
Patterson, Robert B.
Penokie, Charles R.
Powell, Euce B.
Proctor, Thurman A.
Quezada, Carlos R.
Rawlinson, Marvin L.
Richardson, Howard J.
Safran, Jerry J.
Sawyer, Van C.
Schmidt, Herman L.
Snell, Leon C.
Stevenson, James G., Jr.
Stokes, Herman L.
Summers, Clyde S.*
Sunday, Willie A.
Tarleton, Malcom L.
Tucker, Doyle C.*
Voyles, Vernon J.*
Weddel, Orvil R.
White, Henry R.
Wiggins, Christaine W.
Wilson, Elmer R.
Wright, Robert L.
Private
Aasen, Oscar L.

Anschultz, Alfred L.
Carlson, Clifford W.
Carter, George L.
Chavarria, Amador G.
Corley, Eddie F.
Donsbach, Antone K.
Elenbaas, Earl
Ellis, William E.
Fell, George B.
Fowler, Luther M.
Goodson, Legion
Hahn, August G.
Harbiezwski, Frank
Helfrich, Charles W.
Hutchins, Hollis F.*
Isaacson, Dean A.
Krebs, Elmer E.
Letterle, Orvil L.
Lovelady, Oliver L.
Martin, Harold
Martinez, Pablo J.
Mason, Wylie A.*

Maxwell, William E.
McDonnell, William J.
Meyer, Elmond R.
Miller, Lew S.
Millis, Cyril J.
Moore, Warren D.*
Morrison, James B.
Mulawa, Bronislaus
Parker, Leonard J.*
Patterson, James H.
Periman, Alton Z.
Peterson, Albert H.
Pinkston, Earl N.*
Plowman, Rudolph D.*
Pryor, Clarence H.
Raske, Louis C.
Reed, Otis M.
Reynolds, William H.†
Riccardi, George G.
Riggan, John L.
Riggs, Richard A.
Roberts, Johnie

Robertson, Jesse R.
Rogalla, Raymond V.
Samson, Stewart
Skelton, Glen F.
Smith, Jack L.*
Snider, Dale G.
Stone, Dewey H.
Terry, Alfred F.
Vargas, Hector M.
Vaughn, Alton A.
Vire, James A.*
Webb, J.V.
White, Roy F.
Willingham, R.C.
Wood, Walter L.
Wright, Alonzo
Young, Kenneth F.
Zajac, John

(Printed in Reunion Review, *May 1987, No. 56, pp. 731–32.)*

Machine Gun Troop, 112th Cavalry Regiment — USS *Grant* — Passenger List July 20, 1942

Captain
Minter, John L.
1st Lieutenant
Penny, Leonard D., Jr.
Watson, Howell H.
2nd Lieutenant
Prichard, William R.
Waddle, Billy M.
First Sergeant
Colley, Darrell E.*
Staff Sergeant
Barfield, Walter W.*
Sharp, Carlton B.*
Thurmond, Robert L.*
Sergeant
Beckham, Jack W.*
Corley, Alfred D.*
Cornwall, Richard O.*
DeFer, William D.*
Dillingham, Ralph*
Florence, Kenneth N.*
Fyke, Frank C.*
McDearmont, Charles L.*
Smith, Sherwin D.*
Stovall, David C.*
Stovall, James W.*
Youngblood, Jessie J.

Tech 4
Chambers, James D.*
Gamble, Charlie E.*
Corporal
Campbell, Brooks G.*
Chennault, James W.*
Cody, John P.*
Curtis, Roy H.*
Dillon, Jay D.*
Hope, Charles L.
Hopkins, A.P.*
Kobus, Albert J.
Parrott, John, Jr.
Peek, Earl M.
Reese, Ray*
Rich, G.D.
Tech 5
Bass, Curtis B.
Berryhill, Johnie L.
Jennings, Lawrence M.*
Moore, James E.*
Pierce, Christopher K.
Private First Class
Absher, John H., Jr.
Boyd, Willie L.*
Davis, Arthur L.*
Dean, Lee R.

England, John W.*
Faxon, Foster
Fearn, James C.
Fleming, William H.*
Foreman, Randolph*
Freme, Joseph
Garcia, Jesus
Geyer, Donald R.
Giguere, Raymond J.
Gnerlich, Lester L.
Gort, Mitchell E.
Hampton, Donald*
Heldner, Henry A.
Hess, Carl G.
Hulgan, Robert J.
James, George J.
Jones, Arthur
Jones, Robert H.*
Langston, Fred M.*
LaTour, Victor J.*
Lee, Herman
Lee, Raymond E.
Lemley, Anson O.
Lemley, Weldon E.*
McIntosh, Francis H.
McMahan, Jessie K.
Myers, Henry

Najar, George R.
Nelson, Sylvester H.
Nistor, Joseph J.
Ownbey, R.D.
Parker, Joe R.
Parker, Simon, Jr.
Rachwalski, Joseph J.
Radney, Cecil E.
Railsback, James B.
Reiter, Frank
Robbins, Fred H.
Sinclair, Robert V.
Teaver, V.L.
Trevizo, Leonardo S.
Tucker, Roy A.*
Villalobes, Jose V.
Wallace, Judson D.*
Private
Baskett, Robert E.*
Berard, Clarence B.
Bianco, John M.
Blue, Troy W.*
Bogachinski, Simon A.
Bowman, Clynbert L.*
Bryden, Harold C.
Click, Richard S.
Davis, T.D.J.
Easter, Andrew O.
Estrada, Luis
Fears, Jewel R.

Ferenc, Stanley C.
Fontaine, Leonard R.
Fox, Blake R.
Frank, Francis
Frost, Omar
Galindo, Alfonso M.
Garchow, Edward M.
Gawlak, Paul I.
Giaquinto, Nicholas A.
Godfrey, Lloyd C.
Griffen, Wallace M.
Griffin, Howard P.
Grofer, Robert E.
Hambright, Clarence A.*
Hamner, James D.
Hargraves, Alled H.
Hatch, Weldon B.
Hatfield, Clifford C.
Hay, John E., Jr.
Hayes, Harold W.
Hill, Oliver W.
Horner, Noel D.
Howe, James J.
Hurst, Roy A.
Jerrel, Carol O.
Jorgensen, Nels C.
Kazee, William K.
Kizer, John T.
Kovacs, Geza
Lasek, Stanley M.

Lawrence, Howard K.
Lemmer, Francis W.
Lindstrom, Marvin E.
Lockridge, Raymond C.
Marker, Ralph L.
Martin, D.M.*
McGlasson, Burl
McKinney, Everett M.
Milkiewicz, Vincent P.
Moorehead, James
Parra, Bentio
Petty, Leon B.
Porter, Jack C.
Privetera, Alfred Jr.
Radney, George W.
Rut, James G.
Sadler, Sherman T.
Schneider, Marvin Z.
Simons, Ollie D.*
Schoch, Alfred W.
Scott, Richard D.
Tankursley, Delma G.*
Tate, J.C.
Udstuen, Melvin F.
Whitaker, Estel D.
White, Darwin
Wilson, Homzic K.

(Printed in Reunion Review, Christmas, 1990, No. 65, pp. 965–966)

Special Weapons Troop, 112th Cavalry Regiment — USS *Grant* Passenger List, July 20, 1942

Captain
Crews, Sim H.
Houghton, Reeves R.
1st Lieutenant
Stallings, William T., Jr.
2nd Lieutenant
Bird, Russell G., Jr.
Johnson, Leonard L.
First Sergeant
Fenley, George W.*
Staff Sergeant
Brady, Wilson J.
Taliaferro, J.D.L.*
Walters, Vasco L.*
Sergeant
Bouldin, James T.*
Buffington, Oatice E.*
French, Carl

Frost, Harrell C.*
Gamblin, Robert M.*
Gaston, Harry L.*
Humphfus, Martin L.*
Lockett, David T.*
McFadin, Ralph G.*
Moore, James B.*
Nesmith, Warren A.*
Robinson, Wayne P.*
Walker, Jack H.*†
Tech 4
Meadows, Joseph I.*
Corporal
Barnes, Robert V.*
Cook, Benjamin G.
Cryer, Murle J.*
Davis, Crawford B., Jr.*
Fleming, Joe B.*

Hightower, Earl V.
Johnson, Jack A.
Miller, Homer E.
Morgan, Leonard V.
Perry, Davis C.*
Scott, William B.*
Toth, Edward S.
Ware, William A.*
Private First Class
Armstrong, Desmond K.
Baxley, Alvah L.*
Brosch, Joel R.
Hassell, Clinton A.
Holt, Ivers F.*
Locke, Robert M.
Sharp, Henry C.
Abel, Ralph S.*
Abrahamson, Vincent A.

Albright, Thadius T.
Anders, Emil A.
Beinhauer, Elton E.
Boots, Melvin M.*
Brattello, Albert P.
Brown, Erlie V.
Browning, Sally M.
Brzuchalsky, Walter
Buckalew, Elmer A.
Carlyle, Robert W.
Clay Herschael
Denton, M. A.
Duke, Leroy
Eble, Robert L.
Fisher, Kenneth
Grim, Henry L.
Gustafson, Gustaf E.
Hall, Marvin R. J.
Harris, Francis M.
Hawkins, Truman J.
Hedrick, Ralph D.
Hoffman, George S.
Horner, T. J.
Hungerford, Jack W.
Inman, Seth E.
Lee, William E.
Linston, Mack M.
Lynch, Merle F.
Macoviak, Anthony
Mallory, Lloyd J., Jr.*
Pilarczyk, Anthony
Riddle, Milburn T.*
Saenz, Augustine, Jr.
Schmidt, Leon F.
Severson, Danford E.

Taylor, Chester D.
Toki, William V.
Wachter, Carl C.
Wharton, Howard D.
Williams, Wilmot

Private
Basalyga, Mike
Battista, Frank
Brammer, James E.
Campbell, Harley L.
Cantu, Antonio P.
Carrigan, Robert E.
Case, Hursel
Craig, Robert W.
Crawford, Russell P.
Coleman, Bernie H.
Cooper, Eugene A.*
Dabney, Lyman H.*
Dudzinski, Joseph B.
Ehrhardt, Christian E.,
 Jr.
Elmer, Melvin H.
Evridge, William*
Flore, Daniel J.
Gosche, Ervin L.
Hathaway, Emory A.*
Healy, John J.
Howell, Charles R.
Hyde, Earnest H.
Jordan, Earl L.*
Kerr, Raymond P.
Kimble, Clyde E.
Kleinheinz, Victor W.
Kline, J.C.*
Kowal, John

Lawson, Harry L.
Leak, Bernard A.
Livinghouse, Lawrence
 W.
Love, Jimmie*
Mount, William A.
Perrone, Michael J.
Phillips, Jesse N.
Proctor, Johnnie F.
Ribera, Eliseo
Rodriquez, Curtis J.*
Rogers, Barney D.
Rominger, Donald R.*
Schueller, Daniel A.
Shanks, Orville
Shilling, Brondel C.
Sigman, Daniel W.
Smith, Earl C.
Smith, Walter
Stephens, Asland P.
Sykes, Charles H.
Thomas, Paul R.
Treuner, Erwn A.
Underhill, Fred P.
Valent, Teofil P.
Wiggins, David W.
Wilson, Milton T.*
Wisher, Joseph J.
Yuvan, Louis J.

(Printed in Reunion Review, *June 1991, No. 66, pp. 995–996.)*

Headquarters and Service Troop, 112th Cavalry Regiment — USS *Grant* Passenger List, July 20, 1942

Captain
McMains, D.M.*
1st Lieutenant
Albright, Byron W.
Carter, James
Howell, Jack J.
Roehrig, William D.
2nd Lieutenant
Calvert, Hugh W.
Master Sergeant
Campbell, Herbert D.*
Gersling, Earl E., Jr.*

Gray, Jay O.*
Sperry, Walter D.*
Tech Sergeant
Ohinske, Richard*
McDonald, Roy A.*
Stanley, John G.*
Staff Sergeant
Brown, Jacobs*
Harwood, Walter T.*
Hunt, Woodrow W.*
Sergeant
Burgess, Clyde H.*

Chubbuck, Judson
Duncan, William T.*
Irwin, Knox H.
Jones, Merrell M.*
Luttrell, Earl*
Maxey, Edward P.
North, Frank H.*
Sanders, Gilbert B.*
Tomlinson, Maury H.*
Warren, Wilson F.*
White, Willie B.*

Tech 4
Allen, Charles
Brannon, Homer P.
Geb, Ralph N.*
Henry, Loman W.
Law, Billy J.*
Robertson, James J.
Thaxton, Jack G.*
Weber, Richard J.*
Corporal
Bailey, Roy R., Jr.*
Bennett, James E.*
Cannon, Richard A.*
Collier, Pate F.
Etue, Thomas A.
Fittz, Clayton O.
Gabriel, Ernest L.*
Kubic, Arthur J.
Lewis, Albert B., Jr.
Montague, Robert J.
Roberts, John J.*
Sanders, James D.*
Sidle, John A.*
Stanley, Albert E.*
Tech 5
Bailes, Fred O.*
Belotti, James V.
Burch, Fred L.
Burns, James A.
Burson, Earl R.
Caffey, Dee
Cansler, Henry L.*
Carmical, Fred L.*
Cathey, Harmon W.
Cheek, Aubrey R.*
Clark, David T.*
Davis, Thomas O.*
Dillon, Iley B.
Jenkins, Lawrence
McMains, Wallace A.*
Mullee, Peter A.
Nelson, Phillip H.
Payne, Eugene, Jr.*
Phares, Roy A.
Phillips, Loren R.
Plunk, James M., Jr.*
Richards, Kenneth G.
Schell, Dovaul L.
Thompson, William H., Jr.
Tyler, R.B.*
Werner, Frank E.*
Worrell, Jack G.*
Private First Class
Abreo, Santiago
Anglin, Ralph E.

Baker, Charles D.*
Betthauser, Joseph C.
Bolton, Carl W.
Bolton, Herman O.
Bradley, Stewart M.
Brown, Prentice D.
Burbes, William E.
Caffey, John M.*
Calmes, Napoleon B.
Carlson, Herbert A.
Chennault, James R.*
Coats, Roland*
Day, Joyie*
Doyle, Joe P.
Dunfee, Fred E.
Dunning, Harold P.
Ebarb, John
Edwards, Robert E.*
Elliott, Olen B.*
Embrec, Edwin J.
Farrar, Eulice H.
Gidcumb, James E.*
Houser, William E.
Jacobs, Lawrence N.*
Liotta, James W.
Lobello, Kola P.*
Lucero, Ramon
Malcomb, John A.
Marshall, Nathanuel T.*
Martinez, Ysidro
McMurrian, Homer*
McPherson, James W.
Merideth, Clyde*
Moore, Thomas J.*
Nelson, William L.*
Patterson, Vernon L.
Pennington, Otha L.*
Poole, Edgar D.*
Porger, Charles L.
Pye, Jessie Y.
Richardson, Curtis L.
Seay, General F.
Sheppa, John
Shoemaker, Jay M.*
Standiford, Austin A.
Taylor, Louis L.*
Watkins, Lyle P.
Zickuhr, Melvin E.
Private
Abrans, Edwin
Adams, Eswin
Priavte Arp, Walter C.
Banik, Frank E.
Bates, Lennard O.
Becka, Frank J., Jr.
Belcher, James H.

Bell, M.H.
Bell, Robert C.
Blalock, Tommie F.*
Brader, Mack R.
Broun, Ross D.
Broun, William B.
Burden, Billy G.*
Buske, J.F.
Chansler, Frederick L.*
Chennault, Herman H.*
Christensen, Alvin H.
Churchill, Merle L.
Cook, Howard E.
Cooper, Mack R.
Cornelius, Moultrie H.*
Cummings, Edmund A.
Datschefski, Wayne
Davis, James A.
Dennler, Harry C., Jr.
Detch, Alan
Dilbeck, Deriso W.
Donnelly, William E.
Elenbaas, Orrin E.
Fedorchak, Maxim
Galloway, James W.*
Garner, Jimmie L.
Gossett, Earl A.*
Harrison, Bruce C.
Hawley, Johnny M.
Herring, Robert S.
Hill, Henry P.*
Hinderman, Harold
Hollowell, Ivan
Hubbard, Wayne L.
Hyre, Paul W.
Jack, Nathaniel
Jackson, Loys W.
John, Gust
Johnson, Johnnie
Koke, Henry J.
Layne, Paschal S.*
Lewis, Hobert
Losino, Dominic M.
Marsh, Earl W.
Martinez, Jesus O.
McClendon, Alan R.*
Morrell, Clarence A., Jr.
Neaterour, Arthur L.
Nesvig, Frank F.
O'Brien, Ottis T.
Palmer, O.C.
Perkins, Dennis H.
Phelps, Johnie W.
Potter, Harry W.
Riddle, Franklin E.
Seay, John A.

Seitz, Carl R.
Simpson, Keith R.
Squires, Leland
Summer, Lloyd P.
Tillman, Willie B.*
Tucker, William F.*

Turner, Richard Y.*
Wagner, Henry T.
Walters, Ford A.
Welke, Alvin F.
Wiggins, Rufus S.*
Woolsey, Clifford W.*

Wright, Garfield
Yanni, Frank

(Printed in Reunion Review, June 1991, No. 66, pp. 996–997.)

Headquarters, First Squadron, 112th Cavalry Regiment — USS *Grant* Passenger List, July 20, 1942

Major
  Johnson, Rupert H.
Captain
  Carter, John L.
Staff Sergeant
  Hooks, John F.*
  Rhoden, Earl L.*
  Vigne, J. Dell*

Sergeant
  English, John P.
  Gausnell, James D.*
  Fisher, Elmer Jr.*
  Krumm, Herman
  Martin, Homer H.
  Nixon, Woodrow W.
  Roebuck, Raymond

Private
  Garbler, Walter J.
  Manfull, Charles W.
  McCarthy, Joseph
  Leicht, Hugo V.
  Miesch, John C.

(Printed in Reunion Review, August 1991, No. 67, p. 1020)

Headquarters, Second Squadron, 112th Cavalry Regiment — USS *Grant* Passenger List, July 20, 1942

Captain
  Bellinger, Oran R.
  Captain Grant, Clyde E.*
Staff Sergeant
  Barron, Phillip E.*
  Donward, Teddy D.*
  Hitt, Desmond D.*
Sergeant
  Dennard, Olin M.*

Donecker, Frederick W.
Lee, Frank J., Jr.
Moseley, Joseph T.*
Stroud, Grady R.
Underwood, John V.
Private
  Hernandez, Encarnacion J.
  Lambert, Donald

Leper, Michael A.
Limbach, Melvin J.
Molder, Floyd B.
Monogus, Louis J.

(Printed in Reunion Review, August 1991, No. 67, p. 1020.)

Medical Detachment, 112th Cavalry Regiment — USS Grant Passenger List, July 20, 1942

Captain
  Banen, David M.
  Fink, Carl
  Gibson, Hester M. Jr.
  Robinson, Frank B.
  Tascarella, James W.

1st Lieutenant
  Hermel, Mortimer B.
  Kelley, John T., Jr.
  Kothmann, Victor L.
  McCorneck, Rodwin C.

Tech Sergeant
  Parnell, Fred W.*
Staff Sergeant
  Beasley, Lewis*
  Thompson, Hamilton N.*
  Williams, Jessie E.*

Sergeant
Elders, Ted H.*
Holland, Evans C.*
Sutton, Donald C.
Tech 4
Beyer, Charles E.*
Genaro, Robert D.*
Corporal
Dotson, James W.*
Johnson Alfred W.*
Tech 5
Atwood, Otis G.*
Burns, Wiliam T.*
Connell, Riley W.*
Griffith, William M.*
Lankford, Francis G.
Owens, Clifton K.*
Private First Class
Andrews, Carl E.*
Battis, Callan A.

Cline, James P.*
Fortenberry, George E.*
Jenkins, Earl D.
Lawrence, Spurgeon I.*
Matatell, Kenneth I.*
Merritt, John W.*
Pope, Jessie D.*
Salas, Jose G.
Schick, Wilbur L.
Small, Ricahrd M.
Stulgaitis, Anthony C.
Stupora, Felix J.
Tognetti, Emo L.
Trzecinski, Clarence C.
Private
Boyle, Alvin W.*
Cook, Lig
Dunn, Ted M.*
Holden, William H.
Mann, M. C.*

Marquez, Francisco, Jr.
Montes, Cristobal
Nesom, Clarence E.
Ranspot, Richard R.*
Ringel, Fritz
Rolland, Virgil L.*
Schultz, Frank A.
Silcox, Arvin V.
Smith, Lawrence H.
Smith, Ralph H.
Srobernak, Michael J.
Stasewich, Joseph
Swendris, Vincent J.
Vander Vere, Herbert J.
Voklts, Steve

(Printed in Reunion Review, *August 1991, No. 67, pp. 1020–21.)*

Band, 112th Cavalry Regiment — USS *Grant* Passenger List, July 20, 1942

Warrant Officer
Harris, Lester E.
Tech Sergeant
Kreiger, Allen H.*
Staff Sergeant
Lain, Jay W.*
Sergeant
Baker, Hal*
Dunagan, Jack C., Jr.*
Stinnett, McLeod, Jr.*
Suter, William A.
Tech 4
Cruce, James L.
Kreitzer, Lloyd M.*
Corporal
Schafer, Ernest J.*

Sebastian, George T.
Tech 5
Griffith, Paul I., Jr.*
Hammond, Jack E.
Jones, James S.*
Morrell, Lawrence G.*
Ohlson, Leonard E.*
Williams, Fred H., Jr.*
Private First Class
Ambrose, Frank J.
Private First Class
Darby, Robert S.
Private First Class
DuBrock, Paul J.
Lambert, Herbert*
Payne, Haskell L.*

Sergeant
Sergeant, Richard G.
Suggs, John R.
Swift, John R.
Welch, James E.*
Werner, William S.*
Williamson, Henry H.
Private
Eastland, James E.*

(Printed in Reunion Review, *August 1991, No. 67, pp. 1020–21.)*

Appendix B.
Troop A Rubber Boat Assault

In the pre-dawn hours of December 15, 1943, the ancient destroyer USS *Sands* arrived off the southern coast of New Britain some four miles east of the boot of Arawe peninsula. The ship was to unload the 150 members of Troop A, 112th Cavalry Regiment, who were to assail the Japanese held shore line. When it was discovered the *Sands* was closer to shore than the Army plan dictated, the ship had to back out further into the sea, generating engine noise that could possibly be heard by the enemy ashore. After the *Sands* came to a stop, the troopers with their equipment began the descent on cargo nets into fifteen rubber boats floating alongside the transport.

"I was in the first boat of the first wave," wrote Associated Press correspondent Robert Eunson. "We left our ship at 5:08 A.M. A bright moon was shining when the sailors threw our boats into the water. We let out machine guns and my typewriter down off the deck with long ropes. Then we scrambled over the side....

"The sea was black in the moonlight. Our boats were bouncing silhouettes. You could hear little black paddles splashing in the water, lightly at first, then seemingly louder as we came closer to the jungle cove behind the white beach we were heading for. We were in perfect formation when we reached the coral reef."[1]

According to the Army's plan, Troop A, commanded by Captain Edward Wright, Jr., of Dallas, Texas, would land four miles east of the main assault at the Arawe peninsula, climb the cliffs near the village of Umtingalu, and block the enemy's retreat from the main invasion force. Surprise was crucial for the success of their mission because the Japanese had situated two twin-

LCRs on maneuvers off Goodenough Island in preparation for the invasion of New Britain (U.S. Army photograph) (courtesy of the Texas Military Forces Museum).

barreled 25-millimeter antiaircraft guns and several machine guns just to the west of the native village of Umtingalu.[2] It was obvious that if the assault troops were discovered by the enemy before they reached shore, their rubber boats would be sitting ducks.

Less than one hundred yards from shore the fifteen rubber boats were raked by machine gun fire from enemy positions on the cliffs above the beach.[3] The concentration of fire from the machine guns and a anti-aircraft gun played havoc with the rubber boats, sinking twelve of fifteen boats.

The lead boats were only thirty yards from the beach when they received fire and some of the troopers tried to respond with automatic weapons fire, but it was useless. One of the A Troopers said it was "just like a bunch of bees coming at you at one time. You know, every fourth or fifth bullet was a tracer.... All of this coming at you and you knew good and well that you were going to get hit. If you weren't hit, the Good Lord was looking after you the way I look at it!"[4]

Troopers jumped out of the sinking rubber boats that were the target of the guns. Once in the water, the struggling troopers had to remove their packs and abandon the heavy equipment just to keep from sinking to the bottom. Many were lucky enough to have a fellow trooper cut the straps from their body with a knife that the men all carried. There is no way to tell how many men were killed by the enemy's guns or drowned due to the weight of their equipment.

From his position aboard the escort destroyer, United Press Correspondent William C. Wilson saw the Japanese tracers stream into A Troop's rubber boats. "I heard the thump-thump of the rapid-fire Japanese cannon interspersed with the rattle of the machine guns. Then, with the aid of field glasses in the moonlight, I picked out the figures of heavily armed men struggling in the water — rubber boats empty and drifting — other boats with their occupants paddling furiously with the tracers streaking all around them and the cannon shells tossing up geysers of spray."[5]

"They shot most of the boats from under us as the men began trying to make breastworks with their packs," Staff Sergeant W.W. Hughes related later that day. "Quite a few of the men had their rifles shot right out of their hands. I saw four men die. I heard one corporal begging one of his men to shoot him. He got his wish finally. He drowned, although we tried to hold his head out of the water."[6]

Private Charles E. Bell saw that "Our boat was about to go under, so we had to leave. One boy sank once and I caught hold of him and tried to get his pack off. He went to fighting me. His gas mask container was over the pack and I never could get that off. When he started down again I grabbed him by the hair, but he pulled me under twice, so finally I had to let him drown and swim to another boat. Fourteen of us hung on the side with four men who couldn't swim and a wounded man on the inside."[7]

In Robert Eunson's boat, Corporal Homer Jenest started shooting from a crouch as soon as the Japanese opened fire. When his Tommy Gun was emptied he tossed it aside and jumped into the water just as the man next to him fell over dead. Eunson also bailed out and went into water up to his neck. He slipped off the weighty jungle pack full of typing paper when it began pulling him backwards.

When the enemy's anti-aircraft gun focused on Eunson's boat the shells propelled the boat some eighteen feet into the air. The men hovering in the water ducked under the disabled boat until they had to reemerge, gasping for air. Eunson heard a sound from a young trooper behind him.

"'I can't make it,' he said in a tired whisper. I grabbed his arm and pulled him close to me.

"'You can make it,' I kept saying. 'Sure you can make it.'

"But I expected them to open up any minute and kill us."

Eunson saw Captain Wright's boat swing on an arc in an effort to make the beach, but a Japanese machine gun zeroed in on them and sank it with a volley that also mortally wounded Lieutenant Harold Southard.

"When the boy next to me stopped breathing," Eunson wrote, "I let go and his body slid into the water. He just tipped over backward and disappeared.... I'm almost glad I didn't know who he was or whence he came."

The enemy machine guns continued to sweep across the struggling A troopers in the water and their disabled boats. Eunson dived beneath his boat again and when he came up "a bullet hit my typewriter and it flew by my head in two pieces. The machine fire ripped into our boat and we dove under again. When I came up, someone was pulling our half limp boat out so I got behind and shoved.,,, I don't know how many times they shot at us. I remember listening between volleys and hearing them shouting what must have been jeering remarks. The only two words I ever heard clearly were "Tojo's avengers."[8]

Sergeant Hughes' boat sank and he and four other survivors swam over to another boat being pushed out to sea. "I got the men to kick and paddle as well as they could. I was in charge because our platoon commander had just been killed. Finally we reached the channel and drifted with the tide. The boat was full of holes. We used up all our plugs and even stuck our fingers into them. Finally we were picked up."[9]

Eunson's boat sank just after the men pushed it across the reef. They pulled a wounded man off the boat as it went down and spotted another rubber boat off to the left. Corporal Roy C. Jackson directed his boat toward the call for help. When the passengers of the two boats were combined there were seventeen men. The wounded man was placed in the boat and the rest swam alongside, dipping beneath the water when the enemy gunfire came their way. Corporal Jackson worked his way around the boat, plugging bullet holes with wooden screws. "He spoke in a stern voice and never lost his cool," remembered Eunson.[10]

Men clung to the remaining rubber boats overloaded with wounded while others still in the water clung to the sides of the boats awaiting rescue. A pair of medicos named Wickard and Kelly swam from boat to boat giving morphine and caring for wounded men. One of the three boats left afloat picked up Captain Wright, Lieutenant Southard, and a medic. Wright was uninjured but there was a bullet hole in his helmet. However, the lieutenant had suffered a heinous wound in his side and he died on the submarine chaser that picked up the survivors.[11]

Finally the *Sands* moved in and silenced the guns. Three hours after the Japanese guns were disabled, a U.S. Navy sub chaser (the SC-699) moved in to pick up survivors in the water and on three overcrowded rubber boats. The sailors pitched a line to the water logged cavalrymen and they were pulled up one at a time. It was a miracle the losses in A Troop were not worse than they were: twelve men killed, four missing, and seventeen wounded.[12] As it was, Troop A ceased to be a ready combat unit until it could be reequipped. Even the troopers that escaped unscathed had lost all or most of their equipment.

The story about the ill-fated rubber boat assault made the front pages of the Nation's newspapers two days later. The 112th Cavalry Regiment was not mentioned by the National wire services for security reasons, though the newspapers in Dallas and Abilene left no question as to the identities of the soldiers involved. A photograph of A Troop's Captain Edward Wright graced the front page of the *Dallas Morning-News* edition that headlined, "U.S. Troops Storm Ashore on New Britain behind Texas Leaders and Lone Star Flag." *The Abilene Reporter-News* displayed a page one photograph of Lieutenant Colonel Clyde Grant with its story that Abilene members of Troop G, 112th Cavalry, Texas National Guard, were with the invasion force.

Troop A Killed in Action, New Britain, 15 December 1943[13]

Cranfill, Willard PFC
Cox, Donnie PFC
Hall, Hobert L. CPL
Hanna, Ivah E. PVT
Horton, Eugene R. PFC
Lee, George W. 2LT
McKinish, Elmer L. PFC
McMillen, James T. CPL

Ranson, David J. PVT
Sageser, Calvin O. PFC
Sharp, Wallace C. CPL
Southard, Harold D. 2LT
Taulbee, Robert PVT
Tin, Jew H. PVT
Toering, Lester C. PVT
Zeller, Arthur V. PVT

Appendix C.
G Troopers Killed in
the Pacific War

Name	Date/Location	Home State
PFC Elmer Wilson	16 Dec 43/New Britain	Texas
Pvt Raymond Wieber	27 Dec 43/New Britain	Utah
Cpl Guy Griffin	4 Jan 44/New Britain	Texas
Cpl Henry White	4 Jan 44/New Britain	Texas
Cpl Vernon Voyles	4 Jan 44/New Britain	Texas
Pvt Richard Penny*	4 Jan 44/New Britain	?
PFC Eddie Corley	21 Mar 44/New Britain	Texas
Cpl Orvil Weddel	16 July 44/New Guinea	Texas
PFC Forrest Ritter	22 July 44/New Guinea	Alabama
PFC Dewey Barnett	27 July 44/New Guinea	Arkansas
PFC Doyle Tucker	27 July 44/New Guinea	Texas
Pvt Thomas Sullivan	27 July 44/New Guinea	Michigan
Cpl Van Sawyer	2 Aug 44/New Guinea	Texas
PFC Luther Fowler	2 Aug 44/New Guinea	Georgia
SSG Jim Wheeler	3 Aug 44/New Guinea	Texas
Lt Robert O'Briant (Troop F)†	3 Aug 44/New Guinea	Texas
Cpl William Hillson	4 Aug 44/New Guinea	Michigan
Sgt Tom Pat Glass	4 Aug 44/New Guinea	Texas
Pvt Oscar Carlsrud	6 Aug 44/New Guinea	Minnesota
T-5 Walter Wood	22 Nov 44/Leyte P.I.	Texas
Cpt Riford "Rip" Williams (Troop E)‡	27 Mar 45/Luzon P.I.	Vermont
PFC Victor Renischewski	14 June 45/Luzon P.I.	New Jersey
PFC Earl Colee	21 June 45/Luzon P.I.	Iowa
PFC Lewis Krantz	21 June 45/Luzon P.I.	Ohio
PFC John Sexton	21 June 45/Luzon P.I.	Kentucky

*Died later of wounds
†Original member of Troop G
‡Assigned to Troop G at various times

Notes

Chapter 1

1. Christine's father was the son of Scottish immigrants who arrived in America in 1865. A number of her maternal ancestors had served in the American Revolution with the Virginia and the North Carolina militias.

2. Loraine, Texas, a town of less than 1,000 residents, sent more than 20 percent of its total population to the armed services during World War II. The town's first casualty of war was a Navy nurse, Rebecca Britton, who was killed during the Japanese bombing of Pearl Harbor. "Loraine, with 20 Percent of Population in Armed Services..." in *Abilene Reporter News*, June 11, 1944.

3. Enlisted Record and Report of Discharge, Christaine W. Wiggins, 29, June 1945.

4. Robert R. (1884–1971) and Donna Wright (1885–1985) had fourteen children: Lear (1905–1907); William Earl (1907–2001); Vera (1908–2007); Dora Maybelle (1912–1966); Alfred (1913–1985); Alonzo "Pug" (1914–1991); Manuel (1917–1918); Edgar (1918–2005); Andrew Curtis (1920–2003); Aubort Mapes (born 1922); Robert Locke "Pickett" (1922–2007); Mary Girldene (born 1924); Dorothy Virginia (born 1926); Lucille (born 1928)

5. Donna Wright's maternal great-grandfather, John Madison, had acquired his farm in Walker County, Alabama, for his service during the war against the Creek Indians (1813–14). Sixteen-year-old Madison received his father's consent to join the 39th U.S. Infantry and fought under General Andrew Jackson in the decisive battle of the war at Horseshoe Bend, Alabama, on March 27, 1914. Among the wounded from the 39th Regiment that day were Corporal John Madison, with a gunshot wound to his wrist, and an ensign named Sam Houston who was not expected to survive his wounds. He did and became known as the "Father of Texas." For his military service John Madison acquired land grants in Tuscaloosa County, Alabama, as well as in Walker County, and received an annual government pension of $96 from the time of his army discharge in 1814 until 1824 when the yearly payments were reduced to $64. The pension payments ceased at the start of the Civil War and John Madison died in May of 1866. Robert Wiggins, *Generations: Ancestors and Descendants of Robert Wright and Donna Frost* (Lubbock, Texas: privately printed, 1995), pp. 29–31.

Edward B. "Tom" Frost enlisted in the 13th Battalion, Alabama Partisan Rangers, September 20, 1862, and served for the duration of the war. This unit became part of the 56th Alabama Cavalry Regiment (Confederate) on June 8, 1863. Robert Wright served in the 1st Alabama Cavalry Regiment (Union) from September 25, 1863, through September 25, 1864. He had two brothers killed while fighting for the Confederacy.

6. Interview with Aubort Wright.

7. Of the seven Childress recruits, one did not return home. James Hamner (E Troop) was killed in action on Luzon.

8. What happened to "old Ed" was his assignment to a medical battalion with the 36th Infantry Division and he served with the T-Patchers throughout the battles for Italy, France and Germany. He was in almost continual combat from the invasion at Salerno, Italy, September 9, 1943, all the way to V-E Day, May 8, 1945. After the bloody battle of San Pietro, Italy, Ed received a commendation from Major General John Dahlquist of the 36th Infantry Division. It read, in part: "Citation: Edgar Wright, Sergeant, Company C, 111th Medical Battalion, for exceptionally meritorious conduct from 8 to 15 December 1943 in Italy. Sergeant Wright directed litter bearers evacuating wounded during an attack against an enemy-held mountain village. Their route was two miles up the mountainside and under shell fire most of the way. To lessen the burden and speed evacuation, Sergeant Wright spaced his squads in positions to relay the litters to the aid station. By tirelessly directing and supervising his men, when necessary going amongst the front-line infantry companies, he effected prompt treatment and evacuation of injured soldiers. Because of his efficiency many lives were saved." Robert Wiggins, *Generations*, p. 64.

9. Steven E. Clay, "56th Cavalry Brigade," *Trading Post*, July–September 1989, p. 11.

10. The manifest of the USS *President Grant*, July 20, 1942, indicated the regiment's medical detachment consisted of nine officers and fifty-four enlisted men, and twenty-nine passengers were members of the regimental band. *Reunion Review*, August 1991, No. 67, p. 1020.

11. The Abilene, Texas, reunion of the 112th Cavalry in 1989 was dedicated to the eighty-one-year-old Clyde Grant. The ex-cavalry officer and long-time Abilene postmaster died in 2001.

12. Earl Wright served with the 1st Cavalry Division's 82nd Field Artillery from 1936 to 1938. The 82nd's primary piece of equipment was the 75-mm horse-drawn howitzer.

13. Glenn T. Johnston, editor, *We Ain't No Heroes: The 112th Cavalry in World War II, Final Report— History Without Borders*. (Research project of the University of North Texas College of Education: privately published, 2005), p. 145.

14. Perhaps the most unique nickname in the 112th was the moniker acquired by Lionel Carter of Pickett's 1st Platoon. His platoon sergeant at Fort Clark was a tall man with a hawk-like nose and a protruding Adam's apple. Carter, a small slender man, would try to get his sergeant's goat by going "gobble, gobble" from the ranks. Coppy had an idea who the culprit was and after one particular twenty-five mile hike he decided to get even. When Carter let loose with the "gobble, gobble, gobble" as the platoon marched past the stables, the sergeant got his revenge: "You've got a lot to talk about...," he said. "You're not so handsome yourself you god damned Mortimer Snerd looking bastard!" To the rest of the platoon from then on, Carter was "Mort" or "Snerd" for ventriloquist Edgar Bergen's hayseed dummy Mortimer Snerd. *Reunion Review*, August 1974, vol. 18, No. 2.

Chapter 2

1. The term "dog robber" apparently originated at the time of the American Civil War when orderlies were said to eat the scraps from the officer's meals that would otherwise be given to a dog.

2. Carter and the Cavalry, Chapter Three, "Fort Clark, Texas," *Reunion Review*, August 1983.

3. Aubort Wright was assigned to the 222nd Field Artillery Regiment (Utah National Guard). In October 1941 Aubort's unit was designated for overseas assignment, destination the Philippine Islands. On December 5, the regiment's equipment was loaded aboard the SS *Maui* at Pier 7 in San Francisco. His battalion was set to sail the evening of December 7, 1941. The Japanese air raid on Pearl Harbor put the trip on hold.

4. Glenn T. Johnston, editor, *We Ain't No Heroes: The 112th Cavalry in World War II, Final Report— History Without Borders*. (Research project of the University of North Texas College of Education: privately published, 2005), p. 145.

5. Merle Miller, *Ike the Soldier: As They Knew Him*. New York: G.P. Putnam Sons, 1987, p. 323.

6. James Scott Powell, *Learning Under Fire: A Combat Unit in the Southwest* Pacific (dissertation). College Station, Texas: Graduate Studies of Texas A&M University, August 2006, p. 45. http://www.arlingtoncemetery. net/jwcunningham.htm

7. Ibid., pp. 19–20. At the 1994 Midwest reunion of 112th Cavalry troopers, Colonel Hooper told Lionel Carter of an encounter with General Cunningham during the fighting along the Driniumor River in New Guinea. Hooper went to see Cunningham and found the General's tent flaps down. It had been a particularly bad day for losses of officers and non-coms and some of the dead had served under Cunningham since the days at Fort Clark. Hooper thought the General was asleep as he quietly entered the tent, but when his eyes adjusted to the darkness he saw Cunningham with head buried in his hands and crying. The commanding General threatened his exec with "dire consequences" if he ever told anyone. Hooper kept that secret until after General Cunningham's death. "Report of the 1994 Mid-West Reunion," *Reunion Review,* October 1994, No. 76, p. 1277.

8. "Yule Dance to Honor Soldiers Returning Home on Furloughs," *The Centaur,* Fort Clark, Texas, December 6, 1941 (reprinted in *Reunion Review* December 6, 1941).

9. Carter and the Cavalry, *Reunion Review,* Christmas 1984, p. 571.

10. Carter, Lionel, Carter and the Cavalry, Chapter Two, *Reunion Review,* Christmas 1984.

11. Carter and the Cavalry, Chapter Two, *Reunion Review,* June 1985, No. 50, p. 15.

12. "Fort Clark," Carter and the Cavalry, *Reunion Review,* August 1985, No. 51.

13. "J.D. Stallings," *Military Order of the Purple Heart*: Texas Capital Chapter 1919 (Austin, Texas: http://www.purpleheartaustin. org/stallings.htm.) Stallings was wounded four times in New Britain (three of his wounds were sustained during aerial bombardments — twice from bombs dropped by American planes). He was promoted to Captain and was assigned to Second Squadron Headquarters. In the years after the war, Stallings played prominent roles in the 112th Cavalry Association and the Texas Military Forces Museum at Camp Mabry in Austin.

14. Doyle Tucker had two cousins in G Troop, Red and Leonard Parker. Leonard Parker was one of Pickett's best friends at Fort Clark. He was wounded in New Guinea eleven days after Pickett.

15. C.W. mentioned that Robert "Mudcat" Patterson, Jesse Robertson and R.C. Willingham all came from Seagraves, Texas. They joined the 112th at Fort Bliss shortly after Pug and Pickett arrived there.

16. Johnston, *We Ain't No Heroes,* p. 171.

17. In July 1944, the 124th Cavalry Regiment was shipped to India in the China Burma India (C.B.I.) Theatre. The regiment arrived in Burma on October 31, 1944, where it became part of the MARS Task Force with the mission of clearing Japanese forces from the Burma Road, the Allies' lifeline to China. A member of the 124th Cavalry, Audy V. Graham, married C.W.'s first cousin, Hattie Mae Wiggins, in 1947.

Chapter 3

1. Apparently, Riggs and his buddy were celebrating in town when they got into an argument about which one could hit the hardest. They decided to settle the argument and flipped a coin to determine who delivered the first blow. Riggs hit the other trooper so hard he dropped to the pavement and fractured his skull on the curb. The unconscious man was hauled to the hospital and Riggs was detained by the MPs. When the injured cavalryman came to and gave his version of the story, a remorseful Private Riggs was allowed to return to his regiment. "Camp Stoneman and the USS *Grant,*" Carter and the Cavalry, *Reunion Review,* May 1987, No. 56, p. 730.

2. Carter, *Reunion Review,* May 1987. Pug once remarked about the regimental band, "They were litter bearers up there on the Driniumor. Hell, two of them band guys got Silver Stars!"

3. Letter from A.M. Miller to Lionel Carter, November 10, 1987 (printed in *Reunion Review,* April 1988, No. 38, p. 792).

4. Charles L. McDearmont, "My Horse Cavalry Days," 112th Cavalry Association Newsletter, June 1998.

5. Facsimile of President Roosevelt's letter appeared in *Reunion Review,* May 1987, issue 56, p. 737.

6. It was said some soldiers would not take Atabrine because they thought it would make them impotent. Another side effect was the possibility of a yellow-green complexion. When asked if he had a yellowish completion from the medication, the unflappable C.W. remarked without hesitation, "I didn't have a mirror."

7. "New Caledonia," Carter and the

Cavalry, Chapter Four, *Reunion Review*, April 1988, No. 58, p. 798.

8. Letter from David O. Hale, *Reunion Review*, August 1988, p. 803.

9. "Tyler-Based Cavalry Regiment Sees End to Traditional Role in Battle," *Tyler Courier-Times*, April 12, 1994 (reprinted in *Reunion Review*, October 1994, No. 76, p. 1298.

10. "The Band of the 112th Cavalry Regiment," 112th Cavalry Association Newsletter, April 1996, No. 3.

11. Carter, Carter and the Cavalry, Chapter Four, *Reunion Review*, Christmas 1988, p. 843.

12. Letter from Lionel Carter to Girldene and "Bull," dated August 9, 1991.

13. An entry of 29 January 1943 in the 112th's regimental diary noted "We beat 'em" (by a score of 468 to 431) in a rifle shooting match between the cavalrymen and the Marines' 1st Raider Battalion, recently arrived from Guadalcanal. Glenn T. Johnston, editor, *We Ain't No Heroes: The 112th Cavalry in World War II, Final Report— History Without Borders*. (Research project of the University of North Texas College of Education: privately published, 2005), p. 80.

14. James Scott Powell, *Learning Under Fire: A Combat Unit in the Southwest* Pacific (dissertation). (College Station, Texas: Graduate Studies of Texas A&M University, August 2006), pp. 51–52. http://www.arlington-cemetery.net/jwcunningham.htm

15. Photographs of members of the 112th R.C.T. in Japan, 1945. Texas Military Forces Museum, Camp Mabry, Austin, Texas.

16. William J. McDonnell, "Rarin to Go," memoirs, reprinted in *Reunion Review*, October 1994, p. 1304.

Chapter 4

1. General Krueger wanted the troopers to think they may encounter enemy soldiers on Woodlark to prepare them for future landings. However, this lack of information almost cost the lives of a coast watcher and a group of natives before the cavalrymen realized they were not Japanese. Powell, *Learning Under Fire*, p. 55.

2. "Woodlark Island," Carter and the Cavalry, Chapter 6, *Reunion Review*, August 1990, No. 64, p. 951.

3. "Woodlark Island," Carter and the Cav-

alry, Chapter 6, *Reunion Review*, June 1991, No. 66, p. 1005.

4. The phrase came from the title of a 19th-century song about a boy in a faraway land that begins, "Take this letter to my mother, far across the deep blue sea" and the son laments that he may never see his mother again and prays that God will protect "her darling boy." Cary Grant used the title of the song as a sarcastic retort in the 1939 movie *Only Angels Have Wings*. http://library.duke.edu/digital-collections/ songsheets.bsvg401582/pg.1/

5. The landings on Kiriwina mimicked the Woodlark operation. An advance platoon from the 158th Infantry Regiment and an engineer company disembarked from the *Brooks* and *Humphries* about midnight on June 24 and did not find an enemy presence on the island. Seven days later the Kiriwina force (including the 148th Field Artillery Battalion) arrived there in twelve L.C.I.s (Landing Craft, Infantry) although their landing did not go nearly as well as at Woodlark. The L.C.I.s grounded on reefs some three hundred years from shore. The men had to carry their gear ashore and a great deal of equipment and vehicles were lost or damaged because of the salt water. "Jungles of New Guinea: Spring Offensive 1943," *Reunion Review*, August 1995, No. 78, p. 1340.

6. Tokyo Rose was the name American service men gave the Japanese English-speaking female radio announcers. These Japanese propaganda broadcasts played popular western music of the time but their real intention was to negatively affect the morale of the American listeners.

7. Glenn T. Johnston, editor, *We Ain't No Heroes: The 112th Cavalry in World War II, Final Report— History Without Borders*. (Research project of the University of North Texas College of Education: privately published, 2005), pp 233–34.

8. Carter, Chapter 6, *Reunion Review*, Christmas 1990, No. 65, p. 971.

9. Charles Hufstedler: letter to the author, dated July 20, 1992.

10. James Scott Powell, *Learning Under Fire: A Combat Unit in the Southwest* Pacific (dissertation). (College Station, Texas: Graduate Studies of Texas A&M University, August 2006), p. 66. http://www.arlingtoncemetery.net/jwcunningham.htm

11. Powell, *Learning Under Fire*, pp. 57–58.

Colonel Newton, the regimental commander in Norman Mailers' *The Naked and the Dead*, was said to have been modeled after Alexander Miller although the Pulitzer Prize winning author denied it. Newton "was a painfully shy man with excellent manners, a West Pointer," wrote Mailer. "Rumor claimed he had never had a woman in his life ... and was reputed never to have had a thought which was not granted him first by the General (Cummings)." Powell, *Learning Under Fire*, p. 58, Mailer p. 70.

12. The 112th Cavalry Regiment was the primary combat element in the Arawe task force (code name "Director Task Force") that also included the 148th Field Artillery Battalion, 59th Engineer Company, 236th Antiaircraft Artillery, 470th Antiaircraft Artillery Battalion, and A Company, 1st Marine Amphibian Tractor Battalion. The 2nd Battalion of the 158th Infantry Regiment would be held in reserve at Goodnough. John Miller, Jr., *United States Army in World War II, the War in the Pacific; Cartwheel: The Reduction of Rabaul* (Office of the Chief of Military History, Department of the Army, 1959), p. 277.

13. Along with the 131st Field Artillery of the Texas National Guard, Idaho's 1st Battalion, 148th Field Artillery was aboard ship in the Pacific Ocean and bound for the Philippines when Pearl Harbor was attacked. The battalion spent the early part of the war in Australia, losing several men and its 1895 seventy-five millimeter howitzers in the Japanese air attack at Darwin. In February 1943, the battalion received new equipment and 105-millimeter howitzers. Attached to General Cunningham's Director Task Force for the New Britain operation, the 148th would eventually become the artillery component of the 112th Regimental Combat Team. Johnston, *We Ain't No Heroes*, p. 183.

14. John Miller, Jr., *Cartwheel*, pp. 282–83.

15. According to *Operations of the Imperial Japanese Armed Forces in the Papua New Guinea Theater During World War II* by General Kagoro Tanaka, the forces that would oppose the American invasion totaled about 400 men, of which about 190 soldiers of the 115th Infantry Regiment and 30 men of a naval observation team opposed the main landings and an attempt by Troop A to land at Umtingalu. *Reunion Review*, October 1994, No. 76, p. 1334.

16. The author first heard the story of the execution of a traitor on Goodenough during a conversation with Pug Wright and Herman Stokes at the 112th's 1990 Lubbock Reunion. When I presented Pug's story to *Reunion Review* editor Lionel Carter, he responded, "After reading the story about the spy being shot, I scoffed at it. But after thinking about it for a week or so, I seemed to recall hearing this at the time." *Reunion Review*, Christmas, 1990, No. 65, p. 962.

17. It is unclear who planned the rubber boat assault. Some have attributed it to General Cunningham, but Philip Hooper who, as the 112th's executive officer, had a major role in the operation's planning, stated that General Krueger's staff came up with the idea of the diversionary landing at Umtingalu. Powell, *Learning Under Fire*, p. 95.

18. Bill McDonnell to Lionel Carter, reprinted *Reunion Review*, August 1993, No. 73, p. 1192.

Chapter 5

1. *Reunion Review*, Christmas 1991, p. 1060.

2. Powell, *Learning Under Fire*, p. 70.

3. The 112th Cavalry's assault on Arawe was filmed for Frank Capra's "Why We Fight" series that won the New York Film Critics Award as the Best Documentary series for 1944. The film, currently available on DVD, allows later generations to see firsthand the bombardment of the coast, the assault amphibians on their way to the coast, and the actual landings on the Arawe peninsula. *Attack! The Battle of New Britain;* International Historic Films Inc.; 1985.

4. Powell, *Learning Under Fire*, p. 75.

5. "Arawe, New Britain," Chapter 8, *Reunion Review*, June 1992, No. 69, p. 1092.

6. In an article entitled "John Wayne at 70—Still an American Institution," Jim Dean wrote in 1978 that of Wayne's huge collection of memorabilia he was most proud of a letter he kept in a simple black frame: "Your performance meant more than words can express to us particularly since this performance was given within one hundred yards or less of the Japanese outposts," it read. "...The fact that you had everything to lose and nothing to gain was an inspiring factor to us." The letter was dated March 3, 1947, and was signed by Harvey Thompson, Jr., president of Troop G,

112th Calvary Association. *Family Weekly*, April 2, 1978, p. 8.

7. Conversation with Colonel Hooper and Colonel Grant, G Troop Reunion, Abilene, Texas, 1989.

8. It was widely known that the affected trooper often consumed the spirits concocted by the cavalrymen. Men whose systems were already full of Atabrine could easily develop DTs (delirium tremens) from drinking the homemade mixture of grain alcohol and grapefruit juice. Between December 1943 and May 1944, the 112th medical detachment treated ninety-two soldiers for "mental exhaustion" and at least four of these cases were evacuated from New Britain. Powell, *Learning Under Fire*, p. 104.

9. From 15 December, 1943, to 30 January 20, 1944, twenty-one men of the New Britain task force were "wounded accidently" (not in combat). At least thirteen of these wounds were self-inflicted (though not necessarily deliberate) gunshot wounds. Powell, *Learning Under Fire*, p. 105.

10. Address to the 112th Cavalry Association by John Dunlap, 25 September 1994; printed in *Reunion Review*, Christmas 1994, No. 77, p. 1325. G Trooper Lionel Carter mentioned in his memoirs that he witnessed two instances where unarmed Japanese were killed during the fighting along the Driniumor River, New Guinea, in August 1944. The first instance involved a group of wounded Japanese soldiers that wandered into the Americans' lines during the final days of the campaign. Several were killed before the cavalrymen realized they were unarmed and apparently were coming from a field hospital that had received an artillery hit, wrote Carter. "As a second group of four or five Japanese approached with their hands on top of their heads, if their wounds permitted them to do so, there was a general hesitancy among the troopers just what they should do." However, one G Trooper "cut down the wounded Japanese with his Tommy Gun" and received encouragement from an officer. A couple of days later, Carter was assigned to help bury some enemy dead along the river. As the detail completed its grisly task, two soldiers approached carrying a badly wounded Japanese soldier on a stretcher. One of the stretcher bearers said the wounded man "had been moaning and groaning ever since he had been brought in

from a Japanese hospital so that no one at headquarters could sleep, and a decision had been reached 'to put him out of his misery.' The wounded Jap looked at us, looked at the hastily dug grave, tried to smile as if to reassure us that what we were about to do was for the better, but the smile faded from his face to be replaced by apprehension as to how the deed was to be accomplished. The cavalryman rose to his feet, drawing his revolver as he did and shot the Jap through the head. The two stretcher bearers lifted the stretcher from the ground and tilting to one side, slid the Jap off into the grave." Lionel Carter, Carter and the Cavalry, Chapter 29, "Maggot Hill — The Last Battle," *Reunion Review*, July 1980, vol. 24, No. 1. Another former G trooper responded to the latter incident, "the one I saw was rolled into the hole, then shot with a revolver. Who was there or done the shooting I don't recall." "Mail Call," *Reunion Review*, September 1980, vol. 24, No. 2.

11. "Harvey Thompson's Story," *Reunion Review*, August 1993, No. 73, p. 1187.

12. *Reunion Review*, August 1993, No. 73, p. 1187. "Christmas 1942," *Reunion Review*, Christmas 1981, vol. 26, No. 39.

13. Carter, Chapter 8, *Reunion Review*, June 1992, Issue 69, p. 1093. Carter was probably referring to Major Komori's diary. "Smoking to relieve tension was prevalent among men when on patrol where the damp and heavy air made it possible to detect the odor of tobacco smoke hours later when they returned through the area." Lionel Carter, *Reunion Review*, October 1992, No. 71, p. 1122.

14. "Rarin' to Go"; memoirs of William J. McDonnell reprinted in *Reunion Review*, October 1994, No. 76, p. 1335.

15. Powell, *Learning Under Fire*, p. 80. In addition to Voyles (age 23) and White, an overseas replacement named Richard Penny was mortally wounded and Guy Griffin (age 26) of Abilene was killed; Griffin had a thirteen-month-old daughter he had never seen. (*Abilene Reporter News*, January 13, 1944) Apparently the reason that as many casualties were sustained among the second line of machine gunners than the point platoon was because of the terrain. According to G Trooper Robert "Red" Holden, "I (later) checked the terrain and ... there was a slight depression in the ground just enough whereby the firing from the Japs was over me but hit the guys

behind me." "New Britain," Carter and the Cavalry, *Reunion Review*, October 1992, No. 71, p. 1123.

16. Undated article from a Detroit paper posted by Marty Baietty on the Texas Military Forces Museum web site, http://texasmilitary-forcesmuseum.yuku.com/forums/3/t/112th-Cavalry.html, 7/15/2003.

17. Powell, *Learning Under Fire*, p. 83.

18. The Army newspaper (*Yank, Down Under*, February 18, 1944) further reported on the January 16 assault: "The infantry passed through the gaps in the line and deployed beyond it. The only sounds were the shuffle of feet, the clinking of equipment; softly spoken commands.... The men looked back at the road and waited for what seemed to be an endless time. Then they saw what they were waiting for; they yelled back and forth like baseball players talking it up. The tanks came charging up the road, the radio antenna on each tank whipping from side to side like the erected tail of a loping Doberman pinscher dog. The tanks rumbled on through the gaps, deployed and kept going.... The tanks wheeled, spitting tracers from their machine guns, now and again blowing the top off a tree with the heavier bark of their 37s. The infantry fell to the ground, fired, rushed to another position, fired. Occasionally a man would fall, clutching his stomach or head.... Long before evening chow almost all enemy resistance has ceased. All the tanks were operating again. More than a score of Jap machine guns had been captured and a tank had run right over a 75-mm mountain gun...."

19. G Troop Reunion, Abilene, Texas, 1989.

20. McDonnell, "Rarin' to Go," *Reunion Review*, October 1994, No. 76, p. 1336. The final entry in Major Komori's diary, dated 31 March 1944, read "We are very tired and without food." *112th Cavalry Association Newsletter*, June 1998.

21. "Lost on Patrol or How Stupid Can You Get?" *Reunion Review*, August 1974, vol. 18, No. 2.

22. Ibid.

23. Lieutenant Williams became ill and was evacuated on the day after the landing on New Britain, leaving Sergeant Czerniejewski in command of the 1st Platoon. Ray received a battlefield promotion to second lieutenant and would command the 1st Platoon until he was wounded in New Guinea.

24. At the end of his hike across New Britain, after the Marine patrol he was to link up with at the divide of the island never showed up, McMains met with the commander of the 1st Marine Division. "You mean the 112th Cavalry sends out a major on such a small patrol," inquired the General. "In the Marines, we send a captain!" "Yes, and he got lost didn't he," replied McMains. *Reunion Review*, December 15, 1993, p. 1230.

25. Four days after the Japanese signed the articles of surrender in Tokyo Harbor on September 3, 1945, General Hitoshi Imamura surrendered the 135,000-man garrison at Rabaul. Johnston, *We Ain't No Heroes*, p. 211.

26. Talk given by Edward J. Drea, Chief, Research and Analysis Division, U.S. Army Center for Military History, 27 Oct 1990, reprinted in *Reunion Review* June 1992, No. 69, p. 1065. Others put the regiment's losses at a lower number (see Chapter 10 fn5).

Chapter 6

1. *Reunion Review*, October 1992, No. 72, p. 1105.

2. Ibid.

3. Robert Wiggins, *Generations: Ancestors and Descendants of Robert Wright and Donna Frost* (Lubbock, Texas: privately printed, 1995), p. 81.

4. Dorothy Wright Whitley.

5. Childress Air Field was built on farmland west of town. Its bombardier school officially opened on Valentine's Day, 1943, after six months of construction.

6. Girldene Wright Wiggins.

7. Powell, *Learning Under Fire*, p. 137.

Chapter 7

1. Edward J. Drea, *Defending the Driniumor: Covering Force Operations in New Guinea, 1944* (Leavenworth Paper No. 9), (U.S. Army Command and General Staff College, Fort Leavenworth, Kansas; 1984) p. 48.

2. In 1942 the War Department dictated that a cavalry unit in the United States Army would employ 33 .50 caliber machine guns and 56 .30 caliber machine guns. The aggregate number of men in a cavalry regiment was set at 1,650 (officers and enlisted men). U.S. War Department, Table of Organization No.

2–11; Cavalry Regiment, Horse, reprinted in *Reunion Review*, May 1987, No. 56, p. 728; Johnston, *We Ain't No Heroes*, p. 180.

3. Powell, *Learning Under Fire*, p. 109.

4. Author's conversation with Ray Czerniejewski, 1989 Abilene Reunion.

5. Drea, *Defending the Driniumor*, p. 101.

6. Lionel Carter, "Lost Patrol," *Reunion Review*, August 1976, vol. 20.

7. Drea, *Defending the Driniumor*, p. 85.

8. *Reunion Review*, July 1980, vol. 24, No. 1.

9. Another G trooper who traversed the same path a few days later noted "The 112th must have fled in near panic down the trail ... for in their breathless haste every manner and type of equipment had been thrown away to lighten their packs ... except guns and ammunition: steel helmets seemed to be the most prevalent, but there were also blankets, shelter-halves, torn ponchos, mess kits, plus the usual collection of opened and unopened ration cans." Carter, "The Lost Patrol," *Reunion Review*, July 1978, vol. 22, No. 1.

10. Tony Frangella, audio tape narrative, December 1991. Tony Frangella joined the 112th as a replacement in New Caledonia.

11. One veteran trooper remarked that if you "had to go" during the night, you used your helmet and dumped it over the side of the foxhole. This was not only the same helmet the soldier wore, but the same one he used for shaving, washing and cooking.

12. Conversation with Bill Garbo, 1989 Abilene Reunion.

13. Carter, "Lost Patrol," *Reunion Review*, August 1976, vol. 20, No. 1.

14. Ibid.

15. Glenn T. Johnston, editor, *We Ain't No Heroes: The 112th Cavalry in World War II, Final Report—History Without Borders*. (Research project of the University of North Texas College of Education: privately published, 2005), p. 129.

16. Drea, *Defending the Driniumor*, pp. 105–106.

17. On July 20, the 79th Japanese Regiment arrived at Afua with a single Type 94 Mountain gun. They moved it frequently so the American artillery could not locate it. This gun probably fired the round that wounded Pickett.

Chapter 8

1. Doyle Tucker was killed in action only five days after Pickett Wright was wounded. Pickett did not learn of Tucker's death until he read the initial version of this manuscript in 1993.

2. *Reunion Review*, April 1984, No. 47; August 1985, No. 51, p. 5.

3. Drea, *Defending the Driniumor*, p. 113; Powell, *Learning Under Fire*, p. 118.

4. Powell, *Learning Under Fire*, p. 119.

5. *Reunion Review*, July 1985, No. 50, p. 5.

6. "Abilene Aitape Hero to Temple," *Abilene Reporter-News*, September 11, 1944, p. 1.

7. Drea, *Defending the Driniumor*, p. 123.

8. C.W. Wiggins recalled that O'Brient came to the 112th the same time he did. "He had been to one of those CCC camps and already knew close order drill! He left the rest of us way behind. He made sergeant before a lot of 'em made PFC."

9. *Reunion Review*, August 1985, No. 51, p. 610. Dr. Edward J. Drea wrote about the O'Brient relief patrol on page 127 of *Defending the Driniumor* and declared that just before the Americans were fired upon by a machine gun, "A trooper recalled that he heard someone yell, 'Watch Out!'" The inference is that the G Troopers were fired upon by other American soldiers. Three sources for this volume from that rescue patrol, Charles Hufstedler, Pug Wright and Lionel Carter, had no doubt that they were fighting Japanese soldiers.

10. "Seeks Medal for Area Man," by Jane Strbak, clipping from an unknown Ohio newspaper (reprinted in *Reunion Review*, July 1975, vol. 19).

11. Charles E. Hufstedler; letter to the author, dated July 20, 1992.

12. "No one knows what it is like to send men out into combat knowing the chances are that some of them will not come back," an emotional Colonel Clyde Grant told the Midwest Chapter of the 112th Cavalry Association at its annual reunion in 1983. "The person I worried about then and the person I came up here especially to see is Ray Czerniejewski. Word would come down from headquarters to send Czerniejerski out to do this or to do that.... When I heard he had been shot in the hand, I rushed over to the hospital to congratulate him. I told him he had a 'million dollar

wound'!" At that point in his talk Grant broke down, stepped off the stage and walked to Czerniejowski. The two embraced and an observer of the moment noted "there wasn't a dry eye in the room." "Col. Grant & Col. McMains Attend Midwest Reunion," *Reunion Review*, Christmas, 1983, No. 46.

13. By the end of the war only 13,500 soldiers remained from the original 140,000 strong 18th Japanese Army. General Adachi surrendered his command to the Australian 6th Division at Wewak, New Guinea, on September 13, 1945. The Australians tried Adachi for war crimes committed by his soldiers and he was sentenced to life imprisonment in April 1947. Five months later, Adachi used a rusty knife to commit ritual suicide while incarcerated at Rabaul.

14. Carter and the Cavalry, "Going Home," Chapter 30, September 1980, vol. 24, No. 2.

15. Ibid.

16. "Mail Call," *Reunion Review*, August 1987, No. 57, pp. 747–48.

17. Second Lieutenant Dale E. Christensen of Troop E. (k.i.a. August 4, 1944) and Second Lieutenant George W.G. Boyce, Jr., were awarded the Medal of Honor for "conspicuous gallantry and intrepidity at the risk of his life above and beyond the call of duty along the Driniumor River." Boyce was killed on July 23, 1944, when he smothered a live enemy grenade to save the lives of his men during the attempt to relieve a besieged C Troop that included the remnants of the Czerniejowski patrol.

18. Powell, *Learning Under Fire*, p. 162.

19. Ibid., p. 164.

Chapter 9

1. Author's interview with Mrs. Aubort Wright.

2. Glenn T. Johnston, editor, *We Ain't No Heroes: The 112th Cavalry in World War II, Final Report— History Without Borders*. (Research project of the University of North Texas College of Education: privately published, 2005), pp. 130–31. Norman Mailer used his experiences with the 112th to pen his first novel, *The Naked and the Dead* (1948).

3. Johnston, *We Ain't No Heroes*, pp. 240–241.

4. *Reunion Review*, August 1995, No. 78, p. 1348.

5. Ibid., p. 259.

6. While in the Pacific, the 1st Cavalry Division included the 5th, 7th, 8th and 12th Cavalry Regiments.

7. Johnston, *We Ain't No Heroes*, p. 247.

8. "The Memoirs of William J. McDonnell," *Reunion Review*, August 1995, No. 78, p. 1358.

9. Powell, *Learning Under Fire*, p. 189.

10. Herman Stokes of Snyder, Texas, wrote (January 21, 1992) an interesting note about the climax of the Leyte campaign, the Battle of Ormoc Bay: "We stayed on the mountain and watched the Japs load out on ships in the Ormoc harbor. Then our Navy took care of them." Pug was in the field hospital at that time.

11. Powell, *Learning Under Fire*, p. 219.

12. Tony Frangella, audio tape narrative, December 1991. Process about G Troop being assigned as MacArthur's bodyguard also explained in *Reunion Review*, August 1993, p. 1197.

13. Lubbock Army Air Field closed in December 1945 and reopened as Reese Air Force Base in 1949.

14. Between 1942 and 1945, 7,000 Italian prisoners of war were interned at the Hereford Military Reservation, some four miles south of a town of the same name.

Chapter 10

1. Robert Ross, *United States Army in World War II: The War in the Pacific: Triumph in the Philippines* (Washington, DC: Office of the Chief of Military History, Department of the Army, 1963), p. 694.

2. McDonnell, *Reunion Review*, August 1995, No. 78, p. 1360.

3. Tony Frangella, audio tape narrative, December 1991. For another version of the Bataan patrol with MacArthur see Clayton, *The Years of MacArthur*, Volume II (Boston: Houghton Mifflin, 1975, p. 649.

4. Frangella, audio tape narrative.

5. McDonnell, *Reunion Review*, p. 1361.

6. Ibid., p. 1362.

7. The jungle boots with leggings provided the cavalry in New Guinea proved unsatisfactory and the men's feet became susceptible to sores (trench foot). The boots retained moisture once they got wet and it was too dangerous for men to remove the footwear because of the time

it took to unlace the leggings, remove the boots, and allow the feet to dry before putting them back on. Often troopers' feet would swell to the point it became impossible to put the boots back on. The 112th was issued a different style of combat boots in the Philippines. They had two straps and buckles on the outside and could be quickly taken off and put back on. Unfortunately, the boots' rubber cleated soles and canvas construction did not hold up well and fell apart in the rugged and rocky conditions encountered on Leyte and Luzon. Johnston, *We Ain't No Heroes*, pp. 139–42.

8. One of MacArthur's generals wanted to put Manila off limits to the troops because of the spiraling venereal rate among soldiers, but the commander-in-chief wouldn't hear of it: "...I'm not going to put Manila out of bounds to our troops. Besides, they've got some pretty good treatment for that disease now, haven't they?" Clayton, *The Years of MacArthur*, p. 654.

9. In an address to the 112th Cavalry Association on September 25, 1994, historian John Dunlap indicated that through a compilation of the names of the unit's killed in action the 112th suffered 224 service related deaths after it was Federalized. Troop G suffered the lowest number of killed in action with 24 and Troop A had the most with 50. The most battle deaths by the regiment in a single operation occurred on New Britain (88) while New Guinea was second (54), then the Luzon campaign (44), and Leyte (26). John Dunlap's address to the 112th Cavalry Association on September 25, 1994, printed in *Reunion Review*, Christmas, 1994, No. 77, p. 1326.

10. Colonel D. M. McMains, commander of the 2nd Squadron, realized the difficulty of evacuating wounded men in the Santa Ines operation on Luzon. In the rugged terrain, the wounded would need to be transported by litter bearers and front line troopers would be required to go along as guards. "So, I requested Regiment to send a helicopter to carry the wounded out," wrote McMains. "When the first copter arrived the pilot could only carry a wounded person who could sit up in the seat for the ride back.... The pilot was asked if on his return trip he would check and see if there could not be some way that a Navy litter basket could be fixed along the landing brackets of the chopper, therefore allowing two litter patients as well as a sit-up patient for each trip.

The outcome, a contraption was fixed and worked like a charm." Letter from Colonel D.M. McMains, May 14, 1986; printed in *Reunion Review*, July 1985, No. 54, p. 7.

11. Headquarters XI Corps — Silver Star Medal Awards, reprinted *Reunion Review*, August 1990, No. 64, p. 945. Anthony F. Frangella died at the age of eighty-five on May 17, 2006, and is buried in Good Shepherd Cemetery in Orland Park, Illinois.

12. *Reunion Review*, June 1992, No. 69, pp. 1076–77.

Epilogue

1. Caleb Pirtle III and Michael F. Cusack; *The Lonely Sentinel; Fort Clark: On Texas' Western Frontier* (Austin: Eakin Press, 1985), pp. 170–71.

2. Lionel Carter purchased a mimeograph machine for $70 from the bank where he worked and began the *Reunion Review* in July 1957. He typed the newsletter on a used Underwood manual typewriter and transferred the *Review* to stencils that were painstakingly run through the mimeograph, one page at a time. The front side of a page had to dry overnight before the second page could be run. At first, the two or four page newsletter contained announcements and accounts of the annual Midwest reunion of former members of G Troop. Gradually, it was expanded to include letters from fellow cavalrymen, obituaries, and Lionel's experiences with the cavalry, serialized a chapter at a time. As years went by, other 112th cavalrymen contributed their stories and the *Review* republished magazine and newspaper articles about the 112th, accounts from the regiment's historians, and even cavalry cartoons. By the late 1980s he was putting out as many as four issues a year usually of about sixteen pages. Lionel Carter made news in April 2007 when he reluctantly sold the first portion of his collection of over 50,000 baseball cards that he had assembled over the previous seventy-four years. At the auction a 1951 *Bowman* Mickey Mantle rookie card brought the highest price for a single card, fetching $162,000 and the most paid for a set was $285,000 for the complete 1938 *Goudy* series. The cards sold at Mastro Auctions in Burr Oak, Illinois, netted Carter over $1,600,000. Lionel Carter died in an Illinois nursing home on August 28, 2008.

3. Letter from Lionel Carter to Girldene and "Bull," dated August 9, 1991.

Appendix B

1. Robert Eunson. "Japs Open Fire on Rubber Boats," *Dallas Morning-News*, December 17, 1943, p. 1.

2. Glenn T. Johnston, editor, *We Ain't No Heroes: The 112th Cavalry in World War II, Final Report – History Without Borders*. (Research project of the University of North Texas College of Education: privately published, 2005), p. 214.

3. Based on Major Masamitsu Komori's diary the Japanese learned of the American task force when one of their flying boats spotted it more than two hours before A Troop's assault. Johnston, p. 215.

4. Johnston, p. 199.

5. William C. Wilson. "75 of 150 Lost in Diversion Blow," *Dallas Morning-News*, December 17, 1943, p. 1.

6. Robert Cromie, "Enemy Hurls Back First Assault by 150 Commandos," *Chicago Daily Tribune*, December 17, 1943, p. 8.

7. Ibid.

8. Eunson, "Japs Open Fire," p. 16.

9. Cromie, "Enemy Hurls Back First Assault by 150 Commandos," *Chicago Daily Tribune,* December 17, 1943, p. 8.

10. Eunson, "Japs Open Fire," p. 16.

11. *Reunion Review*, July 1994, No. 75., p. 1259.

12. John Miller, Jr., *United States Army in World War II, the War in the Pacific; Cartwheel: The Reduction of Rabaul* (Office of the Chief of Military History, Department of the Army, 1959), p. 285.

13. "List of members of the 112 the Cavalry Regiment Killed in World War II" complied by 112th Cavalry historian David O. Hale. Printed in *Reunion Review*, October 1992, No. 71, pp. 1115–18.

Bibliography

Interviews

Czerniejewski, Raymond — G Troop reunion, Abilene, Texas, 1989.
Garbo, Bill — G Troop reunion, Abilene, Texas, 1989.
Stokes, Herman —112th Cavalry reunion, Lubbock, Texas, 1990.
Wiggins, C.W. "Bull"— multiple interviews between 1987 and 1997.
Wiggins, Girldene (Wright)— multiple interviews between 1987 and 1997.
Wright, Alonzo "Pug"— multiple interviews between 1987 and 1992.
Wright, Mr. and Mrs. Aubort.
Wright, Edgar — multiple between 1997 and 1999.
Wright, Robert "Pickett"— multiple interviews between 1987 and 1992.

Correspondence

Carter, Lionel: multiple with author, 1988–91.
Carter, Lionel to Dr. Edward J. Drea, August 26, 1985 (copy provided by Lionel Carter).
Frangella, Tony: audio tape narrative to author, December 1991.
Hufstedler, Charles: letter to author dated July 20, 1992.

Unpublished Materials

Attack! The Battle of New Britain, International Historic Films Inc., 1985. (VHS)
Carter, Lionel. "Carter and the Cavalry." Unpublished manuscript, serialized in *Reunion Review*.
Carter, Lionel, editor, *Reunion Review*, July 1961–December 1992.
Johnson, Glenn, editor. "We Ain't No Heroes. The 112th Cavalry in World War II," Final Report — History Without Borders. Research project of the University of North Texas College of Education (privately published), 2005.
Powell, James Scott. "Learning Under Fire: A Combat Unit in the Southwest Pacific" (dissertation). College Station: Graduate Studies of Texas A&M University, August 2006.
Wiggins, Robert. *Generations: Ancestors and Descendants of Robert Wright and Donna Frost.* Lubbock, TX (privately printed), 1995.

Wiggins, Robert. *The Wiggins Family: The Story of a Family in Words and Pictures.* Lubbock, TX (privately printed), 1996.

Published Materials

Arthur, Anthony. *Bushmasters: America's Jungle Warriors of World War II.* New York: St. Martin's, 1987.

Cannon, M. Hamlin. *United States Army in World War II. The War in the Pacific. Leyte: The Return to the Philippines.* Washington, DC: Office of the Chief of Military History, Department of the Army, 1954.

Clayton, James D. *The Years of MacArthur, Volume II: 1941–1945.* Boston: Houghton Mifflin, 1975.

Drea, Dr. Edward J. *Defending the Driniumor: Covering Force Operations in New Guinea, 1944* (Leavenworth Paper No. 9). Fort Leavenworth, KS: U.S. Army Command and General Staff College, 1984.

Kinney County: 125 Years of Growth, 1852–1977. Brackettville, TX: Kinney County Historical Society, 1977.

Krueger, General Walter. *From Down Under to Nippon. The Story of the Sixth Army During World War II.* Washington, DC: Combat Forces Press, 1953.

Metz, Leon. *Desert Army: Fort Bliss on the Texas Border.* El Paso, TX: Mangan Books, 1988.

Miller, John, Jr. *United States Army in World War II. The War in the Pacific. Cartwheel: The Reduction of Rabaul.* Washington, DC: Office of the Chief of Military History, Department of the Army, 1959.

Miller, Merle. *Ike the Soldier: As They Knew Him.* New York: G.P. Putnam Sons, 1987.

Moore, John Hammond. *Over-Sexed, Over-Paid and Over Here! Americans in Australia, 1941–45.* Melbourne: Oxford University Press, 1985.

112th Cavalry Association. *The 112th Cavalry Regiment Membership Directory.* 112th Cavalry Association, Inc., 1973.

Pirtle, Caleb, III, and Michael F. Cusack, *The Lonely Sentinel, Fort Clark: On Texas' Western Frontier.* Austin: Eakin Press, 1985.

Smith, Robert Ross. *United States Army in World War II. The War in the Pacific. Triumph in the Philippines.* Washington, DC: Office of the Chief of Military History, Department of the Army, 1963.

Stanton, Shelby L. *Order of Battle. U.S. Army: World War II.* Novato, CA: Presidio Press, 1984.

Steffen, Randy, *The Horse Soldier, 1776–1943, Volume IV, World War I, The Peacetime Army, World War II.* Norman: University of Oklahoma Press, 1979.

Articles

"Address to 112th Cavalry Association by John Dunlap, 25 September 1994," *Reunion Review,* Christmas 1994, No. 77.

"Abilene Aitape Hero to Temple," *Abilene Reporter-News,* September 11, 1944, p. 1.

Boyce, Cpl. Ralph. "Attack on Arawe," *Yank, The Army Weekly,* January 28, 1944.

Boyd, Eve Jolene. "Fort Clark," *Texas Highways,* August 1985, vol. 32, No. 8, pp. 2–9.

Brabham, Charles. "The Band of the 112th Cavalry Regiment," 112th Cavalry Association Newsletter, April 1996, No. 3.

Clay, Stephen. "56th Cavalry Brigade," *Trading Post,* July–Sept. 1989, pp. 11–13.

Cramer, Dusan. "Mantle Fields $165K," in suite 101, May 10, 2007, http://collectibles.siote101.com/article.cfm/mantle_fields_165k

Cromie, Robert. "Enemy Hurls Back First Assault by 150 Commandos," *Chicago Daily Tribune,* December 17, 1943, p. 8.

Dean, Jim. "John Wayne at 70—Still an American Institution," *Family Weekly*, April 2, 1978, p. 8.

Dunlap, Lt. John D., Jr. "Arawe—Prelude to Cape Gloucester," *Officer Review*, December 1993, pp. 5–6. Reprinted in *Reunion Review*, July 1994, No. 75, pp. 1246–48.

Eunson, Robert. "Japs Open Fire on Rubber Boats," *Dallas Morning-News*, December 17, 1943, p. 1.

"Fort Clark," *Handbook of Texas Online*, http://www.tshaonline.org/handbook/online/articles/FF/ qbfl0.html.

Graham, Michael. "Liberating Leyte," *VFW Magazine*, October 1994, pp. 16–17.

"Harvey Thompson's Story," *Reunion Review*, August 1993, No. 73, p. 1186–87.

"J.D. Stallings," *Military Order of the Purple Heart*, Texas Capital Chapter 1919 Austin, Texas. http://www.purpleheartaustin.org/stallings.htm.

"Jap Attacks on Arawe Failure," *Abilene Reporter News*, December 18, 1943, p. 1.

"Japs Open Fire on Rubber Boats," *Dallas Morning-News*, December 17, 1943, p. 1.

"Julian Wallace Cunningham (1893–1972)." http://www.arlingtoncemetery.net/jwcunningham. htm.

"Loraine, with 20 Percent of Population in Armed Services...." *Abilene Reporter News*, June 11, 1944.

McDearmont, Charles L. "My Horse Cavalry Days," 112th Cavalry Association Newsletter, June 1998.

McDonnell, William J. "Rarin' to Go: The Memoirs of William J. McDonnell," *Reunion Review*, October 1994, No. 76; August 1995, No. 78.

O'Connell, T.S. "Mastro Snags Lionel Carter Collection for Auction," Sports Collectors Digest, www.sportscollectorsdigest.com/article/?p._ArticleId=4219.

"Pfc D.O. Tucker Killed in Action," *Abilene Reporter News*, August 12, 1944.

"Reunion of Cavalry Generates Memories," *Lubbock Avalanche-Journal*, July 11–12, 1987.

"South New Britain Area Taken," *Abilene Reporter News*, December 17, 1943, p. 1.

Strbak, Jane. "Seeks Medal for Area Man," unknown Ohio newspaper (reprinted in *Reunion Review*, July 1975, vol. 19).

"Talk given by Edward J. Drea, Chief, Research and Analysis Division, U.S. Army Center for Military History 27 Oct 1990," (reprinted in *Reunion Review,* June 1992, No. 69, p. 1065).

"Tyler-Based Cavalry Regiment Sees End to Traditional Role in Battle," *Tyler Courier-Times*, April 12, 1994.

Wilson, William C., "75 of 150 Lost in Diversion Blow," *Dallas Morning-News*, December 17, 1943, p. 1.

"Xmas Leave to Half Regiment," *The Centaur*, Fort Clark, Texas, December 6, 1941. (reprinted in *Reunion Review*, Christmas 1991, No. 68).

Yank, Down Under, February 18, 1944.

"Yule Dance to Honor Soldiers Returning Home on Furloughs," *The Centaur*, Fort Clark, Texas, December 6, 1941 (reprinted in *Reunion Review*, Christmas 1991, No. 68).

Index

Numbers in **bold italics** indicate pages with photographs.